Alex Zarifis

Leadership With AI and Trust

Alex Zarifis

Leadership With AI and Trust

Adapting popular leadership styles for AI

DE GRUYTER

ISBN 978-3-11-163004-5
e-ISBN (PDF) 978-3-11-163013-7
e-ISBN (EPUB) 978-3-11-163021-2

Library of Congress Control Number: 2025936997

Bibliographic information published by the Deutsche Nationalbibliothek
The Deutsche Nationalbibliothek lists this publication in the Deutsche Nationalbibliografie;
detailed bibliographic data are available on the internet at http://dnb.dnb.de.

www.degruyter.com
Questions about General Product Safety Regulation:
productsafety@degruyterbrill.com

Contents

Section B: Leadership styles and their role in using AI with trust

Section C: **Leadership that builds trust in the age of generative AI**

Foreword

Organisations today across the private and public sector are being offered exciting new opportunities by new technologies. Artificial intelligence (AI) is grabbing most of the headlines, but there are several other exciting technologies such as blockchain, the internet of things (IoT), and even quantum computing. Many technologies that have been with us for some time, such as big data, are being utilised to a far greater extent than before and in different ways. In our personal and professional lives we are experiencing many new technologies, but there is also a cumulative effect of all these technologies that leads to a very different experience. These many opportunities and the cumulative effect of the many changes also create some uncertainties and challenges. It can be argued that we are in the middle of the biggest disruption in business and society since the popularisation of the internet.

In this environment of high uncertainty, an organisation can quickly flourish if the right decisions are made or go out of business. Strong and effective leadership is needed. The modern leader needs to understand AI but also lead mixed teams of people and autonomous AI agents.

Since the dot-com boom, when we last faced such turmoil as we are having now with AI, one of the methods to evaluate and improve businesses was to understand their business model. Many companies took years to make a profit. Other methods to evaluate performance, such as active users, have their limitations and can be manipulated. By identifying the business models that typically succeed and those that typically fail, it becomes possible to do two things: firstly, we can understand which companies face an uphill struggle to succeed, and secondly what steps an organisation can take to move closer to a business model that is often successful. Today, the disruption and digital transformation identifying the successful business and understanding why they are successful while others fail is very useful. While there seem to be hundreds or thousands of different business models, they can be grouped together into a smaller number of groups with common characteristics.

The turmoil of this transitionary period creates some risk, and each technology and new process also adds some new risks. Even if a new process is more effective and less risky in principle, it brings some new risks until it is bedded in and the unknown unknowns reveal themselves. The high degree of the overall risk, but also the variety of different risks, can make people hesitate or even push back on digital transformation. This risk is felt by the organisation but also by all the stakeholders across their ecosystem. To counter this risk, trust is needed in the plan for digital transformation, the business model selected, the technologies and the people involved. The trust needs to be spread across all aspects of the digital transformation to counter all the different sources of risk. Trust is necessary, but this trust should be based on understanding the challenges and finding the best solutions. Unhealthy and unnecessary distrust in some aspects of AI should not be replaced by a blind naive trust. The process of building trust in AI should also be a process of genuinely reducing risk. Risk

https://doi.org/10.1515/9783111630137-203

can be reduced by finding better solutions but also by understanding the risk better and being in a better position to avoid it.

I have worked with Dr Alex Zarifis for almost two decades on these issues and we have published over forty research papers on digital transformation, AI, business models, and trust in technology. Dr Zarifis has worked at some leading universities such as the University of Cambridge, University of Manchester and the University of Mannheim. He has also worked on large industry-focused projects at the Karlsruhe Institute of Technology and Loughborough University. He brings together the insights from his research and the more industry-focused projects together here to provide the best methods to go through digital transformation successfully.

The primary audience of this book are managers and leaders. Leaders with the formal authority, and those that don't have the formal authority but step up to get the most out of AI and other technologies. This book is useful for studying leadership, management, digital transformation, innovation, project management, AI, and business in general.

Prof. Xusen Cheng
Professor of Information Systems, School of Information, Renmin University of China

Acknowledgements

I would like to thank some of the people that inspired, educated, and supported me through my career and the preparation of this book. These are Mr Hugh Cameron, Prof. Peter Kawalek, Prof. Linda Macaulay, Prof. Simon French, Dr Aida Azadegan, Prof. Luis A. Castro, Prof. Alejandro Bernales, Dr Felix Martin Moreno, Dr Alex Rast, Prof. Filippo Sladojevich, Prof. Julia Kroenung, Dr Markus Nöltner, Prof. Richard Ingham, Prof. Uchitha Jayawickrama, Prof. Bryan Zhang, Dr Alexander Apostolidis, Prof. Pierre-Emmanuel Arduin, Prof. Mario Brito, Dr Jaw-Kai Wang, Prof. Larisa Yarovaya, Prof. Ahmad Maaitah, Prof. Manuel Nunes, Prof. Evangelos Syrigos, Dr Agnieszka Stefaniec, Prof. Nicholas Dacre, Dr Iman Taani, Dr Dorrie Chao, Prof. Jelena Petrovic, Prof. Martin Enilov, Prof. Behzad Hezarkhani, Prof. Soroosh Saghiri, Prof. Xusen Cheng, Prof. Costas Christodoulides, Mr Dimitris Mina, Mr Costas Constantinou, Mr Andreas Morales, Mr Teodor Onofrejesuk, Ms Jean Buchanan Armour Onofrejesuk, Ms Janet Zarifis, Ms Stefani Zarifis, and Mr John Georgovski.

https://doi.org/10.1515/9783111630137-204

Section A: **Leadership with trust for people and technology across different stages of a project**

Chapter 1
Leadership in the age of AI and the importance of building trust

1.1 Introduction

1.1.1 The role of the leader in the age of AI

Whatever matters to human beings, trust is the atmosphere in which it thrives. — Sissela Bok, philosopher and ethicist

Leaders shape our socio-economic life. Leadership has a long history, but it never stops evolving. This constant evolution can be a slow gradual shift from one leadership style to another, while other times this shift is far more dramatic. We have been going through the gradual increase in the popularity of transformational leadership at the expense of traditional authoritarian management, but now, due to AI, we are going through a more dramatic transformation. We are talking about AI, generative AI, and autonomous AI agents. Autonomous AI agents use large language models, but they can also plan several steps ahead to complete a task, have a memory of their past experiences, and can choose what specialised tools to use for each task.

This dramatic transformation, often referred to as digital transformation, is also a human transformation. The question arises: How will we lead people, and generative AI including autonomous AI agents? Books on leadership do not sufficiently cover the role of generative AI, and books about generative AI do not discuss leadership and the role people still play. This book comes to fill this gap and give guidance to the modern leader of both people and AI. The ambidextrous leader adapts their processes to fully utilise AI and builds trust in people. Furthermore, the ambidextrous leader understands AI and empathises with people. A leader in AI and trust can understand their context and the stage of a project they are in, the challenges they will face now and in the subsequent stages, and acts accordingly. Trust must be built at the start as it is too late once it is challenged and broken. A leader that is ignorant of these issues will not succeed in the new environment. As is often quoted, Niccolo Machiavelli states that people 'are driven by two principal impulses, either by love or by fear'. While that was probably accurate for his time and context, the modern leader must also know how to lead on information, which means leading on AI, and building trust in people. The effective leader does not think of leadership without thinking about AI and thinking about trust. Going through the process of trying to find ways to build trust creates a more well-rounded leader. The football coach Jose Mourinho famously said he would only go to war with players he could trust. Make no mistake, digital transformation with AI is like going to war.

https://doi.org/10.1515/9783111630137-001

1.1.2 AI and the opportunities new technologies bring

There has been a school of thought in leadership for many years that you do not have to be a subject expert to be a leader. In other words, for example, you do not need to have a degree in computer science to lead a project implementing AI. While there is truth in this, and there are abundant examples of project managers of IT projects who have the least technical knowledge of those in the team, a leader in AI should understand how the application of technology typically affects people and organisations. A leader does not have to be an expert in coding software and developing technology, but they have to be experts in applying it. You are not a leader if you simply follow what your technology provider, consultant, or IT department tell you. The modern leader does not have to be an expert in computer science, but they must have knowledge of some of the key theories from human-computer interaction (HCI) and understand what infrastructure AI needs and how to get the most out of it.

It is more necessary now than ever before for a leader to have some knowledge across these technical issues because there is no education, or profession, that covers them completely. There are many degrees and types of professions that are helpful, but none that are fully comprehensive. For example, a team member with a computer science background will be very beneficial in understanding the inner workings of AI, but they will not necessarily be the best person with the specialised industry knowledge to get the most out of generative AI with prompts. Prompt engineering has become a very specialised role. Getting the most out of generative AI as a user is often more about having the industry knowledge and being a good communicator so that prompts encourage the most useful answers possible. As there is no single professional that is 'perfect' for utilising AI, a leader must have some knowledge across these technical issues to coordinate the 'perfect' team to fully utilise AI.

Generative AI is being used by consultants from the leading firms to produce reports that would have taken ninety hours in five hours. Digital twins of an organisation simulating its operations and external environment in great accuracy can be used to simulate many different strategic decisions and help the leader select the best one. The attraction is very high to shift more and more of the decision making to AI. The risk for over-reliance and loss of skills, control, and eventually reputation is also very high.

Getting the balance right when replacing some tasks humans do with AI can be tricky. For some time the most popular approach was to focus on augmenting a worker's role so that AI takes over some of their more repetitive and standardised tasks. This appeared to be getting the best of both worlds, but it often leads to fragmentation of roles and tasks between the worker and AI that is counterproductive. Time is wasted and errors can be introduced when the task is handed over between the two. On a higher level of abstraction, new business models that were intended to be optimised for AI have in many cases underperformed compared to traditional models.

Therefore, the leader in the age of AI has several roles and is not limited to getting the strategic decisions right. They need to have a positive impact across recruitment, team building, shaping the technology that will be used, and the overall business model. They may also, whether they like it or not, whether de jure or de facto, have to play the role of the 'head auditor of AI'.

1.1.3 Challenges and the need for trust

We should be clear about the scale of the challenge: Not all AI implementations succeed, and a world with AI does not need as many organisations as exist today. The organisations that do not find their place in the new world order, or do not have the leader to lead them there, will disappear. The widely held misconception that adding AI is straightforward, and that the inevitable result will be efficiency, is false. For example, AI needs data and various guardrails. In terms of data, who will negotiate, complete the agreements, and maintain access to the necessary data? Who will get exclusive access to another organisation's data, as part of a wide-reaching partnership? In terms of guardrails, who will decide what kind of multi-agent arrangement is needed to ensure the reliability and transparency of AI. What combination of AI-driven checks of AI, software not using AI, and humans will steer AI towards reliable results? What kind of information and references should a company's generative AI present to support its output? Issues around data and guardrails quickly lead to strategic questions. Who will change the business model so that it fits in with the emerging ecosystem of their industry? It will not be the AI itself, and it will not be an ineffective leader with outdated methods and knowledge either.

A leader may have risen through the ranks for their people skills at a time when the staff were the most critical ingredient in an organisation. For many organisations, the key ingredient may now be the stakeholders trust in how AI is being used. The leader of AI may need to spend less time managing people and more time ensuring AI behaves in a trustworthy way and does not destroy trust and the brand.

This book goes through the popular leadership styles, their strengths and weaknesses, how they can influence AI use, and build trust. The book then offers its proprietary blend of transactional, servant, and transformational leadership that achieves the best results.

Several real-world examples of leaders are used throughout to illustrate. Furthermore, peer-reviewed research is cited to provide support and further reading for the methods discussed.

1.1.4 The proposed approach: Transactional with servant or transformational leadership

This book goes through the popular leadership styles, their strengths and weaknesses, how they can influence AI use, and build trust. The best balance for the current environment is transactional with servant leadership, or transactional with transformational leadership. Servant and transformational leadership approaches are very effective in motivating and inspiring people, but they are challenging to implement and do not necessarily work for every situation. Transactional leadership is usually practical and relatively easy to implement but lacks the motivation and overarching vision the servant and transformational approaches offer. For situations with low uncertainty, transactional leadership is easier to implement, less time consuming, and more effective, but for situations with high uncertainty, servant and transformational approaches often work better. If there is some uncertainty both within and outside the organisation, which is typical for the times we live in, but the leader is clear on what AI-focused business model they want, then applying transactional with transformational leadership is the most effective way to get there.

The organisations that implement an AI-focused business model effectively will get some certainty from the model and gain an advantage over those that struggle to make the transition. Zarifis and Cheng (2024a 2025) propose the six business models proven to be ideal for a modern organisation with AI at its centre are: (1) incumbent focusing on one part of the value chain and disaggregating, (2) incumbent absorbing AI into existing model, (3) incumbent expanding beyond current model to fully utilise the opportunities of AI and access new data, (4) startup disruptor focused on one sector, built from the start to be highly automated, (5) disruptor focused on tech adding a new service like insurance, and (6) disruptor that is not necessarily tech-focused with an extensive user or fanbase.

1.2 The stages of a project: Digital transformation and the challenges at each stage

Trust is the highest form of human motivation. It brings out the very best in people. But it takes time and patience. — Stephen Covey, author on self-improvement

1.2.1 The six stages of collaboration in projects

Whether a leader is a dedicated project manager or a regular manager, they need to implement projects. For example, going through the process of digital transformation can be seen as a series of projects implementing new technologies and changing processes. A good leader must have an understanding of where they are in a journey, and what typically comes in the subsequent stages. A leader must also understand on a micro level how a technology can change specific relationships between people and, on a macro level, how it can fundamentally change business models.

When people collaborate, there are challenges that are dependent on the specific context. For this reason, several models have been developed to improve the collaboration process, especially at the start when the participants are getting to know their roles and each other (Project Management Institute, 2013). Several aspects of the context, such as if the collaboration is online (Cheng et al., 2013), if it is multicultural or from one culture, have an effect.

Research on what motivates people to collaborate shows that there are two typical reasons. Firstly, there is the practical reason that if their work needs them to collaborate, they will, regardless of the social dynamics of the team. The second is the social reason that if they feel there is a collective responsibility, as opposed to an individual responsibility, they will collaborate. Collective responsibility is stronger in the later stages of a collaboration when the team is often referred to as 'mature'. Therefore, a leader must make the team mature with collective responsibility as fast as possible.

There are several models with different priorities that recommend different stages for a collaboration to go through. Despite this variety there is extensive support for a model with four stages (Tuckman & Jensen, 2010). These four stages, with some variations, have been supported in several contexts. A similar model, with five stages, widely supported in project management adds an additional stage at the end of the project called 'project close' (Project Management Institute, 2013). In the current environment, with short contracts and new teams coming together regularly for projects, the fifth stage is important. The fifth stage can involve the leader helping their team members find their next role. A sixth stage post-project collaboration is now more necessary as the formal end of a project does not always mean the end of the collaboration, and some collaboration, possibly intermittent, continues.

The six stages are valid across several contexts, and typical challenges have been identified at each of the stages, as shown in Table 1.1. One of the things a leader must consider is how their actions can mitigate the challenges of the stage they are in and the challenges coming later. Many firefighter-type of leaders have some success, but there is a ceiling these kinds of people reach if they do not develop their ability to see further. For example, while in some teams trust builds as the relationships strengthen moving through the project, for other teams, there is a honeymoon period at the start where trust is not tested, and the trust is tested at the later stages when the credit for the work is divided between the group.

Trust-building tip: Build trust at the start of the project, before the challenges to trust emerge. Use sustainable methods such as establishing shared values.

Table 1.1: Challenges mapped across six typical stages of a project such as digital transformation (based on Zarifis & Cheng, 2024b).

Forming	Storming	Norming	Performing	Adjourning	Post-project
Risk, uncertainty, different priorities, different terminology, different cultures, technology adoption, limited trust.	Conflict		Less conflict	Conflict	–
Lack of loyalty and trust, safety concerns, unclear structure and leadership, and member dependencies.	Conflict		–	–	Unclear structure of new collaboration.
Limited trust in each other.		–	–	–	Limited trust in each other.
Ethical dilemmas.					
Different perspectives on participation and vision including differences in culture, norms, values justice and activism.			–	No new shared vision.	No new shared vision.
Conflict, no shared understanding, culture, values, organisational embeddedness and loyalty. Few or no permanent members.	Disengagement, bad communication, bad coordination, loss of process knowledge, no common place to record knowledge, uncertainty over value of work.		–	No expectation of continuing to work together.	No loyalty.
Geographic divides, social distance, technological challenges.					

1.2.2 The five stages of adopting innovations and what makes us accept a technology

The diffusion of innovation and the technology adoption model are two complementary theories that a leader should apply almost instinctively, like second nature. While they are simple and intuitive, they are a foundation for more sophisticated analyses and strategies. For example, in my research with the University of Cambridge on cryptoasset adoption in Latin America we found two main strategies, to pioneer and lead, or to wait until others have clarified the situation and then follow (Proskalovich et al., 2023). In that situation, the two extremes were considered to be the best choices, but this is not always the case.

Diffusion of innovation

The diffusion of innovation suggests that innovations typically go through five stages: innovators, early adopters, early majority, late majority, and laggards. Understanding who has it in their nature to want to innovate, and who will delay using a new innovation for as long as possible, can inform a leader's approach.

Technology adoption

The widely used technology adoption model is more focused on information technology, as opposed to any innovation in general (Venkatesh & Bala, 2008). It models the role psychology and sociology play in a person's decision to use a technology. The usual norm, usefulness, and ease of use are three of the important factors that typically play a role. This model can be adapted to fit a leader's particular situation. For example, when I was trying to understand how people buying insurance would feel about using an AI chatbot I combined this model with trust in AI (Zarifis et al., 2021). The leader does not necessarily have to collect and analyse data every time they want to use the logic of the technology adoption model to structure their thinking. Simply framing our thoughts with this model can be helpful sometimes.

Post adoption

While most adoption models go up to the point where someone starts to use a new technology such as AI, some issues are also very important after that. Firstly, it is important to appreciate the power of habits when using technology, how long they take to be created, and how hard they are to break. Successful repeated use of technology builds trust. Secondly, just because someone decided they trust a technology enough to use it, it does not mean that is the end of the story. Someone may use a technology without trusting it a hundred percent. This is particularly true with AI due to the opaqueness it often has and the unpredictability of its results. After a person trusts a technology enough to use it, they may still feel vulnerability in several ways. They may feel vulnerable in terms of their personal information privacy, in terms of their money being stolen, or not being credited for their work. A leader must have the sensitivity and empathy to appreciate the level of vulnerability for members of their team feel and build trust accordingly. For example, a new team member may need more support going through the same process as others.

Trust-building tip: Build trust by building social capital. Some followers will not have the psychologic predisposition to trust quickly but will do so when a critical mass is achieved.

Trust-building tip: Be clear about the normal behaviour expected, the usefulness, and ease of use of the technology, along with why it should be trusted. If the leader is clear about these things and prioritises them, it is more likely that the systems will be set up in a way that achieves a positive outcome.

Trust-building tip: Gauge the level of vulnerability people feel when using AI and take the steps necessary to reassure them and make them feel less vulnerable. The necessary steps may be limited to how the solution is communicated but may also require changes to the solution.

1.3 Traditional leadership approaches

Management is doing things right; leadership is doing the right things. — Peter F. Drucker, management book author

Leaders have successfully applied a variety of approaches, the most popular ones being autocratic and authoritarian, democratic, laissez-faire and delegative, bureaucratic, charismatic, and authentic. Some of the leadership styles that were dominant in the past are gradually falling out of favour. The main dynamic in leadership and management is moving away from the management principles of monitoring and control to the typical leadership principles of creating a shared vision and inspiring others. While this shift is inevitable and also beneficial in most situations, this is in no way the end of the traditional management approach. It is important to be clear that the traditional management approach, with an emphasis on control, still has its place. For example, I taught students online for a master's programme at the University of Liverpool who were working on oil rigs where the priority there is safety, so monitoring and ensuring the right processes are followed is greatly important. In that context, the motivation comes primarily from a very good wage and pension, so the managers do not have to prioritise motivating the employees in their day-to-day actions and can focus on monitoring and controlling.

It is therefore important for a leader to know the traditional management and leadership approaches. They may not be the ones a modern leader aspires to use, but context is always king, and they may be the ones they have to use. Furthermore, it is useful to be able to understand what kind of leaders other people are. What is the leadership style of the leader's line manager? Is the leadership approach chosen in line, complementary, or clashing with that of their superior? Experienced leaders can get a feel for the management style in an organisation within minutes of walking into the building. Some leadership styles are easier to identify than others: often, authoritarian, laissez-faire, and bureaucratic approaches are easier to identify; other traditional approaches such as democratic or charismatic can take little longer than a few minutes to identify but they still leave their distinctive mark on an organisation.

Another important point to make when looking at the variety of leadership approaches is that while we would like to believe we can choose from all of them the one we want to apply, our situation and our own personality and skills may limit our choices. The situation might force our hand, for example, if someone is in a highly regulated sector such as education, finance, or health, some bureaucratic leadership is probably inevitable. When we say our personality and skills may limit our options, this does not mean we must be born charismatic to apply that leadership approach, but it means we must be able to convey charisma when we do choose to apply it. Similarly, we must be sure we do indeed have a strong authority – not just on paper but in practice – before relying on an authoritarian or autocratic approach. The typical downfall of many inexperienced leaders is to believe they have, in reality, the power and authority they have theoretically due to their position. When they try to force their will over more experienced employees beneath them in the hierarchy, they quickly discover the real-life limitations of their theoretic authority. The autocratic approach combined with real power has been proven to be successful over the years, but there is less supporting evidence for the success of the leader going to war having overestimated their power.

Authenticity is essential, but you are not married to one leadership style all your life. If you are willing to change, you can authentically embody a different approach. It is a mistake to overestimate the importance of a person's character and underestimate the importance of their values. A quiet leader will make their point forcibly if it is something they truly value. If you decide you value something today, such as the personal development of your team or a democratic approach, you can represent this authentically. Similarly, you can stop having a value today that you had for a long time. For example, if you stop having the value that people perform better when they get the carrot then the stick, you can be authentic about not having that value that you used to have.

Trust-building tip: If you are not using the leadership style that is the norm for your team, you must make the case for it first and explain your approach. Predictable, consistent, and transparent leaders are trusted more.

1.4 Transactional leadership

Transactional leadership focuses on the tasks not the people. The transactional leader is clear that the necessary resources are in place to achieve the goal they will set, and they know what reward they want to give for achieving it. This form of leadership is very easy to understand in principle, but not always easy to implement. Unlike many leadership approaches that focus exclusively on the responsibilities of the follower, the transactional approach covers the responsibilities of both the follower and the leader. Many managers do not like this and prefer to permanently have the 'ask not what your country can do for you, but what you can do for your country' mindset and dynamic in the team. However, putting both sides of the transaction 'down on the table' can be the best way to be fair, transparent and trustworthy.

While people may aspire to more in their professional lives than the immediate reward they receive, not every role can deliver on broader goals such as making the world a better place, environmental sustainability or personal development. The obvious context is a short project or a part time role, where a person wants to be clear on what they are putting in, and what they are getting in return. In many situations a person does not care if their leader is charismatic, visionary, or authentic, they want to know what they are getting for their time and energy. This is one of the reasons why many believe an element of transactional leadership is necessary with many other leadership styles, such as transformational, or charismatic.

If someone is not inspired by the clinical transactional nature of this leadership approach, they should ask people that have been given many promises and visions by charming leaders that never delivered, if they would prefer a clear, transparent transaction. It is often a sign of maturity to appreciate clarity over inspiration. People tend to value broader abstract goals when they are younger and become more individualistic and specific in what they want as they get older. As the transactional approach has clear merit but it is not enough for everyone, at every part of their lives, it should be combined with more inspirational approaches.

From the leader's perspective, this approach is not always easy to apply, as they must be able to deliver on what is agreed, in the timeframe agreed. Furthermore, while the leader may also appreciate the clarity, the leader may also want more from their work. Therefore, it is also beneficial for the leader and their personal development to combine this approach with other more inspirational approaches.

Trust building tip: Transactional leadership, despite its simplicity, can be the most powerful in building trust due to the transparency it offers. When combined with other leadership styles the resulting approach should retain that transparency in what the follower should deliver and receive in return.

1.5 Servant leadership

A servant leader builds relationships, empowers their team, supports growth, and encourages ethics and contributing to the community. While the names of these leadership styles have been chosen carefully through a collective process involving many experts, and they are self-explanatory up to a point, the names on their own do not tell the whole story. One must not assume they understand a leadership style because they understand the meaning of the name. That is never truer than with servant leadership.

Servant leadership does not necessarily mean the leader does whatever the other team members want. The servant leader provides the team with what they need to be successful, but it is not necessarily a subservient role. Many strong leaders that have the authority to be autocratic choose to be servant leaders. This is often because the servant leader acknowledges that they do not have all the information and are not the expert on all aspects of the work being done. Furthermore, this approach can be very motivating and empowering. It is similar in some ways to delegating, but the leader is typically more involved in servant leadership. As with delegating, a servant leader often gets better satisfaction and more creativity from their team (Neubert et al., 2016). Another common benefit of this leadership approach is increased collaboration (Hunter et al., 2013).

The servant leader does not just listen to what their team needs, they also develop their emotional intelligence to understand what their team feels but may not be saying. For example, it is beneficial to understand how extrovert or agreeable team members are, as this can affect what they say, and what they believe but don't say. It can take longer sometimes to understand what an introvert believes. Similarly, someone that wants to be agreeable may hide their true beliefs and want to follow the norm in the group.

Of the many benefits of servant leadership, the most important – and the reason why it is beneficial when combined with other leadership styles – is that it is more focused on morality and ethics. Beyond the inherent value in doing the right thing, more morally focused leadership encourages this in others, creating a positive feedback loop. It is often found that organisations that fail had drifted away from moral behaviour and self-reflection at some point and this contributed to their downfall. While a focus on morality and ethics are not exclusive to the servant leadership approach, this approach has probably been the most effective at encouraging a team to have these values. As a servant leader is typically less narcissistic and is motivated less by personal achievement and more by collective success, this is reflected in the other individuals in the team.

Trust-building tip: Encouraging a degree of selflessness by helping others in the team and the wider community creates an environment where trust can flourish. Selfless people are less likely to intentionally harm someone, so the risk is reduced.

1.6 Transformational leadership

The transformational leader creates a clear vision and communicates it in an inspiring way. They can encourage creativity and disruption with their vision, but also with the time and attention they give to each follower. Their ideas for the future and their general behaviour draw people to them. This approach is similar to charismatic and visionary leadership. Transformational leadership has become very popular over the last twenty years because followers usually respond well to it (Keegan & Den Hartog, 2004). In the years ahead of us, it will be even more popular because the digital transformation process is a journey we will go through where we need to learn and change ourselves. There will be a transformation of leaders, followers, organisations, and society in general. If someone is reading this and is thinking that this is an exaggeration, they should look back at the dramatic journey people went thought in their personal and professional lives during the COVID-19 pandemic.

One common superficial caricature of a transformational leader is portraying them simply as someone that sells a vision. There are many managers that are excellent at selling a vision and making promises to get people to do things, knowing there is a strong chance their followers will not receive the rewards they were led to expect. This is not transformational leadership; this is a fraudster that destroys trust. I have come across many managers like this. They keep looking for new people to trick with their promises. They are like a cancer in an organisation. The transformational leader does not just promise transformation, they go through that transformation with their team and the other stakeholders, creating win-win opportunities.

A second superficial caricature of a transformational leader is portraying them simply as someone inherently charismatic and charming. While convincing people they should be willing to make changes, move out of their comfort zone, and challenge the norm can be made easier with charm and charisma, they are not the main method of achieving these ends. The biggest transformation we are going through is driven by AI and other technologies. This transformation and disruption challenges trust between people and between a person and technology. The transformational leader will therefore have the business acumen and the technical knowledge to identify the AI-focused business model their organisation should move towards (Zarifis & Cheng, 2023, 2024a, 2025).

Trust-building tip: In the age of digital transformation, we will all have to change our roles and what we value at work. Changing ourselves is hard, but having trust in each other when going through this journey will make it easier.

Trust-building tip: We must understand the technology we are using, how it uses data, and how it is applied in business. Case studies on its application are helpful in gaining insight on this. If the leader is in a position to answer questions on the application of a technology the followers will trust them.

1.7 Choosing the right leadership style and priorities at each stage of a project

The leadership styles discussed here all have some strengths when applied correctly, as is proven by their continuing popularity. There may be some we do not find attractive, but they may still have advantages in some situations. Similarly, the ones we instantly feel are a good fit still have weaknesses and are not a silver bullet or a panacea.

A leader must have a core of three leadership styles that are like their belief system, so they have some consistency and authenticity, as shown on Figure 1.1. A leader must build their personal leadership 'brand'. People refer to a leadership toolbox and being a situational leader that picks the right approach for each task. Being a situational leader may be interpreted as being completely agnostic with no personal perspective, entirely rationally picking different leadership styles. A leader must have their perspective based on the most effective leadership styles of today – transactional, servant, and transformational – and must be knowledgeable of the others to use them selectively to compensate for weaknesses in their core leadership styles.

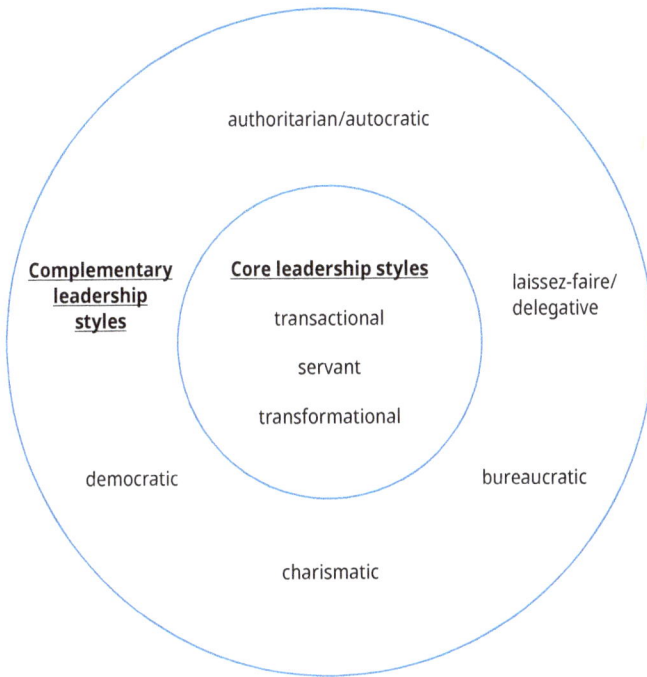

Figure 1.1: The three core leadership styles and the five complementary approaches.

When looking at the popular leadership approaches it is tempting to just pick and use one as it is simpler to learn and implement. However, no single approach focuses on the dimensions that will bring the best results. We need to dig down to the dimensions of the three strongest leadership styles and collect the best ones to focus on. Being a great leader is about knowing the leadership styles, the traits they focus on, the typical stages of a process, understanding their context including their team and competitors, choosing a suitable AI-centred business model, understanding how to build trust, and then deciding what to focus on at each stage. Figure 1.2 illustrates these steps. This might seem like a long, convoluted process, but like many things, once we go through the steps a few times it will start to come naturally, and quickly.

The process of identifying the right dimensions of leadership to focus on at each stage – by following the steps described – is not meant to replace a person's existing experiences and beliefs. This is a way to frame and structure a person's existing experiences and the new things they have learned so that the choices are made faster, and that the right choices are made more often. It will help us be a great leader but not a perfect leader. If there was ever a time when a leader could be perfect, it has long gone as the uncertainty today makes this impossible. Getting everything right over just one day can be challenging enough!

(1) Learn leadership styles, their traits, and the best ways to combine two leadership styles

↓

(2) Learn the typical stages of a project and other key processes such as the diffusion of innovation

↓

(3) Evaluate the context including the team, the competition, the new technologies

↓

(4) Choose a business model and a leadership style

↓

(5) Understand how to build trust with the chosen model and leadership style

↓

(6) Decide what to do at each stage, not doing too much or too little

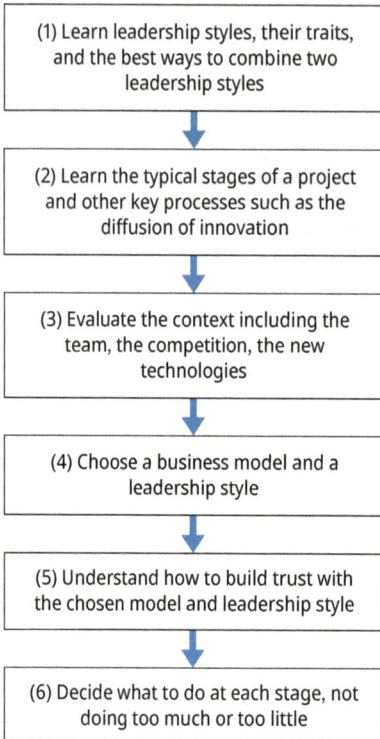

Figure 1.2: The six steps to being a great leader in the age of AI.

We have discussed the specific dimensions of the three leadership styles in detail already. Transactional leadership has three dimensions: a) contingent reward, meaning rewarding good behaviour; b) active management by exception meaning proactively assisting with challenges and solving problems; and c) passive management by exception, meaning intervening only when a problem emerges. For servant leadership these are empowering, encouraging growth, ethical and altruistic behaviour, empathy, authenticity, and integrity. For transformational leadership these are creating a shared vision and inspiring intellectual stimulation, individual consideration, and idealised influence, meaning being a trustworthy and respected role model.

All these dimensions are useful and worth being aware of, but it is impractical and counterproductive to try and apply all of them all of the time. If we focus on the wrong things at the wrong time, we will seem out of sync with the team and destroy trust. What most leaders do is consciously, or subconsciously, pick a subsection to focus on. Can we rely on our intelligence and instinct to always pick the right thing to rely on? Intelligence and instinct can certainly help, but we must structure them by knowing the typical stages, challenges, and things a leader should focus on at each stage.

So, for example, at the start of the project or other endeavour, traditional, transactional, servant, and transformational leadership have a specific role. The same applies to each stage. Table 1.2 illustrates what to focus on at each stage. Balancing the clarity of the short-term extrinsic motivation of transactional leadership with the longer-term intrinsic motivation of servant and transformational leadership is at the heart of good leadership.

Table 1.2: Leadership across the stages of a project such as digital transformation.

Pre-project	Forming	Storming	Norming	Adjourning	Post-project
Traditional leadership					
Decide on selection and goals with others, create buy-in with stakeholders (democratic).	Clarify the necessary processes (bureaucratic).	Give space for people to work, don't be overbearing. Avoid destroying trust with friction (laissez-faire).	Monitor and control (traditional management).	Punish bad behaviour and attitude. Build trust in the validity of the rules (authoritarian).	Continue to promote project achievements and team member performance (charismatic).
Transactional					
Understand requirements and plan project as far as possible.	Build trust with clear agreements.	Maintain trust by not changing agreements (either goals or rewards).	Intervene when problems arise.	Evaluate and share out rewards and punishment.	Find new rewards for new collaboration.
Servant					
Show care and empathy for society.	Show care and empathy for the challenges of starting a project (relocation etc.).	Understand needs of team members and provide what is needed.	Understand needs of team members and provide what is needed.	Show interest in team members' future plans.	Be available for references and anything else former team members need.
Transformational					
Build reputation of transformational leadership.	Build shared vision.	Inspire and motivate, linking actions to vision and trust.	Inspire and motivate, linking actions to vision and trust.	Inspire and motivate, linking actions to vision and trust.	Show that vision goes on beyond project and is genuine.

1.8 What a leader must know about generative AI and digital transformation

People and organisations constantly adopt technologies, but some are far more disruptive than others. Some technologies do not change organisations, or processes, or products and services, they just offer increased efficiency. Other technologies are disruptive with far-reaching consequences. Some of these are the mobile phone, cloud computing, the internet of things (IoT), and blockchain. They can change business models. However, generative AI is bringing a level of disruption that only the internet has brought before, in most people's lifetime. Generative AI, with the help of other technologies such as those mentioned, will change our personal and professional lives, organisations' business models, and whole industries. This will cause anxiety; uncertainty and trust will be challenged further. The leader's role is critical. The leader must be like the calm in the centre of the storm putting people at ease. There is a time to build emotional relationships and use emotion constructively, and there is a time to focus on the tasks that need to be done.

While AI sparks philosophical questions about humanity's role that make us think of servant leadership – and new visions of incredible new capabilities that make us think of transformational leadership – there is a place in this dynamic and exciting new world for the more pedestrian and pragmatic transactional leadership. As many have said, data is the new oil fuelling the economy. In the age of AI, many collaborations and ecosystems are needed to get data from others, and to offer data to them. These collaborations can be with 'friends' or 'enemies'. A leader will often have to turn clear 'enemies' into 'frenemies'. Frenemies still compete against us but are also collaborating for mutual benefit. It is clear that in this scenario what is needed is not to inspire, but to make a deal about a mutually beneficial transaction. As one of the pioneers of transactional leadership states, when applying this approach, there is no relationship between the two beyond the bargaining and the deal made (Burns, 1978). Therefore, the leader in the age of AI needs to have some deep emotionally engaged relationships powered by servant and transformational leadership, and others with no personal relationship beyond a well-crafted exchange of value, skilfully arranged with transactional leadership. They need transactional leadership to satisfy and encourage a follower's self-interest and servant and transformational approaches to encourage them to transcend self-interest.

Trust-building tip: Identify the best business model that is optimised to benefit from generative AI and be clear how your followers fit into this model. Guide them through the digital transformation with clarity and transparency.

Trust-building tip: If you need to make an agreement for one transaction of value, such as sharing data with a competitor so that the services of both organisations run more smoothly, the leadership style should be transactional, and trust is built by crafting a clear, transparent, fair, sustainable, and robust agreement. Emotional engagement can be out of place, seem insincere, and be counterproductive.

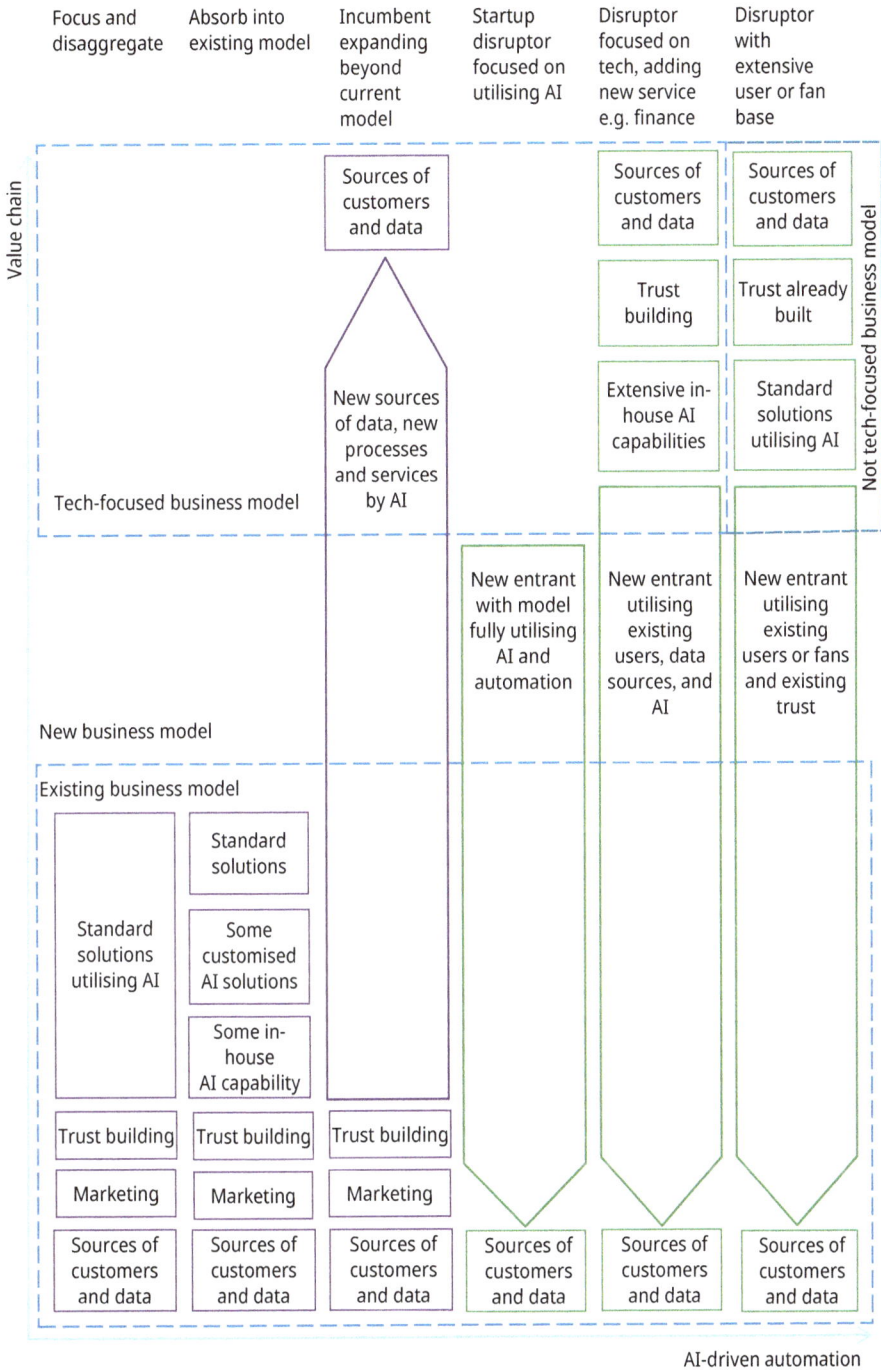

Figure 1.3: The six business models to utilise AI and build trust (based on Zarifis & Cheng, 2025).

Despite the uncertainty and the possibility of the environment changing dramatical, an organisation needs to have a clear model to aim for when going through digital transformation. Adopting AI is a strategic decision. Adding new technologies without having a clear model to aim for will make the organisation fall behind its competitors that have more clarity and utilise AI more effectively. The organisations that implements an AI-focused business model effectively will get some certainty from the model and gain an advantage over those that struggle to make the transition. The six business models proven to be ideal for an AI-centric world are (Zarifis & Cheng 2024a, 2025): (1) incumbent focusing on one part of the value chain and disaggregating, (2) incumbent absorbing AI into existing model, (3) incumbent expanding beyond current model to fully utilise the opportunities of AI and access new data, (4) startup disruptor focused on one sector, built from the start to be highly automated, (5) disruptor focused on tech adding a new service like insurance, and (6) disruptor that is not necessarily tech-focused with an extensive user or fanbase. This model is illustrated in figure 1.3.

1.9 AI leadership and trust leadership: The pillars of trust in AI

The transactional leadership style has a clear incentive structure that not only rewards good performance but also punishes unsatisfactory performance. The leader using this approach also ensures the follower has what they need to complete their tasks. The servant leader is empowering, encourages personal growth, is ethical, empathising, and authentic. It is not just AI that is important at this time, but also environmental sustainability, and the servant leader is aligned to that. A transformational leader creates a shared vision and inspires, offers intellectual stimulation, individual consideration, and idealised influence as a role model. The effective transformational leader makes people want to go above and beyond their tasks but does not mislead them to achieve this.

At this time of uncertainty, a leader that will try to avoid responsibility and do the minimum to get by will fail under the weight of the challenge. They will lose the followers' trust in their drive to genuinely lead. Similarly, an egotistical leader that focuses on promoting themselves and being liked will fail. They will lose the trust in them caring about their followers' future during the great changes we face.

The leader that succeeds will 'stand up to be counted', they will understand how AI is changing businesses fundamentally and how to build trust. They will know when to use transactional, servant, and transformational leadership, and when to use the traditional leadership approaches. They will embody and promote ethics, environmental sustainability, authenticity and empathy, but also determination and grit. They will still listen to their instinct but not act impulsively, instead analysing the situation and their role in a structured way. In conclusion, to lead people today you must lead in AI, and to lead in AI you must lead in trust between people, and between people and technology.

The pillars of trust in AI: Many academics, technology providers, business consultants, and others have identified certain ways to build trust. There is a degree of agreement with some common pillars, but there are also some different opinions and different priorities. Here we take the leaders perspective, not, for example, that of a software engineer. A model from Tata Consultancy Services is adapted for this purpose (Kalele & Subbiah, 2024). A leader should look at these pillars of trust and how they affect them positively in their role. A good leader can know how they should impact these pillars. A software engineer, for example, will see these pillars differently and think about how they can affect them positively from their role. To some degree there is a difference in how you can affect these pillars if you are an entry level manager, middle manager, or on the board of directors where you need to focus more on governance and understanding the risks of AI (Zarifis & Yarovaya, 2025). Trust needs to be built in the AI solutions being implemented. After they are implemented, to maintain trust the AI solutions need to be monitored, whether they are in-house or third-party apps or services.

Trust in an AI business model needs the leader to convey some things, and the AI solution to meet some expectations. The leader must illustrate an up-to-date understanding of AI, choose the right business model to utilise AI, show each stakeholder the benefit to them, and build trust across all operations and stakeholders. In terms of the AI implementation, it needs to have the expected performance, robustness, explainability and reproducibility, transparency, fairness, privacy, security, and sustainability. The two pillars of trust are illustrated in Figure 1.4.

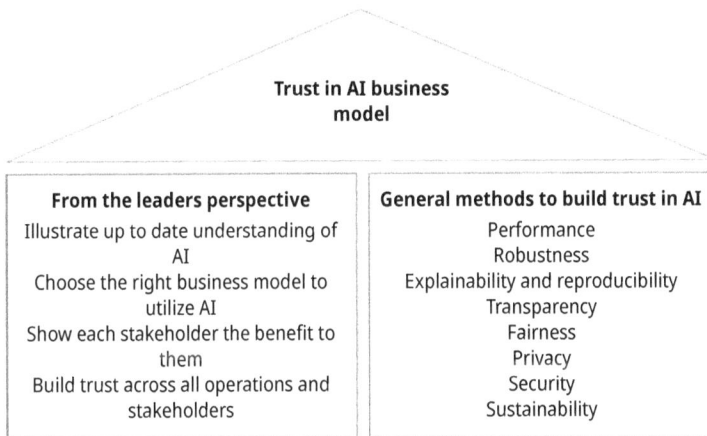

Trust in AI business model

From the leaders perspective	General methods to build trust in AI
Illustrate up to date understanding of AI	Performance
Choose the right business model to utilize AI	Robustness
Show each stakeholder the benefit to them	Explainability and reproducibility
Build trust across all operations and stakeholders	Transparency
	Fairness
	Privacy
	Security
	Sustainability

Figure 1.4: The leader's pillars to building trust in AI.

1.10 Summary

Wise men put their trust in ideas and not in circumstances. — Ralph Waldo Emerson, philosopher

1.10.1 The enduring value of the transactional, servant, and transformational leadership approaches

Digital transformation with AI and trust are vast topics, and choosing the right leadership approach is also quite a large and tricky topic. There is no way to completely avoid this complexity, and there isn't one leadership approach and AI-focused business model that will fit every situation. Even after a business model and leadership approach is identified, each stage of a project has different priorities. However, here the choice of leadership styles to consider is narrowed down to three, and the AI-focused business models are narrowed down to six. Furthermore, the process of going through digital transformation is separated into six distinct steps with different priorities. A combination of styles, and a combination of models, may be needed, but nevertheless what is offered here is at least a starting point for the leader.

While some think the new world with AI at its centre should lead to a deskilling of leaders or even their replacement with AI, here we argue that the role of the leader is elevated. However, at the same time, the leader needs to be very knowledgeable on leadership styles and AI business models to be successful in this elevated role. It is not just about moving quickly with technology. The vast graveyard of companies that failed over the last few years does not just include those that moved too slowly, but also many that moved too fast.

This book recommends using transactional leadership in combination with either servant or transformational leadership. While a leader can take lessons from all three approaches, the best balance for the current environment is transactional with servant, or transactional with transformational. Servant and transformational leadership approaches are very effective in motivating and inspiring people, but they are challenging to implement and do not necessarily fit every situation. Transactional leadership is usually practical and relatively easy to implement but it lacks the motivation and the overarching vision the servant and transformational approaches offer. For situations with low uncertainty, transactional leadership is easier to implement, less time consuming, and more effective, but for situations with high uncertainty, servant and transformational approaches often work better. What is considered high uncertainty is to some degree subjective and down to the leader's judgement. If an organisation knows what business model they want to move towards and they have everything they need to get there, a leader may decide this is a moderate or low level of uncertainty.

If the most suitable approach to lead towards an organisation with AI at its centre is transactional with either servant or transformational leadership, how can we choose which of the two to use? There is a short and a long answer to this. The short answer is that if the leader has identified the AI-focused business model to aim for and believes that if they convince their team of its value their team can get them there, then the transformational leadership approach should be the one added to the transactional approach. If the leader knows that the organisation should utilise AI more but they are not clear on what the best approach is, and they believe a lot of the insight on strategic and tactical issues can come from several specialised experts inside the organisation, then the servant approach should be combined with the transactional approach. This is the short answer – the longer answer involves understanding the three modern and five main traditional leadership approaches thoroughly, their implications for AI adoption and trust in AI, and knowing when to use them.

A transactional leader focuses on the tasks and the exchange of value. We have seen structure-centric approaches such as bureaucratic leadership, and follower-centric approaches such as servant leadership. Transactional leadership is not like either of these as it is transaction-focused. As it is not a people-centric approach, education and personal development are not the priority.

A servant leader is not subservient but supportive. The difference to more authoritarian styles is not necessarily in the leader's position in the hierarchy or degree of authority. A servant leader can have absolute authority like in the other approaches. The difference is that the servant leader believes it is more effective to support, remove obstacles, and give their followers some autonomy in what they do. This is not just about being ethical and kind, but it is also about having an approach that can achieve sustainable results and avoid employee burnout.

For a transformational leader, the inspiration should come primarily from the long-term plan for change and the new business model selected. To create a modern organisation that fully utilises technology, an AI-focused business model should be identified (Zarifis & Cheng 2023, 2025). There are few things in life more intellectually stimulating and inspiring than planning and implementing a dramatically different future. The synergies between the priorities of this approach are what make it so powerful. For all this to work successfully, a transformational leader needs to be able to easily connect with people on an emotional level.

The combination of transactional with either servant or transformational leadership combines practical short-term goals with being emotionally engaged and inspiring. Transformational and servant leadership approaches prioritise this emotional engagement, and not keeping some distance like many traditional approaches prefer. It may not be a coincidence that the two most popular styles, from the follower's perspective, prioritise emotionally engaged leaders.

1.10.2 Transactional, servant, and transformational leadership are the best for AI and trust

Most leadership styles do not prioritise building trust in several ways, and only have a few methods to achieve it. An example is transactional leadership where delivering an agreed reward is the primary way of building trust. For servant and transformational leadership, the whole approach builds trust. These two approaches build trust in multiple synergistic ways and create a more holistic trust in all directions. People trust the leader, the plan, and themselves. When the leader and the plan are in the direction of using AI more, there is trust transference to AI. It is easier to have trust transference if there is a lot of trust to begin with.

The focus on clear goals of transactional leadership makes implementing digital transformation with AI as straightforward as possible. With clear performance measures and performance-based rewards, productivity can be kept at a high level. Having the core operations of an organisation running at a good level offers the platform to try new things and innovate. The modern leader must lead autonomous AI agents collaborating in teams with humans. Transactional leadership is very valuable because it can be applied to mixed teams as it is effective for both humans and autonomous AI agents. The servant leader ensures the effective allocation of resources to digital transformation and AI. Moving to an organisation with AI at its centre is a lot more about allocating resources effectively than being creative and inventive. Servant leadership is a good fit for managing resources as stewardship of resources is central to this approach. So while it is not a very centralised top-down approach, servant leaders don't just care about the people but also the resources. This style has synergies by driving change in the organisation and in the people themselves. In addition to creating a conducive team dynamic, this approach puts individuals in the right mindset to get the most out of AI.

Transformational leadership supports digital transformation with AI in two ways: firstly, they select an AI-focused business model and build consensus around it, encouraging change; secondly, by creating a resilient team, they are better prepared for the far-reaching implications of digital transformation. Strong collaboration with the various stakeholders can implement the change efficiently. Digital transformation has many challenges, and they are not just technical. If the team lose their sense of purpose, this will be a very difficult challenge to overcome. A beneficial consequence of the more people-centric transformational and servant leadership approaches is that they compensate for the loss of humanness due to the use of AI.

1.10.3 Choosing the right business model and the priorities at each stage of a project

The modern leader must identify the most suitable AI-focused business model and then keep the team focused on moving towards that model despite the uncertainty and challenges. For each of the typical stages of a digital transformation project, the leader can resolve or even pre-empt the typical challenges. If the leader can keep the team's confidence in the new model, they can turn the uncertainties they come across into opportunities. The organisation that implements an AI-focused business model effectively will get some certainty from the model and gain an advantage over those that struggle to make the transition.

The six business models proven to be ideal for an AI-centric world are (Zarifis and Cheng 2023, 2025): (1) incumbent focusing on one part of the value chain and dis-aggregating, (2) incumbent absorbing AI into existing model, (3) incumbent expanding beyond current model to fully utilise the opportunities of AI and access new data, (4) startup disruptor focused on one sector, built from the start to be highly automated, (5) disruptor focused on tech adding a new service like insurance, and (6) disruptor that is not necessarily tech-focused with an extensive user or fanbase.

Key concept: The transactional leadership approach should be combined with either servant or transformational leadership. Transactional leadership is usually practical and relatively easy to implement but it lacks the motivation and overarching vision the servant and transformational approaches offer. Servant and transformational leadership approaches are very effective in motivating and inspiring people, but they are challenging to implement and do not necessarily fit every situation.

Leadership tip: If a leader has identified the AI-focused business model they want to move towards (Zarifis & Cheng 2023, 2025), then transactional with transformational styles are the ideal approach. If a leader cannot identify the most suitable new business model to aim for because there is too much uncertainty inside and outside of the organisation, then the transactional and servant approaches may be the most suitable.

Trust-building tip: A transactional leader builds trust with reliable short-term rewards. A servant or transformational leader builds strong resilient trust with its ethical, caring, individualised, and human approach. By combining the transactional approach with either servant or transformational leadership, the leader builds resilient and sustainable trust in a variety of ways.

1.11 Exercises

Exercise 1.1

Scenario: You work for a traditional bank that still has some physical branches but wants to focus more on their online services. They are seeing online-only banks offering a very appealing bundle of services and gifts, including airport lounge access and gym memberships, along with a higher interest rate. The leadership of your bank believe that one of the reasons the online-only banks are achieving this is that they use AI and data more effectively.

Some people argue that the biggest competitive advantage in an AI-centred world is not from having the most advanced AI software and hardware but from having the best access to historical and real-time data. They want you to investigate online-only banks and give them a report on what can be learned from their business model.

Questions

1) Identify how online banks are using data to offer an impressive bundle of services and gifts for the savings account they offer. How can they offer a bundle of services and gifts that costs so much it should make them lose money with every client?

2) Are online-only banks only utilising data to offer more competitive services or are they finding additional ways to monetise their data? Are they also finding new ways to monetise their clients?

3) Is the fundamental difference between a typical traditional bank and the online-only banks that the former still have some branches, or do the differences in the business models go deeper?

Exercise 1.2

The six business models proven to be ideal for an AI centric world are (Zarifis & Cheng 2023, 2025): (1) incumbent focusing on one part of the value chain and disaggregating, (2) incumbent absorbing AI into existing model, (3) incumbent expanding beyond current model to fully utilise the opportunities of AI and access new data, (4) startup disruptor focused on one sector, built from the start to be highly automated, (5) disruptor focused on tech adding a new service like insurance, and (6) disruptor that is not necessarily tech-focused with an extensive user or fanbase.

Elon Musk has had a long career creating and purchasing many organisations. If we focus on the period of his career when his main interests were Tesla and SpaceX, but he also spent a lot of time and money buying and selling Bitcoin and other cryptocurrencies including meme coins, try to answer the following questions.

Questions

1) A leader of a technology company investing heavily in cryptocurrencies is an unusual move, although several other companies such as MicroStrategy have done the same. Do you believe moving into cryptocurrencies is a change in the business model? If so, what are the advantages of this approach? Which of the six technology-focused business models is closest to this move by Elon Musk?

2) It has been argued that if a company holds reserves of cryptocurrencies it stops people short selling that stock (Asgari, 2025). Why do you think short sellers fear companies that hold cryptocurrencies?

3) Some people believe Elon Musk is a transformational leader. Do you agree? Do you think he should adapt his leadership style in some way?

Space for your notes

References

Asgari, N. (2025). The MicroStrategy copycats: Companies turn to bitcoin to boost share price. *Financial Times*. https://www.ft.com/content/f964fe30-cb6e-427d-b7a7-9adf2ab8a457Burns, J. M. (1978). *Leadership*. Open Road.

Cheng X., Macaulay L. & Zarifis A. (2013). Modelling individual trust development in computer mediated collaboration: A comparison of approaches, *Computers in Human Behavior*, 29(4), 1733-1741. https://doi.org/10.1016/j.chb.2013.02.018

Hunter, E. M., Neubert, M. J., Perry, S. J., Witt, L. A., Penney, L. M., & Weinberger, E. (2013). Servant leaders inspire servant followers: Antecedents and outcomes for employees and the organization. *The Leadership Quarterly*, 24(2), 316–331. https://doi.org/10.1016/j.leaqua.2012.12.001

Kalele, A., & Subbiah, R. (2024). *Operationalizing AI: A game of trust and ethics*. Tata Consultancy Services. https://www.tcs.com/what-we-do/pace-innovation/white-paper/building-trustworthy-ai-five-pillars

Keegan, A. E., & Den Hartog, D. N. (2004). Transformational leadership in a project-based environment: A comparative study of the leadership styles of project managers and line managers. *International Journal of Project Management*, 22(8), 609–617. https://doi.org/10.1016/j.ijproman.2004.05.005

Neubert, M. J., Hunter, E. M., & Tolentino, R. C. (2016). A servant leader and their stakeholders: When does organizational structure enhance a leader's influence? *Leadership Quarterly*, 27(6), 896–910. https://doi.org/10.1016/j.leaqua.2016.05.005

Project Management Institute, (2013). *A Guide to the Project Management Body of Knowledge (PMBOK Guide)*. Newtown Square, PA: Project Management Institute, Inc. https://doi.org/10.1002/pmj.21345

Proskalovich R., Jack C., Zarifis A., Serralde D.M., Vershinina P., Naidoo S., Njoki D., Pernice I., Herrera D. & Sarmiento J. (2023). Cryptoasset ecosystem in Latin America and the Caribbean, University of Cambridge – *Cambridge Centre for Alternative Finance (CCAF)*. https://www.jbs.cam.ac.uk/faculty-research/centres/alternative-finance/publications/crypotasset-ecosystem-in-latin-america-and-the-caribbean/

Tuckman, B. W., & Jensen, M. A. C. (2010). Stages of small-group development Revisited. *Group Facilitation*, (10), 43–48.

Venkatesh, V. and Bala, H. (2008). Technology Acceptance Model 3 and a Research Agenda on Interventions. *Decision Sciences*, 39, 273–315. https://doi.org/10.1111/j.1540-5915.2008.00192.x

Zarifis A., Kawalek P. & Azadegan A. (2021). Evaluating if trust and personal information privacy concerns are barriers to using health insurance that explicitly utilizes AI, *Journal of Internet Commerce*, 20, 66–83. https://doi.org/10.1080/15332861.2020.1832817

Zarifis, A., & Cheng, X. (2023). AI is transforming insurance with five emerging business models. *Encyclopedia of Data Science and Machine Learning* (pp. 2086–2100). IGI Global. https://doi.org/10.4018/978-1-7998-9220-5.ch124

Zarifis, A., & Cheng, X. (2024a). The five emerging business models of Fintech for AI adoption, growth, and building trust. In A. Zarifis, D. Ktoridou, L. Efthymiou, & X. Cheng (Eds.), *Business digital transformation: Selected cases from industry leaders* (pp. 73–97). Palgrave Macmillan. https://doi.org/10.1007/978-3-031-33665-2_4

Zarifis A., & Cheng, X. (2024b). A model reducing researchers' challenges in projects: Build trust first for better mental health. *Cogent Business & Management*, 11(1), 1–13. https://doi.org/10.1080/23311975.2024.2350786

Zarifis A., & Cheng, X. (2025). The new centralised and decentralised Fintech technologies, and business models, transforming finance. In A. Zarifis & X. Cheng (Eds.), *Fintech and the Emerging Ecosystems: Exploring Centralised and Decentralised Financial Technologies*. Springer Nature. https://link.springer.com/book/9783031834011

Zarifis A. & Yarovaya L. (2025). How leadership in financial organisations build trust in AI: Lessons from boards of directors in Fintech in Malaysia', In Zarifis A. & Cheng X. (eds.), *FinTech and the Emerging Ecosystems – Exploring Centralised and Decentralised Financial Technologies*, Springer Nature: Cham. https://link.springer.com/book/9783031834011

Chapter 2
The six stages of a project with AI and their implications for leadership and building trust

2.1 Introduction

Remember teamwork begins by building trust. And the only way to do that is to overcome our need for invulnerability. — Patrick Lencioni, author of *The Five Dysfunctions of a Team: A Leadership Fable*

A small number of leaders instinctively build trust with people with their behaviour, either because they have very good judgement, empathy, or some other method. Most of us need to create a trust-building mindset. With the increasing role of AI however, probably for the first time in human history, even those incredibly gifted and talented in building trust in people will have to learn how to do that with technology. Talking about leadership and building trust, without talking about technology and AI in particular, is no longer the best way to move forward.

In recent years, many started to believe that, in most cases, a manager should act as a leader. In a similar way, being a manager or a leader is increasingly becoming about change management and project management. This chapter mainly looks at the stages of a typical project and links them to the common thread throughout this book of choosing a business model to utilise technology better and fully utilise AI. While each project can be different, over thousands of projects, certain typical challenges have been identified for each stage.

Just as a footballer practices for certain typical scenarios, such as taking a penalty, a leader must build their knowledge and be prepared for the typical scenarios they will probably face at each stage. Like a footballer, but also a sailor, or a chess player, they must also get into a position that will be beneficial in the subsequent steps. Several lists of challenges have been compiled over the years, but the ones here are up to date and take into account the technologies such as AI and blockchain. These technologies are disrupting the role of the leader along with many other things. AI is making trust both more important and trickier to achieve. It is becoming more widely accepted that trust is important. An example is the many organisations using some version of a 'trust index' as an indication of the overall positive environment between staff (Aguiar et al., 2022).

This chapter will benefit a leader if they read it in its entirety before moving to the next chapter, but it can also be helpful to refer back to a specific section in the future to keep the concepts fresh in the mind. For example, if a leader is starting a new project with AI they can refer to the first stage – the forming stage. For each stage of a project there is a helpful summary of the key trust-building methods.

https://doi.org/10.1515/9783111630137-002

Of course, a leader can gain experience over years and develop their ability to have the right approach to certain typical opportunities and challenges. However, combining experience with reading about the typical context and journeys a project goes through can turbocharge the learning. A leader that has broad horizons and is constantly comparing different leadership styles, different applications of technologies, different business models (Zarifis & Cheng, 2025), and different contexts will be much stronger.

While there is no simple solution that fits every situation, there is a lot of science behind the popular leadership styles and how they should be adapted. A leader should not feel overwhelmed by the complexity of the modern globalised world, with constant quick innovation. If a leader feels overwhelmed and loses their confidence, or reacts impulsively without a strong plan, then they are truly in dire straits (danger, not the band). Relying on what is proven to work and adapting it to a given context should be beneficial. Some books on leadership or project management will repeatedly tell you that you must create a shared vision and that you do not have to be an expert on the topic to be a leader. This line of thought has some truth in it, in the sense that you cannot know everything related to an organisation. However, a true leader must work hard to understand what they are looking at and build the shared vision, at least partly, with their judgement and insight. We must understand how AI changes our sector, our competitors, and our organisation. That is why traditional leadership issues such as the stages of a project are combined with traditional technology adoption issues here. When Angela Merkel was chancellor of Germany and she had to make a decision on how Germany would move forward with nuclear energy, she did not just follow her advisors, but read about nuclear energy as a technology. She raised her understanding of the technology so she could have meaningful discussions with the experts. Because of the process she took, when she made a decision most citizens bought into her vision. That is the proper way for a leader to move forward.

Leadership tip: A leader should recognise the complexity and accept it. If someone gives a simple answer to the question of how to be a good leader, this will unfortunately be untrue.

Leadership tip: A leader should spend time to understand AI as a technology so its strategic potential becomes clear.

The challenges a leader faces come from many different sources. Some are inevitable, such as human nature, but many challenges come from the misguided strategies of organisations. While a leader may not be senior enough to change a damaging strategy, such as giving short contracts or open offices without allocated desks, they need to recognise how these strategies are flawed and the distrust they create. They need to think about how, and at which stage of the project, bad organisational strategies will have an effect so they are not caught off guard. It is unfortunately human nature that there will always be some managers with large egos that want to push unfairness through and prefer to bully people rather than build trust and win together.

Inconvenient truth: Short contracts = distrust.

Inconvenient truth: Open offices without allocated desks = distrust.

Inconvenient truth: Favouritism and not sharing resources fairly = distrust.

2.1.1 A leader stops the typical problems from happening, they don't firefight

The limited bandwidth of a leader must be utilised on the most important things and to try to pre-empt problems, not be reactionary. When we are talking about integrating technology into a business, pre-empting problems means understanding how innovations diffuse, how technology is adopted, understanding where your organisation is now in terms of their business model, and then deciding what to do. Key issues in the diffusion of innovation are to understand how this process happens and the different stages it goes through. This informs many leadership decisions, such as evaluating whether an innovation will reach a wider audience.

In a famous case in sports, the coach of the New England Patriots was fined for learning opponents' strategies – 'plays' as they call them in American football. Knowing the opponents' strategies did not mean his team knew exactly what an opponent would do, but it may have meant they had some idea of what was most likely, meaning they could focus their limited resources. The obvious benefit is having a better chance of blocking the opponent's attack, but equally importantly, it means they can get themselves into a good position for their counterattack. The leaders that have the luxury to work in dominant companies that shape their industry often have this, but for the majority of leaders that don't work in these dominant companies, they need to use their knowledge and judgement. We cannot predict the future, but a leader that understands their business model, the stages of a project, and how innovation and technology tend to pick up, should be able to identify a small number of likely scenarios.

Leadership tip: Identify a small number of scenarios of what will happen in the future, ideally up to three. Either choose one to focus on or 'hedge your bets' across two or three. Moving forward with AI needs to have a clear plan.

2.1.2 What are your strengths and weaknesses as a person and a leader?

We need to acknowledge what kind of person we are. Some of us have many interpersonal skills, such as interpersonal communication skills, but have limited analytic ability, while for others it is the opposite. We don't have to change our character, but working on our weaknesses will make us a more well-rounded person. If we can have great insight but struggle to make colleagues engage, we should develop some strategies, some typical phrases, to engage people. If our instinct is to dominate a discussion, we can discipline ourselves to give people more time and encourage others to share. One way to judge where we need to improve is to look at our colleagues and think about what they may do better than us. We can resolve our weaknesses in our own way. I know a very talented programmer that used to be socially awkward, aloof, and not able to read people well. He now uses some standard small talk and appears to be very charming, warm, and engaging. He solved the problem in his own way; it is like he created a computer program of how to interact socially.

By looking at the stages here and understanding how to build trust, the idea is that the leader gradually embodies these theories and does not have to consciously think about them as much. These things come with experience if someone makes the effort and their mind is truly awake, analysing situations and learning the lessons. Plenty of managers are in roles for years and they are terrible. In fact, there is a type of manager that gets some kind of perverse satisfaction from getting as many things wrong as possible and getting away with it.

We cannot be a Machiavellian, cunning, scheming, and unscrupulous 'leader' and build sustainable trust. A trustworthy leader's brain works as hard as that of a Machiavellian 'leader' but they have a sustainable win-win mentality, not a smash-and-grab and desperate for an ego boost mentality. As we reflect on the role of the leader across the six typical stages, it is worth thinking about whether a leader can keep tricking colleagues time and time again. However self-confident or even arrogant they are, at some point they will fail. They should also think about what kind of colleagues they will end up having around them if they try to be Machiavellian. 'Soft power' based on good values brings the best talent together.

Key concept: Reflect and try to learn the lessons from each situation. Avoid just blaming others to get off the hook. Even if something was not your fault we can still learn how to avoid it happening again in the future.

The rest of this chapter is as follows. First, we will briefly introduce how AI can support the leadership process and support trust. Then we will go into the six stages of a project in some detail. We will look at the typical challenges at each stage, and how to build trust in people and AI. The theories presented in the rest of this chapter will help the leader frame the situation they are in and make a decision, regardless of what leadership approach they choose.

2.2 How AI can support the leadership process and support trust

Nobody phrases it this way, but I think that artificial intelligence is almost a humanities discipline. It's really an attempt to understand human intelligence and human cognition. — Sebastian Thrun, CEO of Kitty Hawk Corporation

Building trust in AI is often a challenge, but there are also ways in which AI can support a leader and their team when going through a project or managing an organisation's regular operations. There is a period of AI adoption that is focusing on automation and replacing humans that fits in with what many refer to as Industry 4.0. This approach has some negative side effects and the updated Industry 5.0, as put forward by the European Union, is far more appealing. Industry 5.0 emphasises human-centric AI, resilience, sustainability, and ethics. To achieve this, many people will need training to gain the skills to be at the centre of an AI-intensive organisation. While the Industry 4.0 approach is very appealing to senior management, as it is a clear path for them to meet their typical targets, 5.0 should be also attractive to more junior staff. If a leader can illustrate the wider benefits of AI to society and the things most of us care about, this is also beneficial for the organisation.

The use of AI in projects in a human-centric approach will take over many administrative tasks from a leader. The leader will still be in control, but their business acumen, judgement, strategic thinking, and soft skills will become a bigger part of their role. However, this use of AI will only work in situations where the data exists. For example, oil companies have sufficient data to take a data-driven approach to their projects. They can calculate when it is the right time to start drilling at a particular location. Many tasks a leader has to complete will not have sufficient data and they will have to use a more ad hoc approach.

In addition to specialised management virtual assistants, AI can support a project in several ways. It can remove bias from the decision-making process. AI can also monitor progress, anticipating problems coming from less expected sources such as the weather and political uncertainty. This can enable a more proactive approach. Automated reporting can support meeting compliance requirements that often change. Digital twins of the business can be created to test out different scenarios. Digital twins have been used in engineering for many years to predict when parts of a system will fail, but AI makes digital twins very powerful for business also. A leader can use digital twins that cover many different aspects of the business and its environment, including regulation, the economy, and competitors. These simulations can provide the likelihood of certain events, such as the share price going down after a merger, but they can also identify unexpected relationships that a human would not be able to identify.

Fully utilising these capabilities takes time, but it should be worth it in the long run. Typically, being an early adopter of these technologies may end up being a waste of time as they often fail. If an AI tool is relatively mature and widely used, then it is probably worth utilising.

As is often the case, these capabilities of AI make achieving goals easier, but the reduced human involvement in some things, and the increased speed of change, bring risks with them. The metaphor of a plane on autopilot is often used. While the autopilot is mostly beneficial, it might mean the pilot gets distracted, loses situational awareness, and makes mistakes when they are called upon.

While on the one hand AI can take many administrative roles from the leader, freeing them up to focus on engaging with the stakeholders on a personal level, we have to accept that we also have to master the technology and lead with technology. While we want to be human-centric as far as possible, the teams of the future will increasingly involve 'teams' of humans and machines with a degree of autonomy and independent thought. Autonomous AI agents are being used increasingly in teams with humans. Leaders with an engineering or computer science background have often been excellent in these situations, and we need to become more like them.

Key concept: We should aspire for human-centric AI applications while at the same time being realistic and accepting that the growing role of AI may have some negative consequences for people inside and outside of the organisation.

Leadership tip: A modern leader must master the AI tools that can support their role.

2.3 The six stages of a project, their challenges, and how to build trust in people and AI

Age appears to be best in four things; old wood best to burn, old wine to drink, old friends to trust, and old authors to read. — Francis Bacon, English philosopher

As discussed, the project manager should have the framework of six stages in a project. While it is tempting to think that we do not need a structured approach and we can just see how things go, this is not a good idea as the complexity of the situation can become overwhelming without a structure. While the guidance here is for leaders and not limited to project managers, it is useful to mention that project managers in tech companies typically manage five projects concurrently. Being smart and being a 'people person' might not be enough to manage five concurrent projects. Structuring our thoughts and having a 'game plan' helps.

The best version of the project stages for a leader of people and AI is one with six stages that includes the typical five first stages (forming, storming, norming, performing, and adjourning) but adds a sixth stage of post-project collaboration. The 'end' of a project is not a complete end of the relationships but a transition into a different relationship of more informal, occasional, and intermittent collaboration. Research published in reputable journals (Zarifis & Cheng, 2024) and newspapers such as *Times Higher Education* (Zarifis, 2024) has identified the typical challenges to trust at each stage, as shown in Table 2.1.

It is important to focus on different priorities at different stages of the project. There are some typical stages, but not all projects face the same challenges at the same point. While the six stages discussed here are typical, a project may in effect have three or four. For example, if a project team comes together and it includes experienced professionals that have worked together, the early stage may be very com-

Table 2.1: Challenges to trust mapped across the stages of a project (based on Zarifis & Cheng, 2024).

Forming	Storming	Norming	Performing	Adjourning	Post-project
Risk, uncertainty, different priorities, different terminology, different cultures, technology adoption, limited trust.		Conflict	Less conflict	Conflict	-
Lack of loyalty and trust, safety concerns, unclear structure and leadership, and member dependencies.	Conflict		-	-	Unclear structure of new collaboration.
Limited trust in each other.		-	-	-	Limited trust in each other.
Ethical dilemmas.					
Different perspectives on participation and vision including differences in culture, norms, values justice and activism.			-	No new shared vision.	No new shared vision.
Conflict, no shared understanding, culture, values, organisational embeddedness and loyalty. Few or no permanent members.	Disengagement, bad communication, bad coordination, loss of process knowledge, no common place to record knowledge, uncertainty over value of work.		-	No expectation of continuing to work together.	No loyalty.
Geographic divides, social distance, technological challenges.					

pressed, or not really exist anymore, and the team jumps into the performing stage (the green line in Figure 2.1). Alternatively, if a team struggles to build strong professional relationships and trust, they may be, in effect, limited to the three stages forming, storming, and adjourning (the red line). The five first stages have a more typical proven pattern, while the sixth has more variation and is less predictable.

We usually achieve things through teams. While we often work with a similar group of colleagues, some new teammates, a new situation, a change in a person's behaviour, and many other reasons can create a new dynamic in a team. It is not just technology that keeps evolving but people do also. We may think we know what to expect from a colleague we worked with before, but something such as pressure from outside work or health issues may change their behaviour. Therefore, it is good for a leader to have the mindset of the project stages even when working with colleagues they have worked with before.

There are many different opinions on every aspect of management and leadership but there is an awful lot of agreement behind the five stages developed by Tuckman (1965). This is important because in business when we successfully frame something, it does not just help an individual's thought process, but it becomes a shared language that aids effective communication and everyone being on the same page. A classic example is the BCG Matrix, the business planning tool that divides an organisation's products and services into question marks, stars, dogs, and cash cows. When a manager says this service is a cash cow for us, everyone that has had some business education, either formal or reading books in their spare time, should know what they mean.

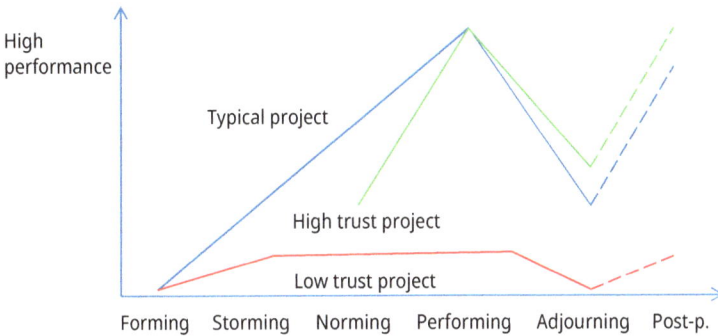

Figure 2.1: The performance trajectories of a typical, high- and low-trust projects.

What a leader does at each stage of a project depends heavily on what leadership style they select. This point was made in the first chapter also. If we take the extremes to illustrate the point, an authoritarian leader will behave differently to a servant leader at the forming stage of the project. Here we have the most typical things a leader would do at each stage. Once we look at the leadership styles in the subsequent chapters, we will be able to form our approach in more detail.

2.3.1 Stage 1: Forming a team with trust

If we look at what researchers or experienced managers say about the start of a project, we see that it is very critical to set things up well at the start. This will increase the chances of achieving high performance and successfully meeting targets. It is equally critical for trust building. We have to handle the challenges to trust the first stage has – and there are many – but we also have to pre-empt future challenges to trust. While one of the points being made here is that there are challenges to trust across all stages of a project, there is no doubt the first stage is the most critical in this regard.

We spoke about some typical ways distrust is built, such as favouritism from senior management. The leader cannot assume they are starting either with some trust 'in the bank', or distrust already weighing them down. While most professionals will go into a new collaboration with positivity and give the leader, their teammates, and other stakeholders the benefit of the doubt for a period of time, there are many different dynamics at play.

What should a leader do in the forming stage?

At the start there is limited trust in the leader, the process, and being rewarded fairly. There may be different cultures, norms, and values, and there may also be a lot of uncertainty (Zarifis & Cheng, 2024). The first step to building trust is usually to be good at our core job. So what does the leader typically have to do as their core job in the forming stage? The team members' feelings at the start tend to run high with excitement and positivity but also some anxiety due to the newness and uncertainty. As we are going through a disruptive digital transformation, this can increase the anxiety further. There are few certainties in the workplace many of us work in.

The shared vision, goals, structure, processes, and roles must be created. Expectations must be calibrated between everyone. We must ensure everyone is clear on these things. Everyone must have the same understanding on their tasks, the goals, and what the priorities are. The popular SMART (specific, measurable, achievable, relevant, and time-bound) goals framework should be used. We should show that recognition of everyone's contribution is a part of the process, and a central part of the culture. Many leaders that over-prioritise collaboration dream that everything will magically happen without a clear plan, but this is naive – we must divide up the work, where possible, to avoid duplication and frustration. We can have a great collaboration by colleagues giving feedback on each other's work. Coming together to give feedback on the parts of the project that were allocated to specific colleagues is often more effective than trying to collaborate and 'hold hands' all the time, on everything. Too much interaction increases the chance of friction.

How do we build trust among team members in the forming stage?

As mentioned, a leader must be good in their role and use that as a foundation for everything else they do to build trust. Trust must be earned by being predictable and consistent. The leader must model trustworthy behaviour. If we want followers to behave professionally, then doing this ourselves by arriving first to work and leaving last will say more than any words someone can say.

If it is a virtual team, it is worth at least having a kick-off meeting face to face, regardless of the high financial cost. Humans should connect on a human level. Face-to-face is a deeper, more emotional and memorable experience that is worth its weight in gold. Most people work best when they are intellectually and emotionally engaged.

In addition to building trust, it is particularly important at this stage to not destroy trust. How can a leader destroy trust at the start before it is built? Many of us, not everyone, but many of us want to believe our leaders and those in positions of authority are trustworthy. Even cynical people want to believe their leaders are competent and benevolent as this gives their life some certainty. In most cases humans evaluate whether to trust someone rationally, but for those that fall into this category, they are looking for reasons, or excuses, to convince themselves that their leader is trustworthy. Some of us are always in this category, looking for someone to idolise and baptise as our new saviour, while others are not always in this category but drift in and out of it depending on our circumstances. Ironically, people who are struggling to stay positive and find motivation are more susceptible to wanting to idolise their leaders. Therefore, while the leader is trying to build trust up, they should not give a strong reason for people to distrust them. I once started work on a new project and on the first day one of the professors was saying how if we do something one way it breaks the rules, but if we do the essentially same thing but in a slightly different way it was alright in the letter of the rules, despite not being in the spirit of the rules. He managed to burn through all my goodwill, my desire to trust leaders, and being willing to give people the benefit of the doubt, within minutes. At the start of the project, the knowledge the followers have of the leader's behaviour is very limited, so it must not be untrustworthy.

There are often colleagues that are free riders, either because this was their plan from the start or because some issue emerged during the project such as personal issues. This needs to be discouraged from the start. It helps to explicitly say that free riding will not be accepted and will be called out. As mentioned, the high emotions at the start of the project should be utilised. The anxiety at the start should be used to discourage free riders. Some anxiety around doing a good job is a good thing. This anxiety is necessary, unlike anxiety over other issues such as being rewarded for our work, which is not helpful (Zarifis & Cheng, 2024).

The positive emotions and excitement should be channelled into the relationships and goals. Often there are questions around the goals, and the leader should have good questions to ask also. The leader's questions can show their empathy for people's emotions and actually be more influential in shaping behaviour than giving orders.

Leadership tip: Resist the urge to control everything, over-organise, and crush people's emotions and enthusiasm. Emotions are powerful and motivating. The leader should channel the team's emotions effectively.

Communication tip: Particularly at the start, a leader should show their personality and vision but also take time to listen, clarify and paraphrase, understand the emotions and motivations, and be kind.

Trust-building tip reminder: Build trust at the start of the project before the challenges to trust emerge. Use sustainable methods such as establishing shared values.

Myth busting: It is a myth, particularly strong in western cultures, that we cannot be genuine friends with the colleagues we work with and we must keep some distance. The best teams are friends. It will be more rewarding if we work with friends. Yes, there can be disagreements, but as Alfred Tennyson famously wrote, 'it is better to have loved and lost than not to have loved at all'. While many of us quote that when a romantic relationship breaks down, it was actually written for a friend of his that died, not a romantic relationship.

How can we build trust in AI in the forming stage?

The risks can be high with such a far-reaching technology such as AI, so some heathy distrust is not a bad thing. However, distrust based on the wrong reasons should be reduced. We must get the vision and the goals right and communicate them well. We must make it clear what will happen if these steps are not taken, and make it clear what will happen when they will be taken. To form a vision it is beneficial to use the six business models that fully utilise AI (Zarifis & Cheng, 2025). The six models were discussed in the first chapter and will be discussed in more detail later.

Training necessities need to be identified at this stage. They may require colleagues to educate themselves, or visits from experts that can give some guidance, or a guest lecture. A leader must illustrate their competence in AI. Creating a strong vision and identifying training needs are an opportunity to illustrate the leader's AI competence.

Box 2.1 How to build trust among team members and AI in the forming stage

Build trust among team members and other stakeholders
- Have a face-to-face kick-off meeting.
- Show a genuine interest in how they are settling in and their wellbeing.
- Get the vision and the goals right and communicate them well. Create a sense of purpose.
- Act in a transparent way and have transparent processes.
- Model trustworthy behaviour. Behave in a trustworthy way so others do the same.
- Make it clear what is expected of them and understand what they expect from the leader. For example, honesty should be expected.
- Divide up the work, avoid duplication and frustration.
- Show that recognition of everyone's contribution is a central part of the culture.
- The goals of the project and the financial rewards are important but not enough. Make it about the people, the journey, and the goals.

Build trust in AI and other new disruptive technologies
- Most important point: At some point in the forming stage we have to offer a convincing vision and strategy to how AI will be used. We can use the six business models that fully utilise AI (Zarifis & Cheng, 2025).
- Identify where in the operations and relationships with stakeholders trust needs to be built (e.g. onboarding). It may not be everywhere.
- Illustrate with examples that it is clear to the leader how AI will be used.
- Clarify what AI will be used for, and what AI will not be used for, and why.
- Clarify how the AI solution will work and what it will do internally to complete a process.
- Clarify what data will be used.
- Offer training or signpost people to where they can find the information they need.
- Ensure performance, robustness, 'explainability' and reproducibility, transparency, fairness, privacy, security, and sustainability.
- Show AI leadership and governance. Project a competence in AI.
- Do not fight a healthy level of distrust based on real or potential problems.

2.3.2 Stage 2: Storming – setting strong foundations to endure the 'storm' of distrust

The storming stage is a natural progression from the forming stage. Some basic things have been resolved but there is still some uncertainty. Challenges around using technology, communicating, and sharing knowledge may get even bigger. The team members may compete to get their ideas adopted. Some may also compete for influence. Those who perceive themselves as alpha may try to become the de facto leaders. It is not just about being competitive. People are comfortable working in different ways, so trying to get what they personally want adopted by the group is normal. Some colleagues want to move forward quickly, while others want to do more brainstorming and 'blue-sky thinking' at the start.

What should a leader do in the storming stage?
Before we go into how to build trust we need to be clear on the other tasks a leader has at this stage. The discussions on what needs to be done need to be facilitated. We can try to keep a level playing field so everyone has the opportunity to make their point. We can also find the common themes between teammates and try to resolve disagreements. For example, one person might disagree with what someone else said because of challenges to the implementation, not the principle of it. In this case, we can discuss ways to overcome the challenges. The way teammates discuss and resolve their differences at this stage will serve as a template for the future, so it is important that it goes well. The process of discussions and bargaining must be allowed to run its course, but some agreements and norms must come out of it.

How can you build trust among team members in the storming stage?
The challenges to trust at this stage are mainly the frictions from the discussions and the fallout from some colleagues not getting what they want. It is helpful if the team are reassured that it is natural to have some disagreements in the storming stage and that it is part of a natural process that will lead to a positive outcome. We all want to hit the ground running and be productive from the start, but we have to accept that there is a journey we must go through.

Building trust at this stage is about projecting the values and behaviours we hope others will have and coordinating the discussions. We should try to be a good listener, be very polite, and show empathy for concerns. We must also be open and transparent. It is helpful to show that we appreciate everyone's input and reflect on it, whether their suggestions are chosen or not. From the start of this stage we should show faith and confidence in the team members and make employee recognition a genuine part of the culture from this stage.

How can we build trust in AI in the storming stage?

In the storming stage, alternative strategies, business models, and technologies are put forward. The AI initiative must be chosen, or we must at least have a shortlist. If there are quick wins, then they should be pursued along with longer-term goals. Small victories help us on the journey to bigger victories. Ideally there will be a portfolio of AI initiatives combining quick small victories and larger transformational projects.

The strengths and weaknesses must be put forward. There are many things to discuss but trust has to remain on the table of discussion when alternatives are contrasted. Firstly, can these alternative solutions be trusted by stakeholders? Secondly, do these alternatives pose a reputational threat, and a threat to the existing trust in the organisation? Thirdly, how much time and money will it take to build trust in them? These are examples of the questions that should be asked. Trust should be looked at at the strategy and business model level, so the discussion should start as early as possible.

There are trade-offs, but these trade-offs are not always clear. Sometimes a more constrained use of AI will build trust, while other times a fully automated process will be more trustworthy. If there was a standardised way to build trust in AI across many situations then this would not be an issue for the leader, but purely a technical or marketing issue.

Leadership still needs to build trust in the team, but more emphasis needs to start being put in building trust in the technology. While many issues will not be resolved at this stage, the right sort of discussions need to start happening. The better understanding of the technology will further clarify what is a healthy level of distrust based on the real risks and what is an unhealthy, unhelpful distrust based on misconceptions.

Not all team members may appreciate the importance of having trust in an AI-centric business model so the leader must ensure the importance of trust is explained to everyone. If necessary, some education on the importance of trust must be made so that everyone in the team has consensus on this central issue.

Box 2.2 How to build trust among team members and AI in the storming stage

Build trust among team members and other stakeholders

- Reassure team members that it is natural to have some disagreements in the storming stage.
- Coordinate the discussions.
- Build trust by projecting the values and behaviours you hope others will have.
- Try to be a good listener, be very polite, and show empathy for concerns.
- Be open and transparent.
- Show that everyone's input is appreciated and reflect on it.
- Make employee recognition a genuine part of the culture.

Build trust in AI and other new disruptive technologies

- Start the discussion on the important aspects of trust in AI.
- Discuss if alternative solutions can be trusted by stakeholders.

- Discuss if alternatives explored pose a reputational threat and a threat to the existing trust in the organisation.
- Consider how much time and money it will take to build trust in them.
- Educate on the importance of trust in AI.
- Build consensus on the importance of trust in AI.
- Further clarify what is a healthy level of distrust of AI based on the real risks, and what is an unhealthy, unhelpful distrust based on misconceptions.

2.3.3 Stage 3: Norming and understanding the risks to trust better

The norming stage benefits from the time the team members have already spent together and the shared understanding they started to create. Most challenges to trust should be getting smaller, but some new challenges may emerge. Some may start to get disappointed about how things are going as they start to be more reluctant to give each other the benefit of the doubt. There can be demotivation, disengagement, and even conflict. If things keep happening that someone does not like, this is usually the time when they try to draw a line and not accept it anymore. Therefore, hopefully the previous steps have gone well and the leader can build cohesion by the end of this period.

What should a leader do in the norming stage?
The leader's role starts to shift from team building to the goals of the project. The leader does not need to be as hands-on, facilitating discussions and worrying about everyone's feelings. If things are going well then now is the time to start letting go a little. 'Let go to grow' as they say.

How can we build trust within the team in the norming stage?
When there is a lack of trust, the leader may be the last to know. Some may keep their distrust private, but it will still have a negative effect on getting things done. By this stage, even if team members have kept their distrust private, an attentive leader must pick up on it.

If conflict is openly happening, or frustrations are about to boil over, the leader must understand what the underlying reason is and resolve it. If it is an injustice then it should be resolved. For example, if based on how things are going someone fears that there will be an injustice in the future, such as not getting credit for their work, and the leader lays out a fair plan in front of everyone in a binding way, this may help. Making a binding plan in front of everyone may also stop the more Machiavellian colleagues from harming others. We can take action, but only after we truly understand the problem.

Experienced team members are usually good at their job, but they are also very good at understanding if they will be unfairly treated in the future. An experienced person will start fighting back as soon as they get a sense of injustice coming their way. Unfortunately, with experience comes a sense of cynicism and suspicion. Along with the more abstract things such as a positive vibe in the team, there is a necessary element of dealmaking. An experienced, cynical teammate will respond far better to something small but concrete, such as paying for some expenses, rather than grand abstract visions of win-win.

If there are specific issues such as disappointment, disengagement, and demotivation, they need to be addressed. One of the biggest fallacies in leadership and management is the idea that a manager should decisively brand someone toxic and ostracise them. Most times, the one branded toxic is the victim of the genuinely toxic colleagues. The colleague branded toxic may be the victim of bullying and people ganging up on them. The leader should stand up for the weak and give encouragement to those that are disappointed. The group dynamics should be stopped from turning into a popularity contest by highlighting everyone's contribution. Ideally, a leader would fix these issues from the start, but some time is needed to understand the different characters and see their mentality in action.

Colleagues have different characters and forms of intelligence. Often, the character of the person that is disappointed is one that is not the strongest in – or has less interest in – the socialising side, so they have not manipulated the group dynamics in their favour. This type of person is useful and worth some extra effort. Often, those that have stronger technical knowledge fall into this category, but more broadly, those that have the mindset of an overachiever and put a lot of pressure on themselves also fall into this category.

How can we build trust in AI in the norming stage?
At this stage, colleagues will have a better understanding of the technology they are using or intend to use. As we go into more detail on the technology and the processes it is used in, all the risks need to be understood. A common mentality is to assume that if other similar organisations are doing the same thing it must be alright. However, AI is not like any other technology, and the other organisation may be reckless or may have found a way to mitigate the risk that is not obvious. Shortcuts should not be sought out and the time should be put in to understand the risks. We must decide what risks are acceptable, and what risks are worth it. If the risk is acceptable and worth it, how can it be managed? Risk is typically seen as: risk = likelihood x impact. The five-by-five risk matrix shown in Table 2.2, is one popular way to categorise risk. It is a simple but effective tool.

Decisions around what should be dealt with in-house and what should be outsourced need to continue happening here. For example, many financial institutions completely outsource the identity verification of their customers because there is a company that does that very well. Therefore, they can pay for that service proportionally to their needs. This is a good time in the project to touch base with other stakeholders as there should be something more concrete than the previous stages. Reporting AI initiatives that are relatively mature will increase buy-in.

These steps are not exclusive to this stage, but this stage is a point where there is enough knowledge of the technologies and cohesion in the team to really make progress on these things before it is too late.

Table 2.2: The popular five-by-five risk matrix.

	Insignificant 1	Minor 2	Significant 3	Major 4	Severe 5
Almost certain 5	Medium 5	High 10	Very high 15	Extreme 20	Extreme 25
Likely 4	Medium 4	Medium 8	High 12	Very high 16	Extreme 20
Moderate 3	Low 3	Medium 6	Medium 9	High 12	Very high 15
Unlikely 2	Very low 2	Low 4	Medium 6	Medium 8	High 10
Rare 1	Very low 1	Very low 2	Low 3	Medium 4	Medium 5

Box 2.3 How to build trust among team members and AI in the norming stage
Build trust among team members and other stakeholders
- Resolve conflict by finding the root cause and coming to a binding solution between everyone.
- If there are issues such as disappointment, disengagement, and demotivation, the leader should stand up for the weak and encourage those that are disappointed.
- Stop the group dynamics from turning into a popularity contest by highlighting everyone's contribution.

Build trust in AI and other new disruptive technologies
- Go into more detail on the technology and the processes it is used in. Understand all the risks.
- Use the five-by-five risk matrix to accurately evaluate the risks AI brings.
- Don't assume that if other similar organisations are doing the same thing it must be alright.
- Decide what risks are acceptable and what risks are worth it.
- Decide what should be dealt with in-house and what should be outsourced. This decision must be made for AI and data.
- If we need to adapt the business model chosen, use one of the six business models that fully utilise AI (Zarifis & Cheng, 2025).

2.3.4 Stage 4: Performing and building trust across the whole ecosystem

There is a gradual shift in focus from the norming to the performing stage. While there is plenty of overlap between the third and fourth stages, there is a clearer difference in focus between the fourth stage and the first and second stages. If the other steps have gone well the leader can show trust in their team at this stage. If the previous stages have truly gone well, less needs to be done at this stage, particularly in terms of building the team, so more time can be spent on the goals of the project and the role of AI. If the previous stages have not gone so well then the leader needs to keep working on the challenges pointed out earlier and resolve them so that they can truly progress to the performing stage.

What should a leader do in the performing stage?
This stage should be the most stable with the least change, so a leader can act more like a traditional manager focusing more on monitoring and controlling. The focus will be on execution. As the team should feel more positive about each other and the task at this point, the whole team must continue to be open to collaborating in new ways. Most of us want individual recognition, but this should not lead to working in silos too much. Many of us want some 'me time' to think, but a balance is needed.

The productivity, morale, and understanding of the task are at their peak, so it is a good time to adjust schedules and make them more ambitious if possible. It might be worth starting to reflect on what can be done after the immediate goals are achieved. For example, if an insurer has automated many of their processes with AI, giving them better performance, does this offer new opportunities? We can use the six business models that fully utilise AI to think about the new opportunities (Zarifis & Cheng, 2025).

How can we build trust within the team at the performing stage?
As a well-functioning team is a prerequisite to truly reach the performing stage, hopefully this has been achieved and the focus can shift to building trust with external partners. This is a good time to do this, not just because there may be more time, but because we will have more confidence in our team and make the case to partners in an honest confident way. Given that some progress would have been made by this point, there will be examples of the team's ability to show partners. These examples will build trust with partners. For example, if we are advising on how to use AI in financial technology (fintech) we can talk about the different types of experts we have in the team and how they cover the topic very well.

How can we build trust in AI in the performing stage?
Hopefully the technology and business models have been chosen at this stage and the focus can go on to how to make the most of them. While many talk about a value chain – and that is still the most accurate way to describe it in many cases – nowadays it is often more like an ecosystem. In the performing stage the team should focus more outwardly to the other players in the ecosystem and how to create solutions and services with better trust. Most organisations, regardless of the AI-centric business model they choose from the six models proven to work (Zarifis & Cheng, 2025), will be dependent to some degree on other partners to use AI in a trustworthy way.

A complex IT solution across many organisations may be watertight in many ways, but one vulnerability or back door somewhere will lead to a data breach. A data breach can put the company in the news for all the wrong reasons and possibly have legal implications. While being a hundred percent secure is unlikely for a large organisation, every effort should be made to be as secure as possible.

Box 2.4 How to build trust among team members and AI in the performing stage

Build trust among team members and other stakeholders
- As the team should have strong trust in each other at this stage, focus on building trust with external partners. Use the capabilities of the team, and their progress until now, to support the case made to partners.

Build trust in AI and other new disruptive technologies
- Shift the focus from how the team can create a trustworthy AI initiative to how external partners can ensure trustworthiness.
- Identify the risks across the value chain or ecosystem and decide on the strategy to build trustworthy solutions.
- If we need to adapt the business model chosen, we can choose one of the six business models proven to make the most of AI (Zarifis & Cheng, 2025).

2.3.5 Stage 5: Adjourning – ending the project but not the relationship

The adjourning (or closure) stage is typically the end of the project when the goals have been met and the team stop working together regularly. However, it is important to appreciate that projects don't always have clear starting points and ends, but having the typical project scenario in our minds helps. With the biggest technological disruptions in our lifetime – the internet and AI – we will probably be involved heavily with these issues throughout our professional lives and across many projects.

There aren't many people that do not appreciate the importance of the leader's actions at the start of a project, but the end is also important. A metaphor to illustrate this is how everyone understands the front of a car helps the aerodynamics and performance, but many people do not understand that the back also has an influence.

What should a leader do in the adjourning stage?
Recognition and closure are the priorities at this stage. It is important not to leave recognition only for this stage; time should be invested in this at many points, but it is one of the two central themes here. As with the other stages there will be a mixture of emotions. Hopefully the emotions can be channelled in a positive way by celebrating the achievements.

As far as possible, some plans must be made for the future. Some plans may be quite explicit and detailed, while others may be more like aspirations or brainstorming for the future. For example, identifying three or four potential scenarios for future collaboration may be helpful.

Future opportunities: This is the time to reflect on what can be done after the immediate goals are achieved. For example, if an insurer has automated many of their processes with AI giving better accuracy and speed, does this create an opportunity to move into new markets? This is not a given as regulation, culture, and many other issues influence this decision. Another typical example is that if a process has been automated and optimised with AI in-house it may actually be a service that can be offered to others in the ecosystem. As mentioned, in the modern partly global world, there are 'friends', 'enemies', but also 'frenemies'. If an in-house service such as AI models that can predict risk more accurately can be offered to competitors, this stops competitors making their own and potentially better systems. Turning a fierce competition into a less fierce competition often increases profitability for everyone involved. If less energy can be used up fighting each other it can be utilised elsewhere.

How can we build trust within the team in the adjourning stage?

There are two key issues for trust at this stage: recognition for work done and future opportunities that may be lined up. Along with these two key issues for the end of a project, the typical ways to build trust throughout the project still apply and should be used. As with other stages, keeping the team in the loop with how the work was received is helpful. Transparency, communication, and feedback all help. If someone did not receive something they wanted, such as an extension to their contract, they should be told the truth as to why it did not happen.

How can we build trust in AI in the adjourning stage?

A more complete understanding of how the AI used has performed should enable a better understanding of its capabilities. An honest discussion about the AI used so far is helpful. Useful lessons can be learned to make improvements in the future. Positive and negative use cases, from both inside and outside the organisation, can be used for discussion and benchmarking. It is not always easy to get accurate information on how other organisations are doing as most will try to sweep anything negative under the carpet. Experienced leaders have a skill at understanding what is happening with competitors' implementations of AI even with very little information. For example, the technology providers a competitor is using can be an indication of what they are trying to do. At the very least we should be able to decipher if they are going for a 'cheap and cheerful' implementation or something more ambitious and groundbreaking. Comparing to competitors and discussing the performance of AI at this stage will also help calibrate what a healthy level of distrust in AI should be.

Box 2.5 How to build trust among team members and AI in the adjourning stage
Build trust among team members and other stakeholders
- Recognise work done.
- Value them as people. Some colleagues' weaknesses are more immediately apparent, but strengths such as perseverance take longer to come through.
- Identify future opportunities that may be lined up. Make plans for future collaboration if possible.
- Recognise the mistakes made in how the team was led and what could have been done better.
- Follow through on commitments made in earlier stages.
- Take pictures of final meeting so those that worked together can remember the friendships they had. Even the most vivid memories fade.

Build trust in AI and other new disruptive technologies
- Have honest discussion about the AI used so far. Learn necessary lessons.
- Find positive and negative use cases from inside and outside the organisation to discuss and benchmark against.
- Reflect on what is a healthy level of distrust of AI based on the real risks and what is an unhealthy, unhelpful distrust based on misconceptions.

2.3.6 Stage 6: Post-project collaboration

As the immediate project has ended, team members will move on to new projects either inside or outside the organisation. Interaction will be far more intermittent. At the same time, many project teams are virtual even when they are working full time together, so not being physically together isn't the decisive end to a professional relationship it used to be. Everyone that worked together has a good understanding of each other's abilities so they can contact them again in the future when necessary.

What should a leader do in the post-project collaboration stage?
The leader's purpose here is to keep the communication channels open and touch base with former members. The leader should not 'hound' former team members but should not 'play it cool' either. We should think of a way we can still add value to former teammates so they also add value to us. For example, sharing experiences on how AI has performed for us since the end of the project may encourage them to share their experiences too. There is a meaningless and hollow way to do networking, but there is also a meaningful and rewarding way to do it.

How can we build trust within the team in the post-project collaboration stage?
It is still worth maintaining trust and repairing any trust that was lost. Keeping the friendships alive beyond the end of the project shows an appreciation, a loyalty, and a genuine interest in the person as a human being. We can use things we have in common to keep the relationship going. This will build strong, sustainable trust on a deeper level.

How can we build trust in AI in the post-project collaboration stage?
Sharing experiences of the use of AI will further help everyone involved understand how to offer trustworthy AI applications. As discussed, modern businesses usually use an ecosystem of services and technologies, so keeping contacts is particularly helpful. We will not always find honest accounts of what happened in an AI implementation on the internet, but we will hear honest accounts from our contacts. By knowing what other contacts are doing we can collaborate to enhance the trustworthiness of AI. When different teams and organisations use similar approaches and this becomes a sort of de facto standard, it is beneficial for trust. The more this happens across the ecosystem we are involved in, the better.

Box 2.6 How to build trust among team members and AI in the post-project collaboration stage
Build trust among team members and other stakeholders
- Keeping the friendships alive beyond the end of the project shows a loyalty and genuine interest that builds strong, resilient, and sustainable trust.
- We should make old teammates feel we are always happy to hear from them so they feel confident that they can pick up the phone when they have an idea about a future collaboration.

Build trust in AI and other new disruptive technologies
- Share experiences of the use of AI so everyone involved understands how to offer trustworthy AI applications.
- Collaborate to enhance the trustworthiness of AI. When different teams and organisations use similar approaches, and this becomes a sort of de facto standard it is beneficial for trust.

2.4 Summary

> *It's always nice working with friends. There's an element of trust there.* — Jeremy Irons, British actor

Before we try to lead and build trust in AI in a project, a good place to start is to find the ways in which AI tools, both the widely available ones and more specialised ones, can help us do our job. While we want to continue to be the masters of our destiny, the more hands-on interaction with AI will help us understand how different machine learning algorithms work and what kind of data we need.

The leader should utilise the framework of a project with six stages and build trust at each of these stages in a targeted way. If trust is built in the correct way at one stage it makes building trust at the next stage easier. Some challenges, such as conflict, can happen in the third or fourth stage, but if we wait for those stages to build trust it is too late. Trust must be built to resolve the immediate challenges of each stage and build a buffer of goodwill for the challenges of the next stages. The complexity of the situation can become overwhelming without a structure. Structuring our thoughts and having a 'game plan' helps.

The best version of the project stages for a leader of people and AI is one with six stages that includes the typical five first stages (forming, storming, norming, performing, and adjourning) but adds a sixth stage of post-project collaboration. When the main project purpose is completed, it is not a complete end of the relationships, but a transition into a more informal, intermittent collaboration. It would be a shame to lose a professional relationship with trust built into it if that can be avoided.

It is important to focus on different priorities at different stages of the project. What a leader does at each stage of a project depends heavily on what leadership style they select. For example, an authoritarian leader and a servant leader will see things very differently.

A leader that has prepared and has at least some insight to offer will encourage a better engagement from all the stakeholders in how to move forward. If we understand the challenges we face at each stage we have a better chance of directing the team discussions towards a clear decision. A passive ill-informed 'leader' may not be given a clear solution and plan on how to move forward by the other stakeholders and will perpetually stay in a state of confusion and indecision.

There is no simple solution that fits every situation, but there is a lot of science behind the stages of a project discussed here. A leader should not feel overwhelmed by the complexity of the modern globalised world with constant and quick innovation. A leader should also not be overwhelmed by the many different characters people in a team have. While no two people are the same, there are some typical challenges, and if the typical concerns are resolved, trust can be built.

The six stages of a typical project provide a strong foundation for leadership decisions. The leader can focus on the core role of a leader at each stage, how to build trust in people at that stage, and how to build trust in AI for that stage. An excellent leader knows how to assess where in the process they are, what they have achieved, and what they need to focus on. For example, if they know the trust has been built between the team, then they can focus on completing the tasks, building trust in AI, and building trust with other stakeholders.

Many people talk about the importance of a leader showing empathy, but when going through the stages of implementing technology, understanding what to show empathy about is not always so easy. We need to understand the process, the technology, and the people to show empathy effectively. By understanding the typical process people in projects go through, the typical process new technology and innovation goes through, and some proven business models, the leader can develop a strategy and a vision to get the most out of their team and AI.

A leader needs to understand how, over several stages, technology changes relationships and business models. A leader that has broad horizons and is constantly comparing different leadership styles, different applications of technologies, different business models, and different contexts, will be much stronger.

2.5 Exercises

Exercise 2.1

Overlay the stages of the project over a technology-intensive organisation's journey
There are many cases of technology-intensive companies that we can learn from. X (formerly Twitter) is a great case study because their journey encompasses all the issues we are talking about. Their journey involved both technology and peoples' perspectives on a variety of issues such as how far should free speech be allowed to go if it is factually inaccurate. If we divide their history to when they were called Twitter and after they were renamed X, let's look at the following questions.

Questions

1) Take the period of the organisation when it was called Twitter and try to overlay the six stages over it. Break it into two stages, setting Twitter up and then running Twitter and evolving it. What were the opportunities and challenges? How was trust built with staff, users, and regulators? Are there any other stakeholders? Were processes too heavily automated with too little human input from staff? What could have been done better?

2) Take the period of the organisation when it was bought and turned into X and try to overlay the six stages over it. As with the previous question: What were the opportunities and challenges? How was trust built with staff, users, and regulators? Are there any other stakeholders? Were processes too heavily automated with too little human input from staff? What could have been done better?

Exercise 2.2

Plan a project for a competitor of X that wants to take advantage of their weaknesses

If you worked for the X competitor Mastodon and you were given the project to attract more users from X, how would you implement that project? What stages would the project have? How would you build trust in stakeholders and AI?

Space for your notes

References

Aguiar, M., Williams, M., Backler, W., Kiderman, J., Candelon, F., Dubner, R., Hammoud, T., Kimura, R., & Marcil, S. (2022). *What AI reveals about trust in the world's largest companies*. BCG Henderson Institute. https://bcghendersoninstitute.com/wp-content/uploads/2022/05/What-AI-Reveals-About-Trust-in-the-Worlds-Largest-Companies-PDF.pdf

Tuckman, B. W. (1965). Developmental sequence in small groups. *Psychological Bulletin, 63*(6), 384–399. https://doi.org/10.1037/h0022100

Zarifis, A. (2024, September 23). Building trust to support researchers' mental health. *Times Higher Education*. https://www.timeshighereducation.com/campus/building-trust-support-researchers-mental-health

Zarifis, A., & Cheng, X. (2024). A model reducing researchers' challenges in projects: Build trust first for better mental health. *Cogent Business & Management, 11*(1), 1–13. https://doi.org/10.1080/23311975.2024.2350786

Zarifis, A., & Cheng, X. (2025). The new centralised and decentralised Fintech technologies, and business models, transforming finance. In A. Zarifis & X. Cheng (Eds.), *Fintech and the emerging ecosystems: Exploring centralised and decentralised financial technologies*. Springer Nature. https://link.springer.com/book/9783031834011

Section B: **Leadership styles and their role
in using AI with trust**

Chapter 3
Traditional leadership approaches and their role in using AI with trust – autocratic vs. democratic, delegative, bureaucratic, and charismatic leadership

3.1 Introduction

I have only one understanding of development and of making success, and that's by going step by step. — Jürgen Klopp, legendary football coach

In 1816 in Loughborough, a town in the UK, some people that were against using machinery fearing it would cost people their jobs attacked a factory that made lace and destroyed all the machinery. With modern life in most parts of the world, the basics of shelter, food, and some safety are provided to a larger degree than before. This creates a civilised society where people are willing to accept many things they do not necessarily agree with. Many things that happen would have caused a violent reaction even a few decades ago, but today will at most lead to an angry post on Mastodon. So why should a leader worry about what their team and their customers think about their plans to restructure their operations for more AI-driven automation? Some technologies benefit society uniformly and nobody has an issue with them, but when a technology changes the balance of power, and takes power away from those that feel they already had very little, there will be a reaction. AI has this potential, so the challenge for the leader is to take the maximum benefit from AI while keeping their team and other stakeholders on their side. There isn't one personality trait, skill, leadership approach, or strategy to achieve that. One must be an effective leader that knows how to handle each situation and show empathy, judgement, and business acumen.

Many people promote one leadership style as the best approach, but this is more because we want to believe that there are simple answers. Someone that has a specific role, such as an operations manager or sales representative, may develop a straightforward approach to implementing their role, but the breadth of issues we must deal with in digital transformation with AI means there are no simple answers. Selecting a suitable AI-centred business model from the six that have been proven to work offers some certainty, but the leader still needs to implement it in their context and overcome many challenges (Zarifis & Cheng 2023, 2025). A good business school rewires people's brains so they don't lazily seek out over-simplistic naive answers, such as being aggressive and 'decisive', but have the determination to do whatever it takes to apply the best-suited approach for each situation.

https://doi.org/10.1515/9783111630137-003

I once witnessed a division of a university preparing to launch a new degree programme. One other division felt this new degree was too close to theirs and that it would 'cannibalise' it, meaning their similar degree would lose students. This could have escalated into a turf war with the disgruntled division managing to block the new programme. The head of the division preparing the new programme could have forcefully argued that they have the right to launch the new programme and that blocking it would be unfair. That would probably be the knee-jerk, instinctive reaction most inexperienced leaders would take. Instead he intentionally appeared weak, downplaying the significance of the new programme and its potential. In a tactic that leaders with big egos would not be able to take, he made himself appear too weak to be a threat. If you think about it, that move was pure genius. Not only did the new programme get accepted, but they did not create any conflict or burn any goodwill in getting there. When the new programme becomes a success, the stature of the leader will increase. The leader will be praised for getting the job done, but also for overachieving. This tactic was not without risk, as downplaying the new programme's prospects may have led to the university deciding it was not worth the trouble offering it. This is where the judgement of a leader comes in. The leader felt he had made the case sufficiently to the university to get it accepted, so they could downplay its significance to avoid ruffling others' feathers.

With the magnitude of the change leaders face, it is a challenge to continue to be leaders and not end up as passengers. If someone thinks this is an exaggeration, they can look at how some of the most powerful people in the world – Mark Zuckerberg, Tim Cook, Jeff Bezos – acted after Donald Trump was elected president of the United States the second time. It could be argued that, in some sense, they became passengers in the change. For example, one of them announced changes such as cancelling moderation in favour of community notes, which had been their preference for a long time. The person that forced these very modern leaders into those changes used traditional leadership approaches. The suggestion is not that old leadership approaches are better, but that we cannot rely on one approach and must understand the main ones.

The traditional leadership approaches discussed here are still useful today, and by understanding them well it helps us understand the modern approaches better as well. For example, the autocratic and democratic leadership approaches may seem too basic or old fashioned for some leaders. However, all leadership approaches lie somewhere on a spectrum from autocratic to democratic. Therefore, by understanding how these two basic traditional leadership approaches affect followers' psychology and team dynamics, it helps us understand all the other leadership approaches better too. Figure 3.1 illustrates where the traditional approaches are on the spectrum from autocratic to democratic.

As with many aspects of management and business, the way to have good judgement and to be able to see what the most likely scenarios going forward are, is to know how things evolved to get to where we are now. Traditionally, leadership was about the effect the leader had on people, but now, due to the central role of AI, the

Transactional   Delegative, laissez-faire

Bureaucratic   Charismatic   Transformational   Servant

Autocratic   Democratic

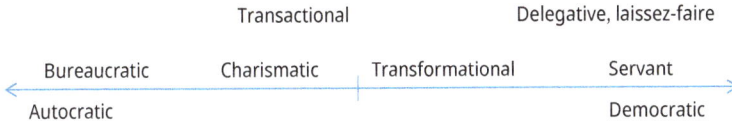

Figure 3.1: Where the popular leadership approaches lie on a spectrum from autocratic to democratic.

leader must also lead on AI with trust (Zarifis, 2024). This includes mixed teams of humans and autonomous AI agents.

We need to develop our ability to understand the interplay between the key issues of leadership, followers and other stakeholders, technology and trust. Even with these four variables we have many relationships that affect each other to think about. In a similar way to a SWOT (strengths, weaknesses, opportunities, and threats) analysis exercise it is useful to note the issues down in the matrix covering the four variables. Some people say business school academics are obsessed with explaining things using two-by-two matrices, but they are wrong, as we have a two-by-three matrix here in figure 3.2.

Human relationships	Leadership and trust issues	Stakeholder and trust issues	Leadership and stakeholder issues
Human–AI relationships to reflect on	Leadership and AI issues	Stakeholder and AI issues	AI and trust issues

Figure 3.2: A two-by-three matrix can be used to note down the main human–human and human–AI issues during a digital transformation.

This chapter will discuss the most significant and useful traditional leadership approaches. These are autocratic and democratic leadership, delegative leadership, bureaucratic leadership, and charismatic leadership. At the end of the chapter, we will have a summary and some exercises to help us reflect on what we covered and try to apply it to our situations.

3.2 Autocratic leadership, AI, and trust

Power has to be protected from scrutiny. That's the principle of every dictatorship, of every autocracy. You hear it from high priests at Harvard and every government department, that power has to be kept secret otherwise it will fade and it won't work. — Noam Chomsky, professor of linguistics

Famous leaders using this style:
Margaret Thatcher, former British prime minister.
Elon Musk, CEO of Tesla, SpaceX, and X.

3.2.1 The strengths and weaknesses of autocratic leadership

It is human nature to get excited about a new technology or approach people are talking about. Having a narrow-minded approach to business in general often leads us to playing 'buzzword bingo' and trying to impress people with our knowledge by using the most popular terms people are excited about. To really understand an issue in business it is necessary to go a little further back, take things from the start and understand the evolution that brought us to where we are today. The best way to understand the most popular leadership styles today, like transformational leadership, is to first understand the leadership styles that were popular before it. Understanding all the leadership styles also gives us a better global understanding, as what is popular or even the norm in one place can be very different to what we are used to and what comes naturally to us.

When we want to understand what leadership style was initially popular from the leader's perspective, there is only one place to start, and that is autocratic leadership. In autocratic leadership, also known as authoritarian leadership, the leader holds the central decision-making power. When we talk about leadership we like to refer to the leader's followers, but in this approach they are quite clearly subordinates with little to no influence on decisions. This style is top-down with clear procedures, rules, and lines of authority. An autocratic leader dictates work methods and sets goals unilaterally.

Typically, this kind of leader will not feel the need to give constructive feedback but will express themselves freely and say what is on their mind. They often have the luxury of being able to offend people without them being in a position to respond. Instead of focusing on positive reinforcement or motivation, compliance and discipline are enforced. As fear of punishment is the main way to get people to do things, subordinates need to be closely monitored.

As power comes from their title or position, autocratic leaders often focus more on protecting their position rather than making a positive difference. Autocrats often drift into focusing on their image and sweeping problems under the carpet rather than finding real solutions to problems.

Interestingly however, while this approach is all about concentrating power in one person, what often happens is that a 'royal court' emerges around the great leader that has influence on them. The royal court may be the greatest minds in the organisation or they may be the autocratic leader's friends, someone that makes them laugh, or someone they have a relationship with outside of marriage. (I have experienced all these things first-hand in organisations I have worked!) Therefore, typically, even in a strict autocratic leadership approach there is some shared leadership, but it is not formally arranged.

While it is easy to create a negative over-simplistic caricature of this approach, it can still be useful in some situations. For example, in times of uncertainty or crisis where unpopular decisions are necessary, this method can be necessary. A recent example was the COVID-19 crisis where difficult and unpopular decisions had to be enforced for the greater good. Before becoming an academic I was an officer in the army infantry engineers and I saw autocratic leadership used not only effectively but fairly, as everyone knew what the rules where. Autocratic leadership can be applied in a very transparent way when there are good structures in place. One night in the army, the unit I was in charge of was under fire for almost two hours. I was given the order not to return fire and that was the order I gave my men. We laid on the floor with our helmets, guns, and all the other equipment hearing the sound of bullets and waited patiently. The decision may have seemed strange, but the senior leadership had probably seen similar provocations and knew that if there was no response they would stop. The autocratic decision passed down the hierarchy almost certainly saved lives. Giving people the freedom to express themselves and make mistakes is not always the best choice.

3.2.2 Autocratic leadership's impact on AI adoption and trust

AI can be used in many ways, but one of its biggest strengths is that it can concentrate power to a small number of people. This is for a variety of reasons, such as needing less staff because of the automation and making it easier to scale the operations. It is not a stretch to suspect that an autocratic leader will find this attractive and try to implement an AI solution that concentrates power to themselves.

The typical character of an autocratic leader will lean on their authority to shape the new business model and AI solutions to give themselves more power. This, however, will be disastrous for trust. The common event that preceded the fall of many dictators is that they constantly increased power to an increasingly smaller circle of people until the circle of the oppressors was no longer large enough to oppress the rest. This process has an almost inevitable evolutionary trajectory; the pride before the fall. Therefore, an autocratic leader should avoid using AI to concentrate their power. They should see AI as an opportunity to have effective operations without the need to micromanage people and have overbearing control.

Autocratic leadership is very effective in implementing AI as long as the chosen strategy and technologies are the right ones. Because of the clear authority and clear plan, the implementation can be swift with standardised solutions and consistency. Resistance will be overcome and everyone can know what to expect. Trust is built with the clarity of the plan and the confidence in the leadership.

There are two scenarios in digital transformation where this leadership approach should probably be avoided. The first is if there is a lack of a clear plan for some reason, for example because of the complexity of the changes and the many potential unintended consequences. The second, related reason is that digital transformation with AI is not about implementing one solution, but rather an ongoing process. There may be a period of very high activity while changing a business model, and once the major changes are made the activity is reduced, but nevertheless it is an ongoing process. If we want to build a culture of innovation, this is not the ideal approach.

It is not impossible to have a culture of innovation with this leadership approach, and there are some examples of this, but it is not the most conducive approach to creating a culture of innovation. It is not always the case that having some rigid structure in how things are done stifles innovation. There are heavily bureaucratic organisations that are excellent innovators. Someone could argue many engineering companies are an example of this. It is the decision-making process in a team with an autocratic leader that will most likely stifle innovation. People don't need to be free to do whatever they want at work to innovate, but they need to feel that they have a say in how things go forward and how their innovation is utilised. What often happens is that an autocratic leader is focused on their personal financial benefit and are not interested in other people's ideas.

An autocratic leader may have that approach to ensure that tasks are done in a specific way, and that the standards are kept. In addition to AI, an autocratic leader can utilise blockchain to ensure that processes are done correctly. Blockchain can be used as an infrastructure layer giving people the right access, executing processes automatically with smart contracts, and providing transparency. While many software solutions can do these things, blockchain has advantages in doing this across the value chain. In some implementations it can also save energy consumption compared to the alternative solutions. The blockchain division of software company SAP have said that in some of their implementations blockchain saves on energy bills. By ensuring things are done correctly through the technology, the autocratic leader will not need to be as hands-on or dictatorial. This may reduce friction and therefore reduce the damage to trust.

While a slower well-planned implementation of new AI solutions may be a positive thing, an autocrat may see any change as a threat and resist it all together. Some autocrats were gifted their position of unquestioned authority, but others used Machiavellian methods to engineer the situation to their benefit. If business models, processes, and roles change, their authority may be diluted. Even something simple like more people having access to certain information can dilute power. For this reason, they may see change as a threat to their position and resist it as much as possible.

We are trying to understand the journey of leadership here, not in depth like a historian, but enough to understand how it is evolving. Autocratic leadership of people is certainly one of the oldest forms of leadership as it comes naturally to many, and it often gets results. Here we also discuss autocratic leadership with AI. We mean leadership in AI in the sense that the leader is not just achieving tasks through other people but also through AI, and they are leading in how AI is utilised. At the same time, we have the increasing dynamic of machines managing people with what could be described as autocratic leadership. We are starting to see technology play the role of an autocratic leader. We need to understand the many implications of this. Technology is not just a tool for monitoring performance, but it actively manages people and enforces specific actions and behaviours autocratically. This can sometimes look like a fitness tracker on steroids. Will this approach have its niche – preferred in certain places such as warehouses – or will it become the dominant approach? Will the dominant approach be an autocratic leader with machines enforcing their will? The strengths and weaknesses of this approach are summarised in Table 3.1.

Table 3.1: Autocratic leadership's strengths and weaknesses in supporting AI and trust.

Autocratic leadership	Strengths in supporting AI	Weaknesses in supporting AI	Strengths in supporting trust	Weaknesses in supporting trust
Concentrates power to a small number of people.	Fast decision making and implementation. Everyone will implement their part of a complex process according to the plan so everything fits together in the end.	No buy-in from the rest of the stakeholders.	Clear message, clear plan, and clear authority.	Makes people believe the motivation will be selfish and not in their interest.
Discourages culture of innovation.	Less deviation from plan.	Without culture of innovation long-term progress will be slower.	Consistency and standardisation reduce risk.	Followers have limited confidence that their ideas will be implemented.
Provide foundation of stability.	Less risk and fewer surprises when implementing new technologies	–	May reduce friction and therefore reduce the damage to trust.	–
Prefer status quo, see change as a threat.	May avoid moving too fast with unproven implementations of AI.	May not innovate fast enough.	Slower progress may reduce risk.	Lack of commitment and confidence in the changes.

3.2.3 The popularity of autocratic leadership in the future

Inevitably, this approach is also very common with smaller and medium-size companies where typically there is a founder of an organisation who has invested their money and wants to make all the decisions. It tends to work well when the national, or organisational, culture is hierarchical with clear lines of authority. It also works better with young people at the start of their career, as being forced into a subservient role is an easier pill to swallow when someone is young. It is also easier to be optimistic and naive when we are young and hope the way we are treated in an organisation will change.

It is also a leadership style that most people can apply if they are in a position of true and undisputed authority. If someone has most of the power in a relationship, such as a manager of people on short contracts, it does not require a specific personality type, particular skills, or traits to apply this approach.

Overall, however, this leadership style is becoming less popular. It will always have a role to play as it suits some situations, but overall, its popularity is fading. Furthermore, increasingly when it is applied it is not the most dogmatic or pure implementation. Modern autocratic leaders often use a blended approach, combining it with some delegation of tasks and democratic decision making for some things. They can delegate where they trust the people involved and have a stricter hierarchy where there is less trust.

This approach is becoming less popular for many reasons, but there are three interrelated reasons that are the most significant. Firstly, leadership that focuses on motiving instead of giving orders often gets better results. Secondly, people want to be involved in the decision-making process. You get more buy-in from people if they are involved in the decision-making process. Even if the final decision isn't what they wanted, they still appreciate being involved. Thirdly the autocratic approach, by design, limits creativity. While this is often the intended goal, if people don't feel like their ideas to improve things will be used, they eventually stop thinking creatively. If an autocratic leader at some point wants to suddenly 'turn on' the creativity, it may not flow. Once habits and attitudes are set, it can take time to change them. While autocratic leadership has its place and is useful in some situations, empowering followers and giving them some autonomy usually brings better results.

Key concept: Autocratic leadership is very effective in implementing change as long as the chosen strategy and technologies are the right ones. Because of the clear authority and clear plan, the implementation can be swift with standardised solutions and consistency. However, as it is a very heavily top-down approach, the reduced communication may cause wrong decisions to be made and a weaker monitoring of progress.

Leadership tip: Autocratic leadership is very effective in implementing a strategy and AI because of the clear authority. Its limitations can be mitigated if it is blended with some democratic leadership to encourage better communication and buy-in.

Trust-building tip: This approach builds trust with the clarity of the plan and the confidence in the leadership. The plan needs to be the right one, and the leader needs a track record of success for this approach to encourage trust between the stakeholders.

3.3 Democratic leadership, AI, and trust

It is acknowledged, namely, that there are in the world three forms of government, autocracy, oligarchy, and democracy: autocracies and oligarchies are administered according to the tempers of their lords, but democratic states according to established laws. — Aeschines, ancient Greek statesman

Famous leaders using this style:
Angela Merkel, former chancellor of Germany.
Mahatma Gandhi, leader of the Indian independence movement.

3.3.1 The strengths and weaknesses of democratic leadership

Democratic leadership is obviously the opposite of autocratic. While we all understand what this leadership approach is, it is still worth reflecting on how it works, what effect it has on people, and how it influences AI and trust. There is a big difference between understanding the basic premise of a leadership approach and having the knowledge and judgement of when, and how, to apply it.

In democratic leadership, also known as participative leadership, the decision making has a shared responsibility and the team problem solve in a collaborative way. The behaviour of the leader is very different to the autocratic approach, as instead of enforcing a top-down approach, the democratic leader tries to encourage everyone to get involved. Hearing different perspectives is perceived as a good thing as it can lead to a more well-rounded decision and avoids surprises in the future. If a strategy is co-created after hearing a variety of perspectives, when it comes to implementing the solution, things should go more smoothly.

There is, of course, the counter argument that when many people get involved and a goal or strategy tries to incorporate all the different perspectives it can end up very muddled. In many, if not all cultures, there are some popular sayings about this, such as 'too many cooks spoil the broth'. We also often hear when something is badly designed without a clear vision people saying it looks like 'it was designed by a committee'.

There needs to be some structure in terms of how democratic decisions are made. Democratic leadership does not mean everyone does whatever they want. Just as democratic countries have a different structure to implement it, the same applies to organisations. Voting is typically limited to important decisions, so the inclusive approach is mainly operationalised through having many meetings to discuss things and share ideas, and shared responsibility in the decision-making process. Democratic leadership is not just about the decision-making process, as the implementation must be transparent so colleagues can see that what was agreed was implemented. Democratic approaches only work when there is transparency.

Central to this approach is delegating responsibility effectively. This is one of the many occasions where we understand something interesting about human psychology while we are trying to become better leaders. It is very interesting, and possibly counterintuitive for some, that followers having a sense of ownership and responsibility can be more powerful than coercion. At least in the long term this often happens; people feeling unfairly oppressed will rebel. The rebellion against being oppressed may be very overt, or simply expressed by working less hard. It is very different, of course, if the rules being enforced are valid. For example, if we are working on an oil rig, the security rules may feel oppressive, but nobody will argue with their validity as their goal is to keep everyone safe.

As was said, good communication is central to this approach. The leader supports the communication channels and is a good listener, but also gives feedback. Younger generations want more regular feedback. The importance followers put on feedback is dependent to some degree on the culture, with some expecting more feedback than others, but the general trend is for feedback to increase. Money and fear are not the only ways to motivate. People want personal development, and feedback is an integral part of that.

3.3.2 Democratic leadership's impact on AI adoption and trust

When it comes to utilising AI, the strengths of democratic leadership can have a very positive effect on implementation and adoption. The emphasis on communication can help us understand people's beliefs on this complex topic and how the implementation is going, so we can adapt accordingly. If people have been included in the process they will not feel AI is against them, and there will be buy-in and ownership. It is easier and more natural for organisations that encourage communication internally to successfully communicate externally also.

A project I was involved in at University of Cambridge tried to democratically get the whole of Latin America to have a common policy and strategy on cryptoassets (Proskalovich et al., 2023). Agreeing on every detail was unlikely, but consultations with both the public and private sector brought everyone together and increased the degree of agreement for a shared vision. The democratic process made everyone see each other's perspective more clearly. There are some opposing interests, so however beneficial the process is it will not resolve everything, but reducing the uncertainty about the various stakeholders' intentions brings people closer.

Digital transformation with AI is changing business models and our professional and personal lives. Because of the far-reaching consequences, there will be many different beliefs on how it should be used. With software and technology, what is usually applied is autocratic leadership, even if the leaders that are autocratic build their personal brand to look very different with charities and telling us how much they care about worthy causes. Despite the public relations, there is no getting away from the fact that most new technologies are either forced onto people or given for free with a good service that then deteriorates after the users are tied in. There are, of course, many exceptions, such as Mastodon that act in a more democratic way.

A genuine democratic leader will also utilise AI in a democratic way. Utilising open-source software as far as possible and not getting tied into oligopolies is the most democratic approach to utilising AI. More democratic leadership internally, and a more democratic relationship across the ecosystem that AI uses, is beneficial. It must be noted, however, that ecosystems are not just orchestrated by the organisations that want to collaborate, but are heavily dependent on institutions such as regulators, the European Union, and technology standards. The organisations' influence may indeed support a democratic approach by pushing open standards, or it might be more rigid and strict. An example of this is the European Union enforcing open standards in banking with the Payment Services Directive. If it is rigidity that is enforced, then, while democratic leadership can incentivise partners to act in a similar way, there are still some parameters of collaborating in ecosystems that must be enforced.

Feedback is needed from staff and partners. In some cases, even a public consultation is necessary. Implementing AI more extensively requires education and building an awareness of the issue. Democratic leadership creates the right environment for education, but it also needs knowledgeable people for the democratic decision making to function well. There is, therefore, a very different dynamic to the autocratic approach. In the autocratic approach some people need to be skilled in making strategic decisions and others need to be strong at implementing. In contrast, by having a democratic decision-making process, a community of professionals with well-rounded knowledge on AI is created.

Leveraging blockchain in a democratic way is far easier than AI, as it is a technology built to decentralise processes. It can be used to actively support the democratic process by providing voting rights and providing transparency on the operations. Democratic leadership is ethical and fair, but that is not enough for it to be successful. The process of how decisions are made can be supported by blockchain that can manage who has voting rights, what they have voting rights on, and the casting of votes. This technology is very useful for identity management, which is one of the things you need if you will have anonymised voting in a large organisation spread across many locations. In terms of the transparency of the operations, various information, such as data on costs or performance, can be recorded on a blockchain ledger so it can be viewed by all staff but cannot be corrupted. The transparency supported by blockchain will support trust because it will not be dependent on one person or a handful of individuals, but a transparent technology. Blockchain can implement decentralised governance and give people a more direct role in the decision-making process in an elegant way. It is not the only way, but it is an elegant and transparent way to do it.

This better understanding of people's beliefs, stronger buy-in, and constant communication can benefit the initial implementation but also the ongoing innovation. Our relationship with AI is definitely a lifelong relationship, not a one-off project of technology implementation. This transparent inclusive process should feel fair, and this will build trust. There will be more trust in the leadership and the technology.

Democratic leadership is more beneficial when the changes to the business model due to AI are significant. For example, it would be a very significant change to the business model if an insurer decides to not do all the processes they used to do and focus on one part of the value chain only, such as the onboarding of clients or risk estimation. If the changes are limited to bringing more efficiency without more fundamental changes, there is less reason to take a vote on aspects of the plan. This leadership approach is also more necessary at the start of a project, where everyone's opinions need to be collected and some brainstorming are required. A leader needs to constantly make an estimation of how much time and resources something will take and what the potential benefits are. Transparency, which is encouraged by democratic leadership, can exist in a way that does not require too many resources. The strengths and weaknesses of this style in supporting AI and trust are summarized in table 3.2.

Table 3.2: Democratic leadership's strengths and weaknesses in supporting AI and trust.

Democratic leadership	Strengths in supporting AI	Weaknesses in supporting AI	Strengths in supporting trust	Weaknesses in supporting trust
Strong communication between all stakeholders.	Find best solutions, get accurate picture of progress.	Decision making is slow and drains resources. Final decision may be a compromise to keep everyone happy but lacks coherence and synergy.	Buy-in from everyone. The more transparent decision making and implementation may reduce the fear of the unknown.	There may be a fear that the plan will keep changing as people change their mind.
People's opinions valued.	Encourages stakeholders to educate themselves in AI. Can create culture of innovation.	–	With enhanced knowledge on AI, the uncertainties and perceived risk are reduced. More confidence in their ability to implement new AI solutions.	–
Can use blockchain infrastructure to support democratic collaboration.	Democratic processes built into the infrastructure to support AI.	May add complexity to the solution.	Blockchain can be transparent to all stakeholders.	People may be overwhelmed by the many new technologies.

3.3.3 The popularity of democratic leadership in the future

Unsurprisingly, this leadership approach is very popular in the modern workplace. While it is a very ethical and a fair approach, it does not always bring the best results, so it should not be seen as a panacea that will lead us to a utopia or nirvana. Unfortunately, the workplace can be very rewarding, full of happy and empowered employees, yet the work being done can be very little and of low quality. Unfortunately, we see this increasingly today. An example is the very democratic decision to work from home, which has decimated productivity and quality for many public and private organisations and is also having a subtle negative effect on the workers themselves.

Democratic leadership is not just popular with the followers, but also with the leaders themselves as it does not require any rare personality traits or skills. It is an approach that most people can apply. Democratic leadership is often combined with other leadership approaches in an effort to get the ideal balance for the situation. It can be made stricter by combining it with autocratic, or less strict by combining it with delegative and laissez-faire.

Key concept: Democratic leadership can have a very positive effect on AI adoption. The emphasis on communication can help us follow the progress of AI adoption closely and adapt accordingly. When people have been included in the process they do not feel AI is against them and there is buy-in and ownership. This buy-in and constant communication benefits the ongoing innovation.

Leadership tip: This leadership approach is very popular with stakeholders. While it is very ethical and fair, it does not always bring the best results. If there are negative, lazy, or less competent stakeholders, the leader needs to blend this approach with a more autocratic approach to get the best results.

Trust-building tip: The democratic approach is ethical, fair, and transparent, so this builds strong sustainable trust. There will be more trust in the leadership, each other, and the technology.

3.4 Delegative leadership, AI, and trust

If you really want to grow as an entrepreneur, you've got to learn to delegate. — Richard Branson, business magnate and co-founder of the Virgin Group

The best way to find out if you can trust somebody is to trust them. — Ernest Hemingway, novelist and journalist

Famous leaders using this style:
Demis Hassabis, founder of Deep Mind, brought together two types of AI deep learning, which uses neural networks that work like the brain, and reinforcement learning that uses a model to make decisions.

Jack Ma, founder of Alibaba.

3.4.1 The strengths and weaknesses of delegative leadership

Delegative leadership is one of the basic, fundamental leadership approaches that come naturally to many people and fit many situations. A leader who delegates typically breaks down a task and assigns sections of it to team members. The team members are given the authority and freedom to make decisions and handle these issues in the way they see fit. This gives team members a sense of ownership and responsibility. The overall philosophy is to encourage team members to feel invested, take initiatives, and move forward quickly.

While this may seem similar to democratic, as it is as far away from autocratic as possible, it is actually quite different. While democratic is about going through a process together and coming to an agreement, when we delegate we want to encourage action not discussion. Of course there are many ways to delegate, and some consider it the same as laissez-faire, but the version of delegating that encourages action is more useful when we are discussing AI adoption and trust.

A leader that delegates does not just offload responsibility. They still give feedback, including constructive criticism, provide support and guidance, and seek out ways for the team members to develop as professionals. These characteristics of this leadership approach are very motivating for people as they feel involved, empowered, valued, and respected. Of course, giving freedom and surrendering some control can cause demotivating problems such as confusion, duplication of work, and incompatible solutions. A leader that delegates still needs the typical leadership skills such as strategic thinking, patience, and being able to resolve conflict.

Delegative leadership is often, but not always, the right approach for the people, the situation, the technology, and building trust. Giving people at work more freedom is often about striking the right balance. Not everyone is self-motivated and inherently behaves professionally.

We argue here that trust goes right through our relationships with each other and technology and is not an issue that can be compartmentalised in one place, such as one person or process. The pervasive role of trust is clearly evident in delegative leadership, as the first step, the trigger that gets the ball rolling, is based on the leader's judgement to trust and their inherent ability to let go and trust, which not everyone has. Therefore, unlike other approaches where trust is built in both directions gradually, here it is like a transaction where the leader gives trust and then the followers give trust back. The way this leadership approach can build trust is one of its biggest strengths. It is one of the most effective approaches at building trust. The downside of that is that trust is entirely necessary for this approach to be implemented. Several leadership approaches, such as bureaucratic leadership, can function with very low trust, or no trust at all. It is not ideal, but they have been proven to get the job done with such low trust. This is an obvious point, but we need to keep all these different dimensions of each approach fresh in our mind so we can compare them and chose the right one.

This leadership approach is implemented to some degree by most managers. How far they go down this road depends on how much trust they have in their people, so if they feel the risk is low, they will delegate, or they might take a leap of faith and hope that people grow into it. In one of my early roles I worked in a small team that started with around five people setting up online programmes. This was before online university degrees became popular. Many people felt online universities were not real universities. Most of us had under five years' experience working in universities and no experience teaching online. The whole project of setting up several programmes was delegated to us. This was clearly a risk, and the people that did this must have believed there was a chance we would grow into this role. The project was very complex and we often changed plans several times in a day. It is unlikely the work would have been completed successfully if responsibility had not been delegated. If we had to have meetings or bureaucracy for every step, we would have ground to a halt.

3.4.2 Delegative leadership's impact on AI adoption and trust

The mentality and philosophy behind delegating may be a good fit for an organisation that wants to fully utilise AI. Utilising AI in new ways can be seen as one more level of delegation. Until now, most of the software used to automate tasks used human logic written into the software. Typically, despite using software, we have not delegated the thinking to a machine, but now with AI, that is what we need to do. Furthermore, a skilled leader that delegates knowns how to motivate and act like a cheerleader for others. Making dramatic changes is scary and needs bravery, so the moral support is beneficial. Having a mindset, or even a philosophy, that can endure through all the dramatic change with AI is very beneficial.

Being successful in digital transformation requires several things to come together. One of the biggest challenges for companies going through this process is for their staff to gain the necessary knowledge to utilise AI (Zarifis & Yarovaya, 2025). As the processes – and even the whole business model – change, so do people's roles. Not every member of staff is fascinated by AI and enthusiastic about leaving their comfort zone. This is not a criticism; it is understandable. Many of us have been in the position where we have resisted change because we preferred the old way of doing things. This leadership approach puts trust and responsibility on staff, and this encourages personal growth in many ways. Firstly, people want to learn new things to complete the tasks, but, equally importantly, they see that their input is valued, so they believe they can benefit from the leader if they improve their skills and knowledge. Therefore, this leadership approach has a very important strength when used for digital transformation, which is that it encourages the personal growth to gain the necessary skills to utilise AI.

Delegating tasks can happen at any stage of implementing AI, but it is better if there is first some shared agreement between all the stakeholders on what the plan is. The motivation and logic behind this approach is clear, but the effect it has on stakeholders and AI adoption is not always what we expect. As the process of implementing and constantly innovating with the application of AI will be a lifelong endeavour – and nobody knows exactly where it will take us – delegating to some degree makes a lot of sense. However, as we emphasise here, some issues, like trust, must be discussed and baked into the business model level (Zarifis & Cheng, 2025). A good leader should delegate where appropriate, but there must be some boundaries to the freedom given. The boundaries should be on issues that affect trust, such as concerns about the privacy of personal information.

Having clarity on the business model is one of the ways to have some boundaries within which to delegate. People can have authority to make decisions, but they cannot change the business model unilaterally. The different stakeholders must be given the certainty that there will not be a deviation from an agreed plan. This certainty is needed so that people can trust the new AI solutions.

If the boundaries of the freedom given are clear, then giving freedom to innovate and make decisions instead of endless soul-searching meetings and bureaucracy can be very beneficial. Our journey to utilise AI is a race, whether we like it or not, and some leadership approaches make faster progress possible. Getting the risk/reward balance right is important, and delegating increases some risks but reduces others. As we move up through the ranks of an organisation, experience and perhaps intellectual capacity may increase, but what those higher up see is often a simplified abstraction of what's happening at the 'coal face'.

For example, I was once an officer at an army base that went through a very thorough audit and got a relatively low score. The audit covered pretty much everything from our knowledge to how clean the base was. While the information they collected was extensive, it was still a subset of the reality I experienced. Some things, like equipment not having a speck of dust on it, are taken as proxies of professionalism. The reality that I was seeing was that there was a very high level of professionalism on the things that really mattered, but some disregard for the formalities, the pomp and ceremony. Some people have it drilled into them in their upbringing that the formalities are important and that you not only have to do your job, but also present the image of what someone in that role should have. Others' minds are wired to focus on getting things done, and they care far less about the image they are presenting. Table 3.3 summarizes the strengths and weaknesses of this approach.

Table 3.3: Delegative leadership's strengths and weaknesses in supporting AI and trust.

Delegative leadership	Strengths in supporting AI	Weaknesses in supporting AI	Strengths in supporting trust	Weaknesses in supporting trust
Giving people the authority to act based on their own judgement.	People are free to be proactive and move forward.	The implementation may be disjointed and chaotic. The final solution may have duplications, incompatibilities, and no synergy.	Stakeholders feel ownership of the decisions. More transparency in what they are doing.	Less transparency in what other people are doing possibly increases the sense of risk. Possibly less clarity in the overarching plan.
Shows confidence and trust in people.	People feel they have the support to move forward and innovate. May feel encouraged to learn more about AI.	Some fear ensures things are done correctly; overconfidence may lead to mistakes. Some people will take advantage of the trust they have been shown.	Stakeholders will reciprocate the trust they receive.	Some boundaries need to be put in place to limit freedom and deviation from the plan. AI may not be used ethically by everyone.

3.4.3 The popularity of delegative leadership in the future

This approach is very popular but it has some limitations that mean it is not always the best approach. There is a trade-off between freedom and control, and if this balance is not right, things start to go wrong with miscommunication and a lack of direction. If the team is not highly skilled and motivated it is unlikely to work. If the team is not used to having less structure, they might grab the opportunity to grow or they may feel they have been left not knowing what to do.

Key concept: A delegative leader typically breaks down a task and assigns sections of it to team members. The team members are given the authority and freedom to make decisions and handle these issues in the way they see fit.

Leadership tip: Having clarity on the business model is one of the ways to have some boundaries within which to delegate. If the boundaries of the freedom given are clear, then giving freedom to innovate and make decisions instead of endless soul-searching meetings and bureaucracy can be very beneficial in implementing AI.

Strength when applied in digital transformation: This leadership approach has a very important strength when used for digital transformation, which is that it encourages the personal growth to gain the necessary skills to fully utilise AI.

Trust-building tip: The pervasive role of trust is clearly evident in delegative leadership, as the first step, the trigger that gets the ball rolling, is based on the leader's judgement to trust. People feel involved, empowered, valued, and respected, so they return the trust they receive.

3.5 Bureaucratic leadership, AI, and trust

Bureaucracy is not an obstacle to democracy but an inevitable complement to it. — Joseph A. Schumpeter, Austrian political economist

Famous leaders using this style:
Jean-Claude Juncker, former president of the European Commission.

Shinji Sogo, former president of Japanese National Railways. Under his leadership, the world's first high-speed train service was offered.

3.5.1 The strengths and weaknesses bureaucratic leadership

Bureaucratic leadership is a tool to support a hierarchy and structure and avoid deviations from it. Everyone must follow established rules and procedures. There are protocols for most things, and before something is done there is a formal process to ask for permission. When I was at a German university, there was one specific person that had to put a physical stamp on my request form to get access to the university internet. Some bureaucracies, such as requiring a physical stamp on a piece of paper to allow a new member of staff to access the internet, were put in place a long time ago, when the circumstances were different. For example, there were fewer short work contracts and more jobs for life, so going through this once was not a big issue. Now, the times are different, with many short projects. It might not be bureaucratic leadership that most people dislike, but outdated and inappropriate forms of it. What is the likelihood that a new member of staff is not granted access to the internet? If a new member of staff needs to accept some terms, can't this be done all in one go when they join?

Some leadership styles are immediately appealing to us and others are immediately unappealing. Bureaucratic leadership instantly creates images of filling in forms, feelings of frustration, and a lack of progress. Certainly not what we want in the age of AI. The weaknesses are obvious: things take longer and there is less innovation, creativity, and flexibility. However, this method does have strengths and still has its place, especially in building trust with stakeholders. Some organisations must have consistency and stability due to regulations or safety requirements. There are other organisations that choose to operate in this way despite it not being entirely necessary.

While many people may prefer more inspiring, dynamic work environments such as startups, what typically happens is that even startups with charismatic, democratic, or laissez-faire leaders add more bureaucracy as they grow in size. Like many issues, there is an ideological and philosophical dimension to it, and there is the practical dimension of coordinating increasingly large numbers of people. It is better to have the structure to stop things going wrong rather than playing the blame game and retrospectively trying to add structure once things go wrong.

A bureaucratic leader spends their time very differently and needs to have different skills to a leader that applies democratic, servant, or transformational leadership. There are similarities to transactional leadership, as it also clearly defines tasks, although it is far less rigid. A bureaucratic leader spends their time defining clear roles, finding ways to formalise processes, and enforcing adherence – a little like a policeman or policewoman. All the leader's actions are aimed at maintaining order and stability.

A bureaucratic leader motivates in a very different way to a democratic, servant, or transformational leader, although once again it does have similarities to transactional leadership. Offering consistent expectations and a clear structure might not sound inspiring, but it is very motivating. It is particularly good at avoiding demotivating situations, such as unfairness due to broken promises and confusion that leads to wasting time. Often, more experienced professionals that know what they want and prefer certainty over inspiration value this approach. When someone starts to doubt that they will be treated fairly, many bad things happen, such as lower productivity and higher staff turnover. Many leaders miss this either unintentionally or try to mask it with other results. I worked in a university that clearly had a problem with very high turnover despite being very highly ranked. The excuses included: 'other universities have worse turnover', 'it used to be worse before I came', and 'the person that left wanted to work closer to their home'. After a while, I started to notice most of those that left were not going to work closer to where they lived. A good bureaucracy that ensured resources were distributed more fairly would have reduced turnover.

3.5.2 Bureaucratic leadership's impact on AI adoption and trust

This approach stifles speed, innovation, creativity, and flexibility. It is more focused on avoiding big deviations from the plan to avoid big mistakes. It tries to ensure the quality does not go below a minimum acceptable level. Therefore, it does not typically help in supporting a culture of constant evolution and innovation. It can, however, support a stop-start approach, where a period of planning is succeeded by a period of implementation. This can work in some situations. It can be challenging to apply this approach successfully in situations where the way to move forward is not clear.

While the word bureaucracy has the negative connotation of a waste of time, several constructive bureaucracies need to be put in place for several important issues. For many organisations, fully utilising AI requires extensive planning on both the business and technology side. While some small and medium enterprises may limit themselves to buying subscriptions to generative AI services, some will need to plan how to implement AI on a large scale. AI needs data, storage, and processing power. While historical data is useful in training machine learning, real-time data from a variety of sources is needed to deliver fast, integrated, and automated services. This not only needs planning, but it needs bureaucracies put in place. Formal contracts with partners with a variety of terms, auditable data, legal and regulatory requirements of different countries, even different regions in some countries, are only some of the examples. Innovation is not just about creative ideas; it is about putting the structures in place to make them happen in a scalable way.

Similarly, in terms of changing a business model and going through digital transformation, agreements need to be made that are binding both within and outside the organisation. Agreements need to be binding as the new business model and the technology it uses is all interconnected and interdependent. You cannot move forward in transforming an organisation if at any point a manager can wake up one morning and decide they changed their mind. There are many interrelated steps and processes that need each other to work successfully. These interrelated processes include both existing and new systems. Existing systems are not a static solution in most cases. What is often referred to as maintenance is usually a constant evolution of a system to adapt to changing requirements and threats. The integration into existing systems needs a structured plan.

There needs to be a standardisation of governance, so policies are always followed correctly. One of the biggest risks AI brings is the shift of responsibility from a person to the opaque AI inner processes. This lack of clear accountability needs to be avoided and there must be always someone formally responsible.

The stop-start approach to innovation mentioned, where planning is followed by action, is a more systematic approach to change management. There need to be clear decision-making frameworks for prioritising what to do and resource allocation. Balancing new expenses against cash flow is a challenge even for successful companies. Even the most successful companies tend to have limited cash flow and often need to arrange loans for large additional expenses.

The planning involved in this approach can also enable staff to specialise, offering them job predictability. The more central technology is to an organisation, the greater the need for people with specialised knowledge. A bureaucratic approach can organise the processes and give people the 'freedom' to focus on their tasks. The dirty secret of more liberal laissez-faire approaches is that people waste time unproductively and must change roles often, wasting the experience they gained in the previous role. The structure of bureaucratic leadership also reduces favouritism.

Having a structured approach to implementing AI will also make monitoring and evaluating the results much easier. Software developers are often too busy to create the necessary documentation, but someone must do it. This starts with comprehensive contracts with the suppliers covering every eventuality and reducing loopholes to a minimum. If the leadership of an organisation is out of the loop at the start of the implementation, they will struggle to catch up and may be permanently left in the dark (Zarifis & Yarovaya, 2025).

Most of these necessary bureaucracies are not needed exclusively when utilising AI, but the use of AI makes them more necessary because of its capabilities, and the far-reaching impact it can have. While this leadership approach may not be the first one that comes to mind when we want to be dynamic innovators, it can provide a stable foundation on which to innovate and collaborate in a safe and sustainable way. If you have the strong structure, you can more easily 'plug in' innovations and collaborations. The supermarket Lidl is an example of that. Their bureaucracies and structure, especially in their supply chain that is very integrated with their suppliers, allows them to innovate with technology. Having effective bureaucratic leadership can be a sign of a mature innovator. The leader puts in the structure so others can innovate.

In terms of building trust in AI, this method is effective, but in a different way to most leadership approaches. Trust is built by offering consistent expectations and a clear structure on how AI will be used, how it will not be used, and avoiding unfairness. Furthermore, by lowering the uncertainty and therefore the risk, less trust is needed. A transformational leader can build trust with a shared vision for change, but the high level of change and uncertainty also necessitates a high level of trust. Bureaucratic leadership in utilising AI does not ask you to take a leap of faith. Furthermore, if we look at some influential tech companies that misbehave from time to time, it is the bureaucracy – both in government and the bureaucracy enforced on organisations – that tries to protect us from the dark side of this technology.

Table 3.4: Bureaucratic leadership's strengths and weaknesses in supporting AI and trust.

Bureaucratic leadership	Strengths in supporting AI	Weaknesses in supporting AI	Strengths in supporting trust	Weaknesses in supporting trust
This approach limits flexibility and is more focused on avoiding big mistakes.	Provides framework and parameters for AI implementation, avoids costly errors.	Speed, innovation, and creativity are reduced.	More predictable outcomes.	Less confidence in the commitment to change.
Bureaucracy mindset enables new structures, procedures, and contracts to be made.	Will make changing business model easier.	–	The new model and structures will be clearer, inspiring confidence.	–
Planning involved in this approach can enable staff to specialise.	Staff will specialise and become experts in their role.	–	Becoming experts in aspects of utilising AI will increase confidence.	–

3.5.3 The popularity of bureaucratic leadership in the future

Some of us will work in organisations that require this leadership approach. Many of us will not feel attracted to this leadership approach and will prefer a more inspiring approach, such as democratic or servant leadership. Broadly speaking, bureaucratic leadership is decreasing in popularity, but it will always have its place. While few people would say it is their first choice in the workplace, with other approaches in theory being more appealing, the strength of this approach is that it tries to avoid the worst outcomes. Some of the more enticing leadership approaches like servant leadership are very effective with the right people, but they can often appear naive and fail to avoid typical problems caused by less professional employees.

Interestingly, many leaders take care of the bureaucratic side of the project when applying servant leadership. In servant leadership the focus is to support the team members with what the team members believe they need. So we see that in a leadership style that has very different priorities to bureaucratic leadership, bringing in some bureaucratic leadership is beneficial. For example, project managers in software development often take care of the administration and bureaucracies so the software developers can focus on their core job. We see here one of the many examples where effective leadership is about combining approaches and not choosing the 'best' approach. The main strengths and weaknesses of this approach are summarised in Table 3.4.

Key concept: A bureaucratic leader encourages everyone to follow rigid structures. Offering consistent expectations and a clear structure might not sound inspiring, but it is very transparent and motivating.

Leadership tip: This approach stifles regular innovation, however, it can support a stop-start approach, where a period of planning is succeeded by a period of implementation. This might be suitable to AI projects where a clear plan can be developed, but it is not suitable to 'playing it by ear'.

Trust-building tip: Offering consistent expectations and a clear structure might not sound inspiring, but it is very motivating, it builds trust, and it avoids unfairness that can create distrust. By lowering the uncertainty and therefore the risk, less trust is needed.

3.6 Charismatic leadership, AI, and trust

There can be no power without mystery. There must always be a "something" which others cannot altogether fathom, which puzzles them, stirs them, and rivets their attention. Nothing more enhances authority than silence. It is the crowning virtue of the strong, the refuge of the weak, the modesty of the proud, the pride of the humble, the prudence of the wise, and the sense of fools. — Charles de Gaulle, former French military officer and statesman

Famous leaders using this style:

Stelios Haji-Ioannou, founder of easyJet.

Michael Portillo, former British politician and cabinet minister.

José Mourinho, football coach.

3.6.1 The strengths and weaknesses of charismatic leadership

A charismatic leader uses their personal strengths to inspire the team. These can include their personality, communication skills, humour, intelligence, and vision. Ideally, a charismatic leader can have a well-rounded personality and skill set, but there are charismatic leaders that lean heavily on one or two of those characteristics. They can communicate in a dramatic way, inspiring people and making them identify with their leader and follow them blindly. While such a leader relies heavily on their personality, it does not mean they lack substance or don't have a good plan. Ideally, they have an excellent plan, but they use their personality rally people around it. When Emmanuel Macron backed Mistral AI and encouraged billions of euros in investment, he used his charisma, but there was also a good plan to build a strong AI tech provider that gave companies using their technology, such as the French army, data sovereignty.

Even the most charismatic leader is not a magician and will not get very far without a plan. People can get excited and inspired by the way a charismatic leader conveys the genuine strengths of a plan. Using charisma to trick people into doing something that they do not want to do is not only unethical but a bad business strategy as it will eventually backfire. Robert Allen Stanford is serving 110 years in prison despite doing an excellent job at creating a charming persona and tricking people. As they popular saying goes, 'You can fool all the people some of the time, and some of the people all the time, but you cannot fool all the people all the time'.

Nobody can doubt that a charismatic leader with a good plan can be successful, but there are two main criticisms of this approach. The first is that many argue that not everyone can be a charismatic leader, and the second is that someone's charisma can fade. What we perceive as charisma can be various things that can include an attractive appearance, high energy, or simply being the right person at the right time. These things may come and go. For example, if an organisation has not evolved or innovated for many years and a leader comes along and eloquently makes the case for the need to innovate and change the business model, they may resonate charisma. They may, in a sense, be a 'one trick pony' and not exude charisma after that.

Being a charismatic leader is tricky even for people with natural charisma. A person having charisma with their friends, their chosen audience, is very different to being a charismatic leader of a team. Being a charismatic leader needs just the right balance of many different things. The difference between getting it right and horribly wrong can be quite subtle. For example, projecting confidence but not arrogance to a range of people with different perceptions of where the line between confidence and arrogance lies is not an easy thing to do. Similarly, the line between having confidence in a project and being insensitive and 'tone deaf' can be tricky. Charismatic leaders are often narcissistic. While they bring success and charm, this can come across as arrogance or swagger, and when the results are less positive, people find it harder to accept.

The second major criticism of this leadership approach is more general and applies to several of the popular approaches. More generally, a concentration of power in one person may work for some periods of time, but there is a very high risk associated with it. The risks of concentrating power in one leader have been illustrated throughout history with family businesses that fail after the founder passes them onto their children. This has happened over decades in many different countries, so it has been proven to be rooted in human nature to some degree. The companies that succeed are typically those that evolve into an organisation with a management structure with many leaders.

There are many examples of charisma fading in leaders, provided one knows how to identify it when they see it. When José Mourinho was the manager Manchester United, some fans told a journalist they wanted a world-class manager. When the journalist suggested José Mourinho was a world-class manager, they said he was not in his prime. Did José Mourinho's ability fade in a few years, after gaining even more experience? He was in his early fifties, so how was he not in his prime as a manager? What had of course happened is that he had not gotten worse, but the situation made him appear less charismatic. Many people struggle to separate the ability, the charisma, and the circumstances.

This is one of the leadership approaches that a small number of people base their leadership on, but many people try to incorporate elements of into their approach. This is why, like with other approaches such as autocratic or bureaucratic, even if our initial reaction is negative, it's worth persevering and understanding them thoroughly. In an age where socialising is diminishing and loneliness is on the rise, people seek qualities in their leaders that resemble those of a parent. Just as a child sees their parents as charismatic figures to look up to, people want to feel the same about their leaders. They want to be able to be proud of them. Many of us want to idolise someone; it gives us hope and some confidence that a better future is possible.

3.6.2 Charismatic leadership's impact on AI adoption and trust

Even critics of charismatic leadership acknowledge that it is useful at times of great change. When an organisation needs to be bold and go through a disruption, having a charismatic leader to 'sell it' can be very helpful in effectively conveying the new vision. When an organisation shifts its business model to fully embrace AI, it often needs to convince all stakeholders, both internal and external. In today's social media-driven world, where people are more inclined to engage with a face rather than a company name, a charismatic leader can be incredibly valuable. There is also the opportunity to prepare before sharing content online, which allows individuals to appear more charismatic than they may actually be. A person who is neither charismatic nor eloquent, and who struggles to think on their feet, can seem otherwise with adequate preparation. This phenomenon is evident in the political sphere, where many politicians hire comedians to write jokes for them, enhancing their appeal and engagement when they speak. Whether it comes naturally or needs some preparation, a charismatic leader can build trust in the transformation by convincing people of its merit.

In addition to conveying the plan in a convincing way, this leader also connects with people on an emotional level, and their confidence and positivity impacts people on a conscious and subconscious level. This emotional level and confidence are often necessary when a big change is going to happen. Feelings such as confidence, positivity, or fear are contagious for most people. In a transition with a lot of uncertainty, we want to hear a logical plan, but we also want to feel a sense of confidence and safety. Confidence is very beneficial for trust as it implies the risks are low.

A charismatic leader can also be a role model, embodying the qualities they want to see in others in a way that is hard for a group of people to convey. They can lead by example with AI. They can use AI more in the workplace and then share their positive experience with others. Leading from the front can create a culture of innovation more effectively than writing reports and books (although books are very useful too). Many people have this fear that their leaders are detached, don't truly say what they believe, or are hypocrites, so leading by example is helpful. Leading by example is especially helpful when it is combined with charisma as it can make people enjoy listening to the leader's plan for digital transformation.

The downside of focusing on the leader is that those who dislike them may perceive the leader's views as representative of the entire organisation, equating the leader they don't like with the organisation as a whole. The risk with charismatic leadership is that there is a concentration of power, and if the person with all the power is wrong, this will cause huge problems. The concentration of power may also deter people from voicing their concerns. A charismatic leader is not necessarily an autocratic leader, but it can have a similar effect. A similar problem can arise for a different reason. While all the followers may be fully on board, this may lead to groupthink and a cult-like, blind devotion.

There is also something I have noticed personally that I have not seen many other people talk about, at least in the context of leadership. Unfortunately, my observation suggests the relationship between charismatic leadership and trust is quite complicated. As mentioned earlier, the charismatic leader may make what they are doing seem effortless, but they actually need to strike a very delicate balance. It is analogous to driving a car fast down a winding road. When it works, it looks effortless and graceful, but a slight misjudgement and the grip of the back wheels is lost and control of the situation is gone. Getting the balance right is crucial to building trust. If a leader shows that they understand the concerns, accept the challenges and the difficulties that lie ahead, and then shows confidence that it will all be good in the end, this will build trust. To the contrary, a confidence in the value of using AI more extensively that does not seem to be grounded in the facts, and a lack of sensitivity towards their concerns, will not only fail to build trust but cause distrust. This is just my personal observation, and it is not backed up with conclusive scientific evidence to the extent of the other points made here. The main strengths and weaknesses of this approach are summarised in Table 3.5.

Table 3.5: Charismatic leadership's strengths and weaknesses in supporting AI and trust.

Charismatic leadership	Strengths in supporting AI	Weaknesses in supporting AI	Strengths in supporting trust	Weaknesses in supporting trust
A charismatic leader can effectively convey the new vision for big changes.	Most of the stakeholders are on board with the vision and move forward together. Can create the necessary partnerships.	–	Everyone understands the new vision, reducing uncertainty.	Some people are suspicious of charismatic leaders and their motives.
Confident and positive, connects on an emotional level.	Can make people overcome their reservations about change.	May make people overconfident and make them underestimate the challenges.	Confidence is very beneficial for trust as it implies the risks are low.	–
A charismatic leader can also embody the qualities they want in others.	Can convince people to change, get out of their comfort zone.	Even a charismatic leader may be disliked by some, and tying the change to them may backfire.	Some people find it easier and more natural to trust a person rather than a plan.	If the charismatic leader has been untrustworthy in the past, some will hold it against them.

3.6.3 The popularity of charismatic leadership in the future

Charismatic leadership is popular but understanding its popularity and how it changes is more complex than for other leadership styles, such as autocratic that gradually decreases in popularity, or transformational that steadily increases in popularity. There are many circumstantial causes to a charismatic leader emerging as a leader of a country or an organisation. What is clear is that when people do not want change, they want a technocrat, a bureaucrat, or a transactional leader, whereas when they want change – or change is forced upon them – they want a strong charismatic leader to give them the confidence that they will get them through the difficult uncertain times.

While it is easy to list personality traits and skills that are helpful for other leadership approaches, this is difficult for charismatic leadership because what is effective is very context specific. Being confident and articulate is usually helpful, but these are basic requirements of any professional. Some characteristics work in one situation but not others. For example, some aggression from a leader might be appreciated if there is anger among people over a scandal or mismanagement. In happier times, humour and politeness are more well-received. The characteristic of a leader that is appreciated is not necessarily something rare or hard to embody. For example, many people value a leader that can be empathetic and connect with them – someone with their feet on the ground. In some cases, the superpower a leader needs is to be 'normal'. Charismatic leadership is therefore not about being incredibly special – someone that can go to the Olympics or get the highest grades at university. Coming across as a charismatic leader is about conveying, either by chance or by design, what people are yearning for.

A leader with personal magnetism and positivity will be seen as the ideal person to drive significant change. Therefore, even if it is not our favourite leadership approach, we need to incorporate some of it to drive digital transformation with AI and trust.

Key concept: A charismatic leader uses their personal strengths to inspire the team. These can include their personality, communication skills, humour, intelligence, and vision. This leader also connects with people on an emotional level, and their confidence and positivity impact people on a conscious and subconscious level.

Leadership tip: Even critics of charismatic leadership acknowledge that it is useful at times of great change. When an organisation needs to be bold and go through a disruption, having a charismatic leader to convey the new vision effectively and build confidence can be very helpful.

Trust-building tip: Charismatic leadership with a bad plan for digital transformation will temporarily build trust, but trust will then inevitably nosedive along with the bad plan. Charismatic leadership with a good plan will engage people emotionally, give positivity and confidence, and build trust.

3.7 Summary

It's not about changing people; it's sometimes about changing a situation. How can we build an even better situation for them? — Jürgen Klopp, legendary football coach

3.7.1 The enduring value of traditional leadership approaches

The leadership approaches discussed here all have something to offer in driving digital transformation. The key, apart from implementing them effectively of course, is to strike the right balance. Success in business, technology, and many other areas is usually about how the key pieces of the puzzle fit together. The key pieces of the puzzle used to typically be leadership, people, and technology. Now, the key pieces of the puzzle are leadership, people, AI, and other technologies not based on AI. This change in what the key pieces of the puzzle are also changes what the role of leadership is. Leadership now must have synergies with AI, not just the people and the other technologies not based on AI.

Some people say that Jürgen Klopp adopted his famous high-pressing 'heavy metal football' tactics after a game against the team of coach Ralf Rangnick. The story goes that he was so impressed by Rangnick's team that he told his players they should play like that. Klopp has often acknowledged that he was influenced by Rangnick. However, Klopp had the experience of other tactics, and this enabled him to appreciate the one he finally adopted. His experience enabled him to understand the tactics his competitor was applying. A football coach must learn how the most popular formation was the four-four-two and then the four-two-three-one, before more recent tactics, such as having inverted fullbacks or three-four-three with wingbacks. While the style he adopted necessitated one of the key ingredients of high energy, his implementation married it with clear communication, accountability, and showing emotional intelligence.

3.7.2 Which one of the traditional leadership approaches is the best for AI and trust?

Autocratic leadership is arguably the most historic of all the leadership approaches, preferred by kings and dictators, but also family businesses, inventors, and startups. It can provide fast decision making and implementation. The standardisation and consistency can build trust in all the stakeholders. Democratic leadership is fair, ethical, and transparent, creating buy-in and trust, but it can also be slow and disjointed across the transformation. Delegative leadership gives people the authority to act based on their own judgement. This gives people the confidence to move forward and innovate with new AI services. Stakeholders will reciprocate the trust they receive. Bureaucratic leadership limits flexibility and is more focused on avoiding big mistakes. This may not be the first leadership style that comes to mind when we want fast far-reaching innovation, but it has its benefits. It can ensure more predictable outcomes, and the planning involved in this approach can enable staff to specialise. Charismatic leadership can effectively convey the new vision for big changes, thus reducing confusion and uncertainty. Connecting emotionally and embodying the change can overcome people's reservations. Having one person push the change heavily can backfire if that person has been untrustworthy in the past.

3.7.3 Choosing the right leadership style and priorities at each stage of a project

If we consider that a project typically goes through a series of stages, and that those stages have different priorities, it is worth reflecting on which leadership styles are more beneficial at each stage. A leader going through a process to implement new AI capabilities will typically have six stages: forming, storming, norming, performing, adjourning, and post-project collaboration. A leader must select a suitable AI-centred business model from the six that have been proven to work and then create a plan of how to implement it in their context. The six business models are: (1) incumbent focusing on one part of the value chain and disaggregating, (2) incumbent absorbing AI into existing model, (3) incumbent expanding beyond current model to fully utilise the opportunities of AI and access new data, (4) startup disruptor focused on one sector, built from the start to be highly automated, (5) disruptor focused on tech adding a new service such as insurance, and (6) disruptor that is not necessarily tech-focused, with an extensive user or fanbase (Zarifis & Cheng 2023, 2025).

While a dogmatic autocratic leader will adopt that approach from beginning to end, a more flexible leader may start with a democratic approach for brainstorming and developing a plan and shift to a more autocratic approach for the implementation and when evaluating people's performance. Similarly, a charismatic leader may choose their moment to turn on the charm and inspire people. A dogmatic delegative leader will show trust in the team from the start to empower them and hope they repay them. A more flexible leader will choose their moment when they truly trust their team and their ability to implement an AI-centric model to delegate. Table 3.6 suggests the two most suitable styles for a flexible leader to apply at each stage.

Table 3.6: The most suitable leadership for each stage of a process to implement new AI.

Forming	Storming	Norming	Performing	Adjourning	Post-project collaboration
Democratic, charismatic	Democratic, charismatic	Delegative, bureaucratic	Autocratic, bureaucratic	Bureaucratic, autocratic	Democratic, delegative

However, some leaders will prefer to have a consistent style in implementing AI so that people know what to expect from them. Some will find it hard to start more democratically so everyone comes together to make the plan and then move towards a more autocratic approach. The next three chapters focus on the three most prominent modern leadership approaches.

Key concept: The traditional leadership approaches discussed here help us better understand the new more popular leadership approaches, but we can also apply elements of them in combination with our preferred leadership approach. Being a great leader is not usually about dogmatically applying one leadership approach, but is about getting the right blend for a given situation. The situation can be shaped by many factors, including the business model and the stage of the digital transformation we are in.

Leadership tip: Being a great leader in digital transformation is about knowing how to combine the traditional and more recent leadership styles to give people confidence, belief, and trust in AI. It is not about one moment of achieving success, but a process of creating the right culture for sustainable innovation and the right business model to fully utilise AI.

Trust-building tip: The leadership approaches discussed here can all build trust if applied effectively at the right time, and they can all create distrust if they are applied ineffectively at the wrong time. The relationship between these approaches and trust have some proven certainties, but it is also about delicate and nuanced handling of the situation.

3.8 Exercises

Exercise 3.1

Are the priorities of a leader different in an organisation with AI at its centre?
In the past, leaders focused on leading people. Understanding the role of trust in the relationship between the leader and the follower was not too hard, and building trust was more straight forward.

Questions

1) In an AI-centric organisation, does the leader still need to focus on getting things done through people, or do they also need to lead in utilising AI?

2) Have the key attributes a leader should have changed? In your opinion, which are the most important key attributes now?

3) Many aspects of what happens in an organisation influence trust in AI. A leader's time is limited. In your opinion, what three things should a leader focus on to build trust in the processes of using AI across all the organisation's operation.

Exercise 3.2

Applying autocratic leadership and its impact on AI adoption and trust
The weaknesses of autocratic leadership are obvious. It can often be demotivating, not encourage buy-in, discourage people from professional growth, and discourage innovation. It also has strengths, such as being practical, simple to implement, and it usually gets things done. It is also often the most suitable approach when there is very high risk to people's safety.

Questions

1) Can this leadership approach be effective in the context of going through digital transformation towards an organisation with AI at its centre?

Exercise 3.3

Applying democratic leadership and its impact on AI adoption and trust
Democratic leadership is one of the approaches most focused on operating in an ethical way. An effort is made to be fair with everyone, and it is an approach that followers and other stakeholders appreciate.

Questions

1) Should this leadership style be implemented in every situation across all the stages of a project? Does it fit in with all the types of organisations? What are the challenges?

2) How can this leadership approach encourage people to adopt AI more extensively, and for more risky tasks?

3) How can blockchain technology support democratic processes and decentralised governance?

4) Is this a leadership approach that requires particular traits or skills? Can anyone apply it?

Exercise 3.4

Applying delegative leadership and its impact on AI adoption and trust
Delegative leadership is a very simple approach that is often effective. It is popular with followers as they feel respected and empowered. Many followers feel encouraged to learn more and improve when they are led in this way.

Questions

1) In what ways can this leadership style support an effective implementation of extensive, far-reaching AI?

2) Does this leadership style have any particular strengths or weaknesses for building trust in AI?

3) Are there aspects of using AI where this approach is not suitable? What alternative leadership approach would you prefer in those situations?

Exercise 3.5

Applying bureaucratic leadership and its impact on AI adoption and trust
An online retailer selling luxury products has a leader who is very passionate about having a delegating leadership style, very close to the laissez-faire approach. He values giving people freedom, and because of this the organisation has attracted staff that thrive in that environment. As the organisation changes their business model to put AI and trust at its centre, he has been advised that some structure and bureaucracies are needed. He is reluctant to go against his instincts, especially since the organisation has been so successful thus far.

Questions

1) Try to convince him of the benefits of using bureaucratic leadership in this context. Identify three bureaucracies that are needed to fully utilise AI with trust.

2) Find three possible ways bureaucratic leadership can overcome challenges in trying to fully utilise AI with trust.

Exercise 3.6

The impact of applying charismatic leadership on AI adoption and trust
A charismatic leader uses their personal strengths to inspire the team. Charismatic leadership is harder to understand than other leadership styles and certainly harder to replicate. Arguably it is more about psychology than business or technology. It is about understanding how some people are thinking and how to influence them. Ideally, a charismatic leader can have a well-rounded personality and skill set, but there are charismatic leaders that rely heavily on one or two of their characteristics.

Questions

1) For your profession or the profession you aspire to follow, if someone wants to be a charismatic leader, what personality traits or skills do you believe would be appreciated most?

2) If you wanted to be a charismatic leader, what personality traits or skills that you have would you build on?

Exercise 3.7

Which traditional leadership style would you choose for digital transformation with AI
Based on the information provided here and your personal experience with traditional leadership approaches, it is worth reflecting on the advantages and disadvantages of these leadership styles for digital transformation with AI and trust.

Questions

1) Which of the leadership styles best fits your personality and skills?

2) How would your chosen leadership style encourage the right culture for innovation with AI? What would that culture look like? Is there a way for the culture to support trust?

Space for your notes

References

Proskalovich, R., Jack, C., Zarifis, A., Serralde, D. M., Vershinina, P., Naidoo, S., Njoki, D., Pernice, I., Herrera, D., & Sarmiento, J. (2023). *Cryptoasset ecosystem in Latin America and the Caribbean*. Cambridge Centre for Alternative Finance (CCAF). https://www.jbs.cam.ac.uk/faculty-research/centres/alternative-finance/publications/crypotasset-ecosystem-in-latin-america-and-the-caribbean/

Zarifis, A. (2024). Leadership in Fintech builds trust and reduces vulnerability more when combined with leadership in sustainability. *Sustainability*, *16*(3), 5757. https://doi.org/10.3390/su16135757

Zarifis, A., & Cheng, X. (2023). AI is transforming insurance with five emerging business models. In J. Wang (Ed.), *Encyclopedia of Data Science and Machine Learning* (pp. 2086–2100). IGI Global Scientific Publishing. https://doi.org/10.4018/978-1-7998-9220-5.ch124

Zarifis, A., & Cheng, X. (2025). The new centralised and decentralised Fintech technologies, and business models, transforming finance. In A. Zarifis & X. Cheng (Eds.), *Fintech and the emerging ecosystems: Exploring centralised and decentralised financial technologies*. Springer Nature. https://link.springer.com/book/9783031834011

Zarifis, A., & Yarovaya, L. (2025). Building trust in AI: Leadership insights from Malaysian Fintech boards. In A. Zarifis & X. Cheng (Eds.), *Fintech and the emerging ecosystems: Exploring centralised and decentralised financial technologies*. Springer Nature. https://link.springer.com/book/9783031834011

Chapter 4
Transactional leadership and its role in using AI with trust

4.1 Introduction

I only go to war with those I can trust. — José Mourinho, football coach

Transactional leadership is a relatively old but popular approach that may not seem like the first choice for digital transformation with AI. However, in the workplace where we are moving towards multi-agent teams comprising of people but also several autonomous generative AI agents, having a process that focuses on the exchange of value can be helpful. While the humans in the team may value other things such as inspiration and an overarching goal to improve the world around them in some way, for the autonomous AI agent, these issues are irrelevant to its performance. The autonomous AI agents will be more effective when they have clear tasks that make the most of their capabilities. A leadership approach that is effective for both humans and autonomous AI agents is very valuable as it can be applied to mixed teams.

Transactional leadership has a long history, but it is still often misunderstood (Weber, 1947). While it is a relatively simple approach that most people should be able to implement, it is not quite as simple as some people believe. Transactional leadership has many variations. At one extreme, there are transactional approaches that involve a highly consistent reward and motivation structure to elicit certain behaviour. At the other extreme, there are transactional leaders without a structure or a detailed plan, moving from one deal to another trying to maximise their return. Some people consider that Donald Trump's approach of focusing on maximising the immediate benefit from the deals he makes, as opposed to an overly detailed long-term plan, is a form of transactional leadership. If we focus on the overarching plan, we may prioritise keeping stakeholder 'A' on our side because they will be needed later, whereas with a dealmaking approach, we try to get the most out of our deal with stakeholder 'A' now, regardless of the knock-on effects on the overarching plan. So while many people associate transactional leaders with a structured, stable reward system, this is not necessarily the case. It is also worth noting that as we try to understand a leadership approach, it does not take us long to recognise how it should be coherent and conducive to the strategy, overarching philosophy, and values of the organisation. It might just be a leadership style, but it is also the mechanism of turning plans into reality.

As there are several ways to apply this approach, what then is the common characteristic across all transactional leaders? We can say with certainty that it is clear that all transactional leaders focus on the tasks, not the people. We have seen struc-

https://doi.org/10.1515/9783111630137-004

ture-centric leadership approaches such as bureaucratic leadership, and there are several leadership approaches that are more follower-centric, such as servant leadership. Transactional leadership does not necessarily focus on structure or people, but on the exchange of value. This focus makes it very easy to apply when there is a clear direct benefit from the work that will be done so that a clear reward can be given to the person that does the work. For example, if we pay someone two thousand pounds to set up some internet routers in an office, there is a clear exchange of value. This approach is harder to apply at times of great disruption when there is only a vague direction, such as wanting to automate more extensively and gain deeper insight from our data. For example, what exact financial value would we put on a consultant explaining some capabilities of AI more clearly to our team? As it is not a people-centric approach, the education and personal development are not the priority, so it is not easy to decide what gaining some knowledge is worth.

Focusing on the exchange of value may seem very dry and not as engaging as the approaches that encourage personal development and making the world a better place, but, in fact, it is not necessarily less ethical. Many of the leadership approaches that focus on inspiring do not always reward followers with something of substance. The obvious example is the many generals throughout history sending young men to an almost certain death with many vague promises of glory and making history. Just as with the soldiers, many followers in the modern workplace get disillusioned when they do not get rewarded. Transactional leadership is more transparent in terms of what people get. A similar point is that we all want freedom at work and most of us do not like being told what to do, but when we do not have sufficient structure and at least some fear of punishment, it actually makes it harder for us to have self-control and we can drift into negative time-wasting habits, such as watching short videos (Cheng et al., 2023).

This form of leadership is relatively easy to understand in principle, but not always easy to implement. Unlike many leadership approaches that focus exclusively on the responsibilities of the follower, the transactional approach covers the responsibilities of both the follower and the leader. So, in this sense at least, it is actually more complicated. Unsurprisingly, many managers do not like this and prefer to permanently have the spotlight on the follower's performance. However, focusing on both sides of the transaction can be the best way to be fair, transparent, and trustworthy.

As there are successful leadership styles that focus on structure, such as bureaucratic, there are approaches that focus on the leader, such as autocratic, and approaches that focus on the follower, such as servant, why do we need an approach focused on the exchange of value? Furthermore, why has this approach become so popular? Someone new to the topic of leadership would probably not expect this approach to be one of the three most influential approaches at the moment. There are many reasons for its popularity, but the nature of modern society and work are definitely two of them. With the proliferation of short contracts and the gig economy, there are many business models that necessitate this approach. More broadly, even if we just compare it to ten or twenty years ago, money has become everything for many people. The majority of people today want money above all other things, and they want it now. Trying to inspire followers with visions of a better future has become harder. It is also because of the near-absolute collapse of trust in many societies. People don't trust that they will be appreciated, they don't trust that they will get a promotion, and they don't even trust that the currency they are receiving will hold its value (Zarifis & Fu, 2024).

If the context is a short project or a part-time role, a person wants to be clear on what they are expected to be putting in, and what they are getting in return. In many situations, a person, quite frankly, does not care if their leader is charismatic, visionary, or authentic, they want to know what they are getting for their time and effort. This is why many believe that an element of transactional leadership is necessary with many other leadership styles, such as transformational or charismatic.

As the transactional approach has clear merit but may not entirely fulfil everyone in every part of their lives, it should be combined with more inspirational approaches. People may aspire to more in their professional lives than the immediate reward they receive, but not every role can deliver on broader goals, such as making the world a better place, sustainability, and personal development. In Maslow's famous hierarchy of needs, the simple point is made that you need to cover the more basic needs first before someone starts to seek the higher goals such as self-actualisation.

To be clear, young people and less cynical people, do get more motivated and driven by wanting to make the world a better place, but, rightly or wrongly, we become more individualistic and inflexible in what we want as we get older. When I was doing my PhD at the University of Manchester, there was a popular saying third year PhD students would tell the first year PhD students: In the first year you try to save the world, in the second year you try to save your area of science, and in the third year you try to save your arse. More experienced people tend to be more individualistic and value clarity over inspiration. It is not just cynicism, and many would argue it is not primarily cynicism. At least, it is not a general cynicism about life, but a cynicism about the motivation of the senior management.

If we go to a nice hotel's breakfast, many children and some adults that are young at heart will try to experience everything on offer, while someone more seasoned and mature will have a more razor-sharp focus on what they know is their favourite. Not only do the more mature people know what they value from the buffet of life, but they also have had negative experiences with some of the other options. Regardless of what we personally value more – and the more philosophical discussion of what should be valued more – a leader will have to get the most value out of both types of people. We must lead people of both types, and the many that drift between them.

4.1.1 Personality traits and skills

In terms of applying this approach as a leader, no particular personality traits or skills are prerequisites, so in that sense, it is simple and anyone can apply it. In practice, however, it is not always easy to apply, as we must be able to deliver on what has been agreed within the agreed time frame.

While it is clear that the follower may not feel inspired by poetic visions of a magical future, the leader may also feel constrained and like they are lacking in personal development. They may feel tied into an endless cycle of transacting value. Therefore, while a leader may also appreciate the clarity of this approach, they may also want more from their work. It may also be beneficial for the leader's personal development to occasionally combine this approach with more inspirational strategies.

While there are no prerequisites, in terms of personality traits and skills that would completely exclude someone from applying this approach, there are some skills that typically help. These are the kind of skills any professional should be able to develop. The ability to make clear and beneficial exchanges is central to this approach. Focusing on the exchange only has benefits if both parties are clear on the details of what is being exchanged. Being able to organise people and implement some structure and hierarchies is also necessary. In reality, many transactional leaders find sufficient structure already in place and need to focus more on the clarity of the message. As this approach focuses on the carrot of rewards and the stick of negative consequences, they need to be chosen effectively to get the desired effects. Short-term realistic goals must be set and achieved effectively and efficiently.

4.1.2 What does an effective team using this leadership style look like?

Due to its focus on follower compliance, this approach is not the most natural fit for innovation, but it is often effectively used by innovators like tech companies and pharmaceutical companies to ensure regular, predictable, and measurable progress.

Everyone in a team led by this approach will have clear roles, and as far as possible, ambiguity and uncertainty around what they need to do will be reduced. The operations are orderly and focused on the results with little or no interest in any other aspect of the work. Everyone's communication is centred on the targets and how to achieve them. There are regular reviews of performance where staff are judged, and feedback is given.

4.1.3 Transactional leadership examples

We increasingly talk about ecosystems and organisations not having clear boundaries. This obviously applies to the private sector, but more than ever it also applies to the public sector. For example in England, whether you are interacting with the police, a hospital, or many of the other traditional public sector services, you will probably engage with a sequence of different organisations. Some will be clearly public, some clearly private, and many somewhere in between. It is hard to have a coherent vision and belief system across these diverse organisations. It is also hard to inspire people in dramatically different organisations. Therefore, what is best suited to this situation is for transactional leadership to organise a chain of effective transactions to implement the value chain needed to implement a single, yet complex, service.

4.1.4 How this leadership style builds trust in people

As has already been touched on, this leadership approach does not show a particular interest in a person's dreams or personal development. It therefore does not try to engage emotionally and create a deep personal connection or bond. While a deep personal connection and bond are the ways people typically build trust in each other, particularly in a social setting, this is not what happens with this approach. However, the clarity of the role, the clarity of the goal, the overall transparency, and delivering on what is promised builds trust extremely well. Not only does transactional leadership build trust effectively, it builds it on strong foundations in a sustainable way. Importantly, it avoids destroying trust and encouraging distrust.

Key concept: Transactional leaders focus on the tasks and exchanges of value, not the people or the structure. This focus on exchange of value makes it easy to apply when there is a clear direct benefit from the work that will be done so that a clear reward can be given to the person that does the work.

Leadership tip: Due to its focus on follower compliance, this approach is not the most natural fit for innovation with AI, but it is often effectively used by innovators like tech companies and pharmaceutical companies to ensure regular, predictable, and measurable progress.

Trust-building tip: Due to the transparency it offers, transactional leadership, despite its simplicity, can be the most powerful in building trust. When combined with other leadership styles, the resulting approach should retain that transparency in what the follower should deliver and receive in return.

4.2 The strengths and weaknesses of transactional leadership

4.2.1 Strengths and opportunities

In this section, we will first discuss the strengths of transactional leadership from the follower's perspective, followed by the leader's perspective, and the opportunities it creates. We will then move onto the weaknesses from the follower's perspective, then from the leader's perspective, and finally the broader challenges that emerge.

4.2.1.1 The strengths of transactional leadership from the follower's perspective

The leadership approach applied can have both intended and unintended consequences on the followers that need to be understood. Learning the process of this leadership approach and its intended consequences is a good starting point, but we need to understand how things typically play out when this approach is applied.

We live in a time where people have very different visions of what kind of workplace and society they aspire to have. Leadership is not separate from the turmoil in society – it is completely engulfed in it! A leader in an organization cannot also be a great sociologist and psychologist, but the more we understand about these issues the better. In many societies there is a huge trend towards virtue signalling that is often empty of any substance. People that present themselves as leaders are often consumed with virtue signalling instead of focusing on making improvements to the reality we live in. This has gone far beyond an ideology or a new religion. The need to do empty virtue signalling to get attention and an ego boost has become an addiction to some people, stronger than any drug we have seen. In addition to the ego boost, the second attraction of the virtue signalling drug is that it makes laziness virtuous. The virtue signalling leader says something that sounds nice, so with their logic, even if they do not affect reality, they are alright. There are many leaders who build their image while doing very little in the real world. Often, the only real effect is managing decline as opposed to moving things forward. Their current role is simply a springboard to something else and they do not truly care about what they are doing. The virtue signalling leader is celebrated by followers that do not have the intellectual capacity to understand the complexity of reality and prefer to operate purely on the level of saying things that sound nice.

The explosion of virtue signalling that is empty of substance has made many people very suspicious of leaders in terms of both their motivation and their ability to create positive change. This suspicion from followers makes it harder to communicate and engage with them effectively. What would have been inspiring in the past is treated with suspicion. A leader that would have been perceived as charismatic is now considered out of touch and unconvincing.

This widely spread mood and mindset among followers is one of the main reasons why transactional leadership is being received positively. The weaknesses in other approaches to get people to act means that the leadership approach that focuses on the transaction of value between the leader and the follower is a strong choice.

The follower is in a particularly weak position in many ways, with their bargaining power often reduced. This is due to many reasons, including the prevalence of short contracts and high migration – both legal and illegal – of people willing to work for less. On the other hand, in some ways the follower is in a stronger position than before. The follower now has more choice, as relocating is easier and many roles can be fulfilled from home online. Additionally, a shift towards quality of life as opposed to climbing the corporate ladder at any cost, makes followers less willing to endure unfairness. Therefore, while the power has not necessarily shifted to the follower, the follower needs to be convinced by providing something of real value to them.

The transactional leader can make their offer and calibrate based on the response. While a charismatic leader can also calibrate if their first offer is not appealing, they are more exposed to losing credibility. Typically, a transactional leader can negotiate and calibrate as much as necessary without losing face.

Clear structure, rewards, and accountability

Having a clear structure with clear expectations may not be exciting, but it has many benefits: it reduces uncertainty and the unnecessary anxiety that comes with it. From a follower's perspective, transactional leadership offers several key strengths that can contribute to a positive and productive work experience. Putting a well-defined structure in place reduces confùsion, uncertainty, and anxiety. Coordination is easier as everyone knows what to expect from each other. The streamlined coordination reduces disagreements and friction. Everyone's roles are clearly defined, and they have a more predictable career laid out in front of them. At times of stability, even a badly run business may be able to provide staff with specific goals. Achieving this at times of dramatic change is harder, but also more valuable. Each person can plan their time and not be consumed by constant firefighting.

The employee will feel that the transparent process is more ethical and fairer, and they will believe their work will be recognised and appreciated. Giving employees some inner calm will motivate them to work harder and gain the necessary skills to use AI. If additional work is needed above and beyond what an employee's contract requires then additional rewards and bonuses can be provided. The constant flow of rewards creates a positive work environment that is sustainable. Intrinsic motivation is always good, but there are often times when a person's intrinsic motivation is reduced, so having regular extrinsic motivations helps.

When the leader repeatedly delivers their part of the bargain, this increases how much they can hold followers accountable. This process focuses on a series of short-term goals so the employee will feel like they are achieving something. Other approaches that focus more on the vision may be initially exciting, but if achieving that vision is years away and there is a lack of small victories along the way, the situation may end up being demotivating. Most people prefer tasks that take a few days or two to three weeks at most. There is a sweet spot that can be different for each person, but typically if the tasks are very small and short, people feel micromanaged, and when tasks are very large and take too long, they run out of motivation before they are completed. Getting regular rewards builds a strong work ethic and a culture of accountability. A typical team member will also feel more motivated to hold themselves accountable, both because there are less excuses left and because they will feel the responsibility of reciprocating. In addition to the positive mindset this approach gives a follower, it also makes feedback easier. The clear career path for advancement provided by this approach is also helpful in this respect. Clear goals, feedback, and career advancement make it easier for an employee to identify the skills they need to gain. So, while personal development is not at the centre of this approach, the constant setting of goals and clear feedback on the performance can guide a follower to constantly improve.

This is one of the good examples of how, while there are many aspects of leadership that are straightforward, there are some that are a little more nuanced. We see that a leadership style that does not put personal development at its centre does have some advantages in terms of personal development. This, inevitably, leads to the tricky question: Can a leadership that does not prioritise personal development, under some circumstances at least, be more effective at improving professionals than an approach that prioritises personal development? The answer is clearly yes. Truly great leaders that manage to consistently deliver high performance have the ability to get the main issues in leadership right, but they also get these nuances right. Lesser leaders get the main issues right and are sometimes lucky with the nuances that they haven't fully grasped playing out favourably for them, while on other occasions they are unlucky with the nuances going against them.

For most people, this predictability and clarity is worth more than having an exciting and dramatic – or melodramatic – leader. They appreciate having a predictable work environment that will reduce their anxiety and stress at work and allow them to take less stress home. The structure does not hold them back, but it helps them thrive. The detailed plans of a transactional leader can lead to positive outcomes on time without the need for overtime and heroics, so everyone can have a better work-life balance. Another important nuance of this leadership is how putting some structure, and in a sense reducing freedom in the workplace can in the end be empowering due to the progress and clarity achieved.

The strengths of transactional leadership for Generation Z and Alpha employees
There are many negative stereotypes about Generation Z and Alpha, such as them having a short attention span, spending a lot of time socialising online, having a heavy emphasis on their personal wellbeing, and that they are less focused on work and more on having a good quality of life.

The benefits of transactional leadership discussed, such as the clarity, helps people from these generations achieve the balance they want between work and their other interests. They also value the regular feedback and praise. The feedback helps them plan their personal development. These generations are more comfortable online in the sense that they are happy to spend more time online, and they do not have the urge to meet face-to-face to get motivated. These generations also value flexibility, which is not a priority of this approach, but effective organisation and division of labour can make flexibility easier to achieve in some cases.

4.2.1.2 The strengths of transactional leadership from the leader's perspective

In an age when complexity is often increasing, a leader that can simplify things is a true blessing. This approach is time consuming, but it is usually straightforward to implement. All leadership styles need to be adapted to each context, but the principles of this approach stay the same. The short-term measurable goals enhance control and improve decision making and planning. More data-driven decision making can be made. We talk about the need for a leader to be in the loop in terms of AI. At the very least, this approach ensures the leader is involved with day-to-day operations and re-mains proactive. The measures in place, the regular performance updates, and the attentiveness of the leader help minimise risks, while streamlined operations reduce errors and mistakes.

Having a clear structure to motivate people is a useful tool for the leader. The leader has the option to increase motivation by giving higher rewards if necessary. The reward structure can also be used in recruitment to encourage people to choose this team over other more ambiguous offers. The onboarding can also be more straightfor-ward. The onboarding is often problematic for organisations in many ways, and time, money, and talent can be wasted.

4.2.1.3 The opportunities of transactional leadership

As we have seen, this relatively straightforward approach that may seem old-fashioned and unimaginative is actually as powerful as ever. Applying it correctly cre-ates many opportunities. Firstly, it can be used to leverage technology. Its focus on clear goals makes implementing plans such as digital transformation as straightfor-ward as possible. With clear performance measures and performance-based rewards, productivity can be kept at a high level. Having the core operations of an organisation running at a good level offers the platform to try new things and innovate.

This leadership is easy to understand, relatively straightforward to apply, and it has clear benefits. This makes it a very strong candidate to be combined with other leadership styles. Along with transformational and servant leadership, it is arguably one of the three most popular leadership styles today, and elements of all three can potentially be combined.

Key concept: From a follower's perspective, transactional leadership offers sev-eral key strengths that can contribute to a positive and productive work experience. Putting a well-defined structure in place with everyone's roles clearly defined reduces confusion, uncertainty, and anxiety. Coordination is easier as everyone knows what to expect from each other. The streamlined coordination reduces disagreements and friction.

Leadership tip: The leader is proactive and in the loop with day-to-day operations. The short-term measurable goals enhance control and improve decision making and planning. More data-driven decision making can be made. The measures in place, the regular information on performance, and the attentiveness of this leader minimise risks. The streamlined operations can reduce mistakes due to insufficient information or simple errors.

Trust-building tip: The regular process of first setting short-term goals and then both the leader and the follower delivering on what was agreed builds trust in a cumulative way.

4.2.2 Weaknesses and challenges

We have seen throughout history that when measuring people's performance, no measure is perfect, and as soon as a new way of evaluating performance is created, some people try to find its weaknesses to game the system. A recent and high-profile example of this is when people spread controversial and shocking fake news on social media platforms to gain more views, thereby earning money from them. In some cases, the more unrealistic and shocking the fake news, the more views it gets, so if the poster is paid based on views, there is a perverse incentive to be dishonest. A leadership approach that relies so heavily on measuring performance needs to grapple with this challenge.

4.2.2.1 The weaknesses of transactional leadership from the follower's perspective

The weakness most people raise about transactional leadership is that it can easily drift into micromanaging people. If the planning and oversight get to the point that they feel like micromanagement then this is clearly going to feel overbearing and stifling. It is one of the most basic human needs for us to want to express ourselves. When I teach young adults, I try to prepare them to be more successful, because with success you tend to get more opportunities to express yourself, which is in my opinion one of the greatest benefits of having some success. When I was in the army, a huge effort was made to indoctrinate people and rewire their brain so that they no longer have this need to be creative and make their own decisions. In the context of the army, along with some other contexts that have very high risk, that is understandable. However, in most jobs, people need to be given some freedom to express themselves through their work. Interestingly, even in the army, while soldiers did learn to follow the rules through the initial training, they still found very subtle ways to show their personality that would not break the rules and go mostly under the radar. As there was so much conformity, you could notice these subtle small expressions of different personality. A less subtle attempt at expressing oneself was to leave a moustache because soldiers had to shave every day, but they were allowed to do that. In a way, you could interpret that action as a form of weak or pointless protest against conformity, but it is yet one more example of how people need that freedom to express themselves.

Even for this relatively straightforward approach to management, success and failure can be very close. Many of the weaknesses are a different side of the same coin compared to the strengths. For example, focusing on short-term goals has benefits, but this often leads to not focusing sufficiently on long-term goals. It is easy to focus on one or the other, but it takes some planning and skill to optimise for both. Achieving long-term goals is not just a series of short transactions; usually, some step changes and more fundamental changes are needed. We see the huge challenges and failures in moving towards electric cars. Bringing them in slowly has its weaknesses, such as not having the incentive to create the infrastructure of charging stations, and there isn't the courage to make a step change, such as banning vehicles with internal combustion engines. A short-term focus can limit how much the people in the organisation are developing the knowledge they need to make a big step forward. If a person gets rewarded only for the tasks they complete, that is what they will focus on. This can also be detrimental to the development of new leaders with a new vision. Having a culture of conforming to rules and targets is mostly a good thing, but it can hold potential leaders back. Often an upcoming leader in an organisation is someone that is seen as a safe pair of hands – which this approach encourages – but other times, the upcoming leader is someone that made breakthroughs and found new ways of moving things forward.

The transactional approach is in some ways fairer, as it has the reward of the employee at the centre of its logic, but it can be very top down. This approach does not just use rewards to motivate, but also punishments. This typically creates fear and a risk-averse environment. Many people, of course, believe you need to have some fear in your leader; they need to have a stick also, not just a carrot. While leaders have used fear successfully throughout human history, we aspire to get things done without more fear, anxiety, and stress than is necessary. As we have said already, if you do not create the environment, culture, and mindset for innovation, it is not necessarily something that can be turned on, like flipping a switch, when needed. While there is a risk that people feel they are not appreciated and their work is not recognised in general, in a culture that does not encourage innovation, people will feel particularly unappreciated when they do actually innovate, despite the odds not being in their favour.

It is in most people's nature to want to be at peace with their environment. While some may fight against it like revolutionaries throughout their life, most people will try to accept the cards they have been dealt and find happiness in their reality. The focus on reward and punishment, similar to how we discipline a dog, eventually creates a resistance to change where people's comfort zone is their routine, and they do not want to take it upon themselves to proactively solve problems. By putting faith in the process, this approach does not put faith in the people, and they will not feel very empowered. Without this empowerment and proactive mentality across the organisation, reacting to unexpected events will be slower.

The focus on reward and punishment can make competition too fierce, creating hostility and friction, and it is not the best way to create a sense of community. It can create a win-win mentality in some situations, but as the focus is on results and not behaviour, people will be willing to behave unethically to get the results. It is usually shared beliefs and a strong culture that create a win-win mentality. For many organisations the overriding shared belief is the love of money, but ideally some ethical and environmental sustainability values should also be involved. Staff fiercely competing with each other in a cut-throat manner may have some benefits, but it does not encourage collaboration. In the modern workplace collaboration is a priority for many obvious reasons, so we need to find a way to encourage it with this approach.

These weaknesses do not impact all employees in the same way. There may be a higher turnover of the more ambitious or creative people, and this will make the organisation weaker in some areas.

The weaknesses of transactional leadership for Generation Z and Alpha employees

While transactional leadership can benefit someone with some of the typical characteristics of Generation Z and Alpha indirectly, it can be unappealing in a very direct way. There are ways to apply this approach to get the best out of these generations, but it does not have many synergies with them and is not a natural fit. It is not a natural fit in theory, but of course, if it is implemented better than one of the leadership approaches that are a more natural fit, then in the end the results will be better.

The lack of meaning and purpose is something that will make many from these generations feel unfulfilled. While the clarity of this approach can potentially help people organise their free time better, the short-term targets may present a lack of flexibility and clash with the work-life balance they are trying to achieve. Even if people from these generations with these priorities are determined to make it work, the bad fit may leave them unsatisfied and burned out mentally. I met many people that worked in call centres selling services over the phone and earning a commission on each sale, and there was a clear division between those that thrived in that environment and loved the challenge, and those who were completely demoralised and depressed.

4.2.2.2 The weaknesses of transactional leadership from the leader's perspective

This approach does not necessarily require any specific personality traits or skills, but it puts a large burden on the leader to constantly set targets and evaluate. Even when micromanaging is avoided, this is still a very hands-on approach. Of course, some aspects can be automated with AI. When people reflect on the weaknesses of this approach, they often take it as a given that the short-term targets being set are neither overly ambitious nor too easy. I have looked at a lot of literature and it mostly takes this for granted. Regularly setting short-term targets that are going to sufficiently cover the time people have can be challenging. Anyone that has been in a managerial position knows this is tricky, and it will not be perfect every time. Most professionals that finish their tasks early will fill any additional time they have left over by doing something useful. This is normal and not too much to expect. Academics usually fill any time they have left over by reading to keep their knowledge up to date. This is clearly useful for their university. All the leadership approaches need the follower to be honest and hard-working, so many of them have a similar vulnerability if a follower is not willing to give one hundred percent. However, if the culture is too focused on the exchange of work with a reward, then a follower may feel they are justified to not work more once the specific task is completed.

There are two potential solutions for this. The first is to set the tasks very accurately, which is indeed feasible in some professions, but not in every situation. The second solution is to combine this leadership approach with a more inspirational one, so that there is some overarching inspirational vision in addition to a series of transactions. Many leaders that identify as transactional but are not too dogmatic do this, whether consciously or subconsciously, as putting all your eggs in one basket, by relying on one motivational tool is risky. Just as it is hard for even a competent charismatic leader to be charismatic every day across their whole career, it is hard for a competent transactional leader to consistently set the ideal short-term targets.

Football is a great example because we see the successes and failures unfold before our eyes and we try to find the reason behind them. Personally, I have learned as much from watching games and playing games as I have from my formal education. The point being made here is not to undermine formal education, but to emphasise that playing games adds special skills to us that are hard to develop in another way. The Nobel laureate Demis Hassabis encourages us to play and create games in order to learn more. In football, we see that there are some dogmatic managers who will not change their style even if it is going very badly. Some football mangers will insist on playing out from the back even if they keep losing the ball and conceding goals from this tactic. Other managers adapt to the situation. Carlo Ancelotti is an example of a manger that is willing to adapt and is not married to one strategy. The 'gaffers' that are not flexible are trying to get as close to perfection as possible in one strategy. Leadership of people outside of sport is the same in this sense. A transactional leader can be fully committed to implementing that approach and hope the benefits will outweigh the drawbacks in the long run. This dogmatic commitment can work, as it builds stability and skills, but it often sacrifices the present to build a better future.

4.2.2.3 The challenges of transactional leadership

There are many potential weaknesses to transactional leadership. These weaknesses are not fatal for this approach, and they can be avoided or at least mitigated. However, we need to understand them to be able to navigate them effectively. If we are captaining a ship, it is definitely worth taking some time to identify were the icebergs lie ahead, rather that powering forward in the hope that our confidence and machismo will melt them away.

Based on the weaknesses discussed, there are two main challenges. The first challenge is to implement transactional leadership effectively by identifying the ideal short-term goals, rewards that resonate, and hopefully not many punishments. The second challenge is to have an awareness of how all the weaknesses discussed play out in the current situation the leader is in, and what actions they can take to mitigate them. For example, if transactional leadership typically rewards short-term goals and people do not put time into preparing for longer-term targets, a percentage of people's time can be allocated for blue-sky thinking. One of the large audit and consulting firms gives some of their employee's fifteen percent of their time to spend on whatever project they want. While they have strict targets for the rest of their time, this time is theirs to utilise how they see fit. They can spend the time doing some training or launching a startup – whatever they want. One tax advisor I spoke to utilised this opportunity to learn how to create apps with generative AI. Whether he creates apps for the company or not, clearly that knowledge will be useful to his employer as they go through a prolonged digital transformation.

An important way to mitigate the weaknesses of transactional leadership is to combine it with either transformational leadership for more inspiration and big visions, or servant leadership for a more caring, supporting, and ethical element. By combining it with one of these two approaches we are combining hard power with soft power. Hard power can get things done, but it can cause friction and gets demotivating over time, so combining it with some soft power is beneficial.

If there will be some soft power used alongside the predominantly hard power used, then this should be done from the beginning, so it is received as genuine. If it is left too late to try and use some soft power, it will come across as fake and the followers will not believe that there are win-win motivations behind it. An example from history that people from Britain might be familiar with, but others may not know, is William the Conqueror, originally known as William the Bastard. He was the ruler of Normandy in France and when he came to England to attempt to become king, he was very brutal and heavy-handed, killing, burning, and stealing people's land. At some point he saw that the resistance to him as leader in Britain would not go away, so he tried to also implement some soft power, but unsurprisingly at that point this was received with suspicion and did not work.

Key concept: When measuring people's performance, no measure is perfect and as soon as a new way of evaluating performance is created, people try to game the system. A leadership approach that relies so heavily on measuring performance needs to grapple with this challenge.

Leadership tip: Transactional leadership needs to be implemented effectively, and its typical limitations need to be mitigated. To implement transactional leadership effectively, we need to identify the ideal short-term goals, rewards that resonate, and hopefully not many punishments. To mitigate its limitations, we need to understand how all of its typical weaknesses play out in each situation, and what actions we can take. Often the solution is to have some elements of servant or transformational leadership, without going too far.

Trust-building tip: Despite the weaknesses of transactional leadership, the focus on the exchange of value and the clarity do actually build sustainable trust. If this approach is going to be combined with other leadership styles, such as transformational leadership, it is important that one of the two is the dominant approach so people know where they stand. A good blend of two leadership approaches can get the best of each, while a bundled-up mixture will leave followers in 'no man's land' not knowing what to expect.

4.3 Transactional leadership's impact on AI adoption and trust

Not taking a risk also brings some risk. — Thomas Frank, football manager

4.3.1 How this leadership style can support AI and digital transformation

Can be applied to mixed teams that have humans and autonomous AI agents
When thinking about how to be a great leader in an organisation with AI at its centre, we cannot just look at how to get the most out of AI through other people. The modern leader can lead autonomous AI agents that are collaborating in teams with humans. Sometimes we talk about AI in an organisation as if it is one entity. However, there is an increasing number of independent AI systems. Some of them have a narrow focus to perform a specific task, such as analysis or automation. In addition to this, with AI in a specialised role, we increasingly have autonomous AI agents that are set up to be more flexible, with more well-rounded capabilities that can collaborate in teams in a similar way to humans. This relationship between humans and machines that seemed imminent for decades is now here. We are finally in teams with autonomous AI agents that can help us in similar ways to what we imagined with C3PO and R2D2 from *Star Wars*. Just as we have seen with the fictional character Marvin the Paranoid Android, an autonomous robot that felt the tasks he was given were too far below his ability, a leader faces the challenge of fully utilizing these AI agents.

Having a leadership style that focuses on the exchange of value can be helpful in the workplace we are moving towards, with multi-agent teams comprising of several people but also several independent autonomous AI agents. Humans in a team may value an inspiring overarching goal but inspiration has no influence on the autonomous AI agent's performance. The AI agents will be more effective when they have clear instructions. The transactional leadership style is very valuable as it can be applied to mixed teams as it is effective for both humans and autonomous AI.

Even if a leader is hugely charismatic, effortlessly charming, and wildly in-love with the sound of their own voice, they will need to adopt a transactional leadership approach to lead autonomous AI agents. While leading AI is a relatively new challenge, it is an example of how transactional leadership is in a sense a great leveller between people. Regardless of whether someone is charming or not, whatever their appearance may be, it is about communicating goals clearly and making skilful exchanges of value.

Staying on top of the finances and risks and dealing with crises

It surprised me personally for many years that innovation was a lot more about planning and ensuring the finances are in place than creative thinking. As many academics teaching innovation will say in the first lecture, innovation is not invention. Invention is creating something new, while innovation is implementing the novel idea in the real world. Typically, innovation involves successfully commercialising a new idea. The reason why this distinction is important to remember at this point is that transactional leadership is definitely not the best suited for invention, but it may be helpful in innovation and digital transformation. Organising and financing innovation is far from straightforward. Unless someone with deep pockets is backing us, we need to accurately evaluate the likelihood of certain scenarios and the various risks. Once we have done this we need to stick to the budget for each step. A digital transformation of this magnitude does not just raise questions about what the business model of the organisation should look like in five years, but it also raises questions about how the transition to that new model will be financed.

AI does usually bring efficiencies and reduced costs, but as with most technologies, there are some upfront costs. Even if the AI used will be provided as a service on the internet, paid for by subscription, there are still some upfront costs. In this simplest scenario of AI adoption, there are still upfront costs to change processes, train people how to use AI, arrange the contracts, etc.

The structure and predictability encouraged by transactional leadership can make risk management much easier. It comes more naturally to a transactional leader to plan in detail and follow established protocols and regulations. The different scenarios of how the digital transformation may unfold will need to be modelled to accurately evaluate the risk. The financial implications of the best- and worse-case scenarios at some key point must be estimated. When we say transactional leadership can provide the foundation for digital transformation with AI, staying on top of the financial dimension and not running out of money is a big part of it.

If despite the best efforts to avoid problems there are some crises during the adoption of AI, a transactional leader may be in a good position to steady the ship due to their hands-on approach and understanding of the day-to-day operations. While there is a strong trend in leadership to empower followers and not micromanage them, at a time of crisis a leader needs to step in. If there are urgent problems, a leader that has the overarching understanding of the operations and the environment, and also has the gravitas and authority, should step in. A leader with a more laissez-faire, delegating, or democratic approach may not be sufficiently engaged or inclined to take the bull by the horns.

Providing enough stability and control at a time of change

The overall complexity of digital transformation can be daunting, with potential risks and unintended consequences lurking in every corner. It may seem counterintuitive, but providing stability at a time of great change is beneficial to digital transformation. Transformation is not about going forward as fast as possible; it is about going forward as fast as possible without losing control. A more structured implementation with more control can counterintuitively enable transformation to go faster. The obvious analogy is a sports car. Those that watch *Top Gear* will know that often the way to make a car go faster around a racetrack is to fit bigger brakes, a bigger splitter, a bigger rear wing, and wider tires, all of which make the car slower but give more control so it can go faster without skidding off the track. To have effective control in digital transformation the monitoring needs to be sufficient. If we continue with the metaphor, the monitoring is analogues to a sports car that, through its steering, suspension, and tyres, gives the driver an accurate feel of the road so that they can react quicker and better.

Furthermore, as utilizing AI, blockchain, and other new technologies almost inevitably involves engaging with technology providers and other partners for data, being strong in planning, monitoring, and controlling is very valuable. By setting clear performance standards internally and with partners, it will be easier to make quick corrections, stay on the front foot, and be proactive. At a time of dramatic change, when everything has been geared towards moving forward, small problems can quickly snowball out of control if not dealt with quickly. It is important in terms of the business model and plan to not only change what is intended to change, but to also keep the things that shouldn't change the same. If, for example, an auditor is seen as traditional and risk-averse, at least some of that is worth keeping. We should always be conscious not to 'throw the baby out with the bath water'. In addition to the value of genuinely delivering some stability, by consistently applying policies, this sends a message internally and externally and gives stakeholders a sense of familiarity and security.

Working with several partners across an ecosystem makes it hard for leadership styles focused on inspiration to be effective for all the partners. Transactional leadership can be used to arrange a chain of effective transactions to implement the value chain needed to implement a single, yet complex, service.

A related point is that at times of stability, holding people accountable is more straightforward. Even with leaders that are less hands-on, roles and expectations are clear. It is easier to monitor and evaluate, because people know how much work is needed for a certain level of output. At a time of change things aren't so clear. Many people in many different professions see this. For example, at universities, academics often find it more challenging to evaluate students' reports due to the use of generative AI. A transactional leader who has been hands-on and in the loop throughout and has developed their ability to set regular goals and evaluate performance, will be in a better position than most. A transactional leader may not have all the answers immediately either, but they will have the proactive mindset and experience to find new ways to set goals, offer rewards, and evaluate performance. The way a transactional leader operates in an organisation with AI at its centre may be quite similar to today, or it might be different in a way we cannot even imagine right now.

In addition to AI, blockchain offers many useful solutions to automate processes in a reliable and transparent way. If we are talking about a sophisticated solution with blockchain, and not simply launching a meme coin on the 'Pump.Fun' website, it can be quite a daunting task. Processes can actually be more inefficient and problematic at the start until it hits its stride. A sophisticated blockchain project is usually about replacing an old infrastructure utilised by many organisations to coordinate some processes with a new infrastructure. This is not usually a simple project. The first efforts to sell bonds on blockchain are an example of the slow initial progress that is typical with this technology. The structured approach of this leadership style and the discipline it encourages in leaders, followers, and all the other stakeholders can help navigate the challenges.

Being able to motivate people to change and keep their role manageable
The inspirational approaches are popular nowadays and seem a more natural fit for digital transformational as they can inspire people to value change and work towards a new vision. What happens, however, if some people, despite all the charm and charisma of the leader, are not inspired to use AI more? They may not be inspired for many reasons, including that they see the new changes and automation as a threat, or they believe the transition will be difficult. As transactional leadership has a simple method to reward and punish, it can incentivise people even when the broader vision is not inspiring. The regular communication, active listening, and feedback will help the leader understand people's reservations and think about how to bring them back on their side. The regular communication can also help 'prime the push' in a less 'pushy' way than an announcement or a presentation. By discussing the process regularly, people that had reservations initially will slowly feel more comfortable with embracing the new technologies. If enthusiasm cannot be created by inspiration, people need to be incentivised to achieve specific milestones and be given recognition when they do. Beyond the rewards that are agreed, celebrating successes is also beneficial in motivating people. Celebrating success can be a deeper emotional experience that brings something different to people's lives and breaks their routine. Chasing targets can feel like being on a hamster wheel, constantly running without going forward.

The changes will typically get people out of their comfort zone and reduce efficiency for a period. The inevitable turbulence should be kept to a minimum. If there is too much extra confusion and additional work, even those that were on board with the change may start to desert the cause. Keeping the transition as smooth as possible and keeping workflows streamlined is an area where a transactional leader can excel.

4.3.2 How this leadership style builds trust in AI and digital transformation

Interacting with AI for important issues, particularly when money is on the line, creates some challenges to trust and privacy concerns (Zarifis & Fu, 2023). The characteristics of this leadership approach that build trust in other situations also build trust in digital transformation with AI. Some of the ways it builds trust are even more valuable in an AI-centred organisation. The issues already identified, such as the leader giving a reward for each goal, consistent enforcement, early intervention to solve problems, transparency, structure, and relative stability, all hugely benefit trust. Accountability is put on both the leader and the follower to deliver on their side of the bargain, which is fairer than most approaches. One typical reason for some to hold back from change is a lack of trust in the motivations behind the change, so a more transparent approach should avoid that. As the risk increases because of the magnitude of the change, people need some familiarity, predictability, and routine to act as their comfort blanket.

In addition to these core principles of transactional leadership, there is no reason why a leader applying this approach cannot also lead by example, further building trust. This can involve doing something high-profile and heroic like getting a huge new contract for the company, or it can be something more mundane like not rewarding themselves if a target is missed. Regardless of whether from the leader's perspective the behaviour they embody is central to their role, such as in charismatic leadership, or not, it is one of the things that stay engrained in the follower's mind. There are few things more destructive to trust than the combination of bad performance and bonuses to the leaders. It is the kind of behaviour revolutions were triggered by in the past.

As discussed, transactional leadership is a style with the rare characteristic of being effective at assigning clear short-term tasks to both humans and independent autonomous AI agents. This creates a genuine team dynamic. The humans and AI agents can receive guidance in a similar way, and the humans will see the real performance of AI in their context and on their tasks. This will create a sustainable trust in AI based on real performance. As the leader is proactive, hands-on, and in the loop, and the rest of the human team is involved in working with AI, they will have an accurate and up-to-date understanding of its capabilities and avoid giving AI tasks that would 'set it up for a fall', damaging trust in the process.

The weakness of this approach, in terms of trust, is that having an overarching inspirational vision for the project is not central. There is nothing stopping a transactional leader having an inspirational overarching vision, but each approach prioritises certain things. If a leader tries to do everything that will potentially benefit the project, it will be a muddled mess that will leave everyone confused and bewildered. Therefore, the best approach is often to make sure the inspirational vision does exist, even if it is not where the leader spends most of their time.

4.3.3 The business models that work well with this leadership

Not limited to stable operations but probably not suited for the start of a project
When someone first learns the basic principles of this leadership approach, they will probably consider it to be a good choice for stable operations. As discussed, when applied skilfully, it does not necessarily hold back innovation but supports it. Certainly, if we consider the stages of a project, it may not be possible to apply it from the start as there may be too much uncertainty. Even a confident leader should probably hold their horses a little and listen to what the rest of the team think before charging forward. Taking some time to collectively, as a team, process and analyse what is happening before choosing the new business model is necessary. A leader that knows when to keep their powder dry will be more effective when they do act. This leadership style is mostly a top-down approach, but it is not autocratic and dictatorial.

Can be used with all six business models optimised for AI
There are business models that will help organisations already active in an area fully utilise AI, and there are business models for organisations that use the new opportunities created by AI to move into new areas (Zarifis & Cheng, 2023, 2025). The six business models proven to be ideal for an AI-centred organisation are: (1) focus on one part of the value chain and disaggregate, (2) absorb AI into existing model, (3) incumbent expanding beyond current model to fully utilise the opportunities of AI and access new data, (4) startup disruptor focused on one sector, built from the start to be highly automated, (5) disruptor focused on tech adding a new service like insurance, and (6) disruptor that is not necessarily tech-focused with an extensive user or fanbase.

This leadership approach can be adapted to all six business models, but it is particularly well suited to the first: an organisation operating as part of a wider ecosystem providing services (Zarifis & Cheng, 2023, 2025). These complex dynamic business models need this approach more than the relatively simple models. For example, a company that sells products through a platform and has a relatively simple business model is not in such burning need of clarity and could adopt any number of leadership styles. For example, if you are part of a complex ecosystem, a delegating leadership approach may not offer sufficient control.

Key concept: Digital transformation with AI is not about going forward as fast as possible, it is about going forward as fast as possible without losing control. Transactional leadership can deliver a more structured implementation with more control and predictability and can counterintuitively enable transformation to advance faster.

Leadership tip: The modern leader can lead autonomous AI agents that are collaborating in teams with humans. Transactional leadership is very valuable as it can be applied to mixed teams because it is effective for both humans and autonomous AI agents. Having a leadership style that focuses on the exchange of value can be helpful. While the humans in the team may value other things such as an inspiring overarching goal, for the autonomous AI agent, these issues are irrelevant to its performance. The autonomous AI agents will be more effective when they have clear tasks that make the most of their capabilities.

Trust-building tip: The priorities of a transactional leader, such as giving a reward for each goal achieved, consistent enforcement, early intervention to solve problems, transparency, structure, and relative stability all hugely benefit trust.

4.4 The popularity of transactional leadership in the future

4.4.1 The trends in the popularity of this approach

While transactional leadership was used more extensively in the past, there is no question that it is still widely utilised today and will continue to be very popular in the future. It should not be grouped with leadership approaches that are falling out of favour, such as the autocratic style. While the autocratic leader may see a very high turnover of staff and be forced to change their approach whether they want to or not, a transactional leader can be successful even if they are quite dogmatic in how they apply it. The question is if most leaders will use it as their primary method or their secondary method. Many leaders consider it to be practical but not the best way to strongly engage and motivate people. Many people believe it may be less effective with Generation Z and Generation Alpha, who value flexibility and more meaningful work.

4.4.2 How does transactional leadership compare to other leadership styles?

For Generation Z and Alpha, human-centred approaches resonate strongly. This does not mean that there is no place for transactional leadership, as the more human-centred approaches have their own weaknesses. It is easy to conclude that some kind of blend is necessary, but it is much harder to identify and implement one ideal blend for every situation. Table 4.1 summarises the main strengths and weaknesses of this approach when it is used on its own, or in combination with either servant or transformational styles.

Key concept: The practical and transparent process of transactional leadership is still useful, but it needs to be combined with the more human-centric approaches to get more engagement from Generation Z and Alpha.

Leadership tip: Transactional leadership's weaknesses in supporting AI and trust can be mitigated by combining it either with servant or transformational leadership, but not both, as trying to apply three leadership approaches will send confusing signals to followers and they will not know what to expect.

Table 4.1: Transactional leadership's strengths and weaknesses in supporting AI and trust.

	Strengths in supporting AI	Weaknesses in supporting AI	Strengths in supporting trust	Weaknesses in supporting trust
Transactional leadership	Can be applied to mixed teams that have humans and automated AI agents collaborating together, staying on top of the finances and risks, dealing with crises, providing enough stability and control at a time of change, being able to motivate people to change and keeping their role manageable.	As uncertainty and complexity increases it might be harder to apply. Chasing targets often leads to whatever is not being explicitly identified in a target getting ignored.	The leader giving a reward for each goal, consistent enforcement, early intervention to solve problems, transparency, structure, and relative stability all hugely benefit trust.	An overarching inspirational vision for the project is not central and therefore builds trust less.
Primarily transactional leadership, with some servant leadership	It will support experts working on technologies the leader does not fully understand. Avoids overly focusing on targets that are unlikely to be perfect and comprehensive. Encourages free thinking and creativity.	–	Illustrates an overarching inspirational, caring, and ethical vision of the organisation.	–
Primarily transactional leadership, with some transformational leadership	More emphasis on change and motivation can encourage digital transformation.	May lose some structure.	Promotes overarching vision in the value of innovation.	May increase uncertainty.

Trust-building tip: Transactional leadership builds trust very effectively, but it is worth having a meaningful, inspiring, overarching vision and not rely too heavily on the short-term targets.

4.5 Summary

I will leave my position only if I lose player's trust. — José Mourinho, football coach

4.5.1 The enduring value of the transactional leadership approach

Transactional leaders focus on the tasks and the exchanges of value. They do not focus on the structure or the people. We have seen structure-centric leadership approaches such as bureaucratic leadership, and there are several leadership approaches that are mainly or partly follower-centric, such as servant leadership. The focus on exchanges of value makes it very easy to apply when there is a clear direct benefit from the work that will be done so that a clear reward can be given to the person that does the work. This approach is harder to apply at times of great disruption when there is only a vague direction. As it is not a people-centric approach, education and personal development are not the priority. It is not always easy to put a financial value on the benefit of education and personal development. This can make it harder to see the short-term benefits of it.

4.5.2 Is the transactional leadership approach the best for AI and trust?

Applying this approach correctly creates many opportunities. Firstly, it can be used to leverage technology. Its focus on clear goals makes implementing plans such as digital transformation with AI as straightforward as possible. When there is clarity on how the current operations are running it is easier to innovate.

Increasingly, the modern leader must lead autonomous AI agents collaborating in teams with humans. Transactional leadership is very valuable because it can be applied to mixed teams as it is effective for both humans and autonomous AI agents. Having a leadership style that focuses on the exchange of value can be helpful. While the humans in the team may value other things such as an inspiring overarching goal, inspiration has no value for the autonomous AI agents. The autonomous AI agents will be more effective when they have clear tasks that make the most of their capabilities.

José Mourinho famously said he would only go to war with players he could trust. Make no mistake: digital transformation with AI is going to war. Even at times of change, this approach builds trust between all the stakeholders with the structure it offers.

4.5.3 Choosing the right leadership style and priorities at each stage of a project

This leadership is easy to understand and apply and it has clear benefits. This makes it a very strong candidate to be combined with other leadership styles. It is arguably one of the three most popular leadership styles along with transformational and servant leadership, and elements of two of the three can be combined.

An important way to mitigate the weaknesses of transactional leadership is to combine it with either transformational leadership for more inspiration and big visions, or servant leadership for a more caring, supporting, and ethical element. By combining it with one of these two approaches we are combining hard power with soft power. Hard power can get things done, but it can become demotivating for followers over time, so combining it with some soft power is beneficial.

Key concept: With clear performance measures and performance-based rewards, productivity can be kept at a high level. Having the core operations of an organisation running at a good level offers the platform to try new things and innovate.

Leadership tip: Transactional leadership can be used to give clear tasks to both humans and autonomous AI agents.

Trust-building tip: This approach builds trust with the structure, stability, consistency, fairness, and clarity it creates, even at times of change.

Best blended leadership approaches using this style: (a) Primarily transactional with some transformational leadership where necessary. (b) Primarily transactional with some servant leadership where necessary. We should choose to utilise some transformational leadership if we want to drive the change and choose the servant style if we want to support the team, so they drive the change. Transactional leadership takes centre stage because it is effective in communicating short-term goals to humans and AI agents.

4.6 Exercises

Exercise 4.1

Improving transactional leadership's trust-building
Scenario: You are a middle manager in a company that requires leaders to be transactional. There is a formalised process of setting short-term goals and giving rewards. This process must be documented. Your organisation is going to change its business model to focus on the advertisement of the service and the onboarding of clients. The rest of the value chain will be covered by partners and coordinated through APIs. The purpose is to automate most of the processes and rely heavily on generative AI. Most of your followers are from Generation Z and Alpha.

Questions

1) You are asked by senior management how the transactional leadership approach can be augmented in four or five ways to engage your followers more in the digital transformation.

2) Senior management also asks you to identify four or five ways to augment transactional leadership to build your follower's trust in AI and blockchain technologies.

Exercise 4.2

The benefits of transactional leaderships in business ecosystems
Scenario: You work for a startup that wants to provide a specific service through an API to other organisations. Your role is to go out and find partners. You will need to explain the value of the service and then, once an agreement is reached, integrate the startup's systems and processes with the new partner. You are reflecting on what kind of leadership style to apply.

Questions

1) What are the typical strengths and weaknesses of transactional leadership in this scenario?

2) What steps would you take to make the most of transactional leadership in this context?

Space for your notes

References

Cheng, X., Su, X., Yang, B., Zarifis, A., & Mou, J. (2023). Understanding users' negative emotions and continuous usage intention in short video platforms. *Electronic Commerce Research and Applications*, *58*, 101244, 1–15. https://doi.org/10.1016/j.elerap.2023.101244

Weber, M. (1947). *The theory of social and economic organizations*. Free Press.

Zarifis, A., & Fu, S. (2023). Re-evaluating trust and privacy concern when purchasing a mobile app: Re-calibrating for the increasing role of Artificial Intelligence. *Digital*, *3*(4), 286–299. https://doi.org/10.3390/digital3040018

Zarifis, A., & Fu, S. (2024). The second extended model of consumer trust in cryptocurrency payments, CRYPTOTRUST 2. *Frontiers in Blockchain*, *7*, 1–11. https://doi.org/10.3389/fbloc.2024.1220031

Zarifis, A., & Cheng, X. (2024). The five emerging business models of Fintech for AI adoption, growth and building trust. In A. Zarifis, D. Ktoridou, L. Efthymiou, & X. Cheng (Eds.), *Business digital transformation: Selected cases from industry leaders* (pp. 73–97). Palgrave Macmillan. https://doi.org/10.1007/978-3-031-33665-2_4

Zarifis, A., & Cheng, X. (2025). The new centralised and decentralised Fintech technologies, and business models, transforming finance. In A. Zarifis & X. Cheng (Eds.), *Fintech and the emerging ecosystems: Exploring centralised and decentralised financial technologies*. Springer Nature. https://link.springer.com/book/9783031834011

Chapter 5
Servant leadership and its role in using AI with trust

5.1 Introduction

Servant leadership always empathizes, always accepts the person but sometimes refuses to accept some of the person's effort or performance as good enough. — Robert K. Greenleaf, founder of modern servant leadership

There are various ways to define servant leadership, with some emphasising the role as a servant in a more subservient way. However, the more popular definition is that of a leader that focuses on supporting their followers and removing obstacles from their path so they can excel. Someone might ask what the difference is between a subservient servant leader and one that focuses on supporting their team. There is an important difference. The definition supported here is that the servant leader is not subservient or weak, but as supportive, with their support directed towards achieving the goal. Being a servant leader does not mean you make coffee for your followers and let them order you about. A servant leader can, in many ways, be like a traditional leader with the highest wage, the largest office, and absolute authority. The difference is not necessarily in their position in the hierarchy or their status. The difference is that the servant leader believes it is more effective to support, remove obstacles, and give their followers some autonomy in what they do. Many narrow-minded leaders don't like this approach as they do not get the dopamine hit or ego boost from ordering people around. It is also not an appealing approach for control freaks. That is their loss.

Another common misunderstanding relating to this approach is that it is fixated on ethics. It is true that in this approach moral authority based on principles is applied, as opposed to formal authority coming from the leader's position and ego. A servant leader is indeed ethical, but they are not fixated on helping people like a charity worker. Based on discussions with the team, they take the necessary steps to put the things in place that the followers need to be successful. They may listen to a team member's problems outside of work, but that is not the focus.

As with the other leadership styles discussed, the names are very informative and they put us on the right track to understanding them, but they don't tell the whole story. Once we dig beneath the surface, things get a little trickier – but also more fascinating. With leadership, the big ideas are important, but the devil is in the detail. It may be frustrating at times that we need to spend so much time just to fully understand the different approaches, and then we also need to make a big effort to apply them correctly. However, the challenge leadership gives us is also an opportunity to

https://doi.org/10.1515/9783111630137-005

learn more about human nature, society, business, and, increasingly, AI. Servant leadership is definitely one of those approaches that someone can get the main points about how it works in a few minutes but can spend a lifetime trying to understand the nuances of where, how, and why it works.

When some people talk about leadership, they like to go back to the start of an approach because it gives us a sense of a grounding of our understanding and a sense of completeness. For leadership approaches it is not always significant or particularly useful to know who popularised or framed the approach first, because these approaches have been used for as long as humans have existed. Certainly, Jesus Christ embodied servant leadership by putting others first but still had a strong impact at the same time. Servant leadership is one of the cases where it is indeed worth learning about the people that popularised the term in modern times. The first academic to use the term servant leadership was Robert K. Greenleaf in the 1970s (Greenleaf, 1970), but the first to popularise the concept was the famous author Hermann Hesse back in 1932 (Hesse, 1932/1933). He wrote fictional novels and won a Nobel Prize for Literature, making him an unconventional source for an important business theory. As we said, there have been servant leaders for as long as there have been humans, but because the stereotype of the macho, alpha-male leader was so powerful, it took a particularly gifted author writing a fictional tale to convince people that you could be a leader by being a servant. In his book, a group of fictional and historical characters, including Plato, embark on a fantastical journey. However, once a person who acted as their servant disappears, friction begins to develop between them, and they stop functioning as a team. The author is not making the case for servant leadership too overtly but lets the reader understand the value for themselves by reflecting on what is happening in the story. You cannot help but think that if someone pushed the concept of servant leadership onto people in the 1930s it might not have been accepted. It might say something that we had to wait until the 1970s for someone to make the case for servant leadership more directly. Today, this approach is not only popular, but it is expected at least to some degree by employees.

We must accept that less caring and ethical approaches, such as authoritarian leadership, are indeed effective and may be necessary in some cases, but we should also aspire to achieve great things while keeping people as happy as possible and with a minimal amount of stress. This is not just about being ethical and kind, it is also about having an approach that can achieve sustainable results and avoid burnout. Therefore, wherever this more caring approach can be used, it should be. Furthermore, by understanding the mechanics of why this approach works, we can apply it to contexts that a less skilful servant leader would not be able to.

In the 1930s it took someone incredibly gifted with words to make people understand that someone can be both a leader and a servant, but people and society have moved on, and we can now apply this approach to people that will appreciate it and will play their role for it to be a success.

5.1.1 Personality traits and skills

This approach does not include every leader that served people well, but only those that apply the servant leadership style as it has been defined by Greenleaf in his seminal 1970 article. Many people assume they understand what this approach involves, but they are often wrong. Servant leadership is often grouped together with authentic leadership and coaching. While an authentic leader may not prioritise being a servant leader, a true servant leader has to be authentic. There isn't really a way to be a true servant leader without being authentic. If you want to support people but you aren't genuinely interested, or you are not honest and transparent, this approach will not work. For many people, their personality will be a natural fit for servant leadership, but this does not mean its use is restricted only to those with a matching personality. Someone that does not have a personality that has natural fit to this approach but understands its value can adapt their behaviour and thought processes as they learn more about it. So while this approach will be a more natural fit for some and they will apply it more effortlessly, anyone that genuinely appreciates the value of this approach can apply it. To fully implement this approach we need to value its philosophy. A leader can implement elements of this approach without necessarily believing its philosophy, but if it will be someone's only leadership approach, or their primary approach, they need to believe in it.

The overall approach is more humane, which is very well received by most people in a period when targets have dominated management. This leader is selfless and willing to sacrifice themselves, caring and empathetic, a good active listener, and committed to the team members' work-related self-development. Mentoring and coaching are part of this approach. If more authority is delegated to the followers, it is especially important that they are as capable as possible, and they have the mindset of lifelong learning.

A leader applying this approach provides support and leads by example with their professionalism. The people that will try to imagine what this approach involves without reading about it may miss that a servant leader should also be a role model with their behaviour. This leader can be gentle to others, but they have the determination of an Olympic athlete. A second point that is not obvious from the name of this approach is that it emphasises foresight and persuasion. Someone reading the name will certainly not expect it to involve coercion, but they may think the servant leader is really a follower and not a true leader. The emphasis on leading by example and utilising persuasion are examples of how the servant leader is still a genuine leader and not weak or subservient to team members. While this leader does not apply a top-down approach and tries to empower followers and create consensus, if they can have the greatest foresight after drawing insight from the whole team, this will make people want to follow them. As the leader does not rely on formal authority, they need to prove themselves on an ongoing basis so the team has confidence in them.

5.1.2 What does an effective team using this leadership style look like?

The servant approach – as is the case with most of the successful leadership styles – matches a very natural human need to achieve things with people by genuinely helping them. It is analogous to a parent that may occasionally give their children orders but mostly strives to put everything in place for them to succeed in the way they want. When this approach works, it creates a very positive work environment. Most people appreciate this positivity and reciprocate. A culture of empowerment, high engagement, collaboration, and trust is created. People feel empowered and collaborate more openly because they are all treated fairly without favouritism. Also, they are not pitted against each other to meet individual targets in an overly pressurised environment. All these things together typically lead to everyone involved being more satisfied.

However, as with every leadership style, if the work goes badly, the disappointment and negative consequences of that will override any positive experience. Therefore, all these positive vibes should not come at the expense of getting the job done. If achieving the necessary tasks is at risk, then a servant leader may need to adopt alternative approaches to take corrective action. As many managers, lecturers, and other professionals know, it is easier to start strictly and gradually become less strict than to start less strictly and try to tighten things up later. This is one of the weaknesses of this approach that suggests that in many cases it needs to be combined with another approach, such as transactional leadership, to get a good balance. Personally, I would love to be friends with all my students, but this can backfire for a variety of reasons and some distance is necessary. This risk of the kindness and closeness backfiring is always present with servant leadership; it's like the elephant in the room of this approach.

5.1.3 Servant leadership examples

Effective servant leadership is displayed in both the private and public sector. Many successful politicians are considered servant leaders. An example is António Guterres, the secretary-general of the United Nations, who worked to support the weak and vulnerable. This came at a great personal cost, as he sacrificed an easier life to stand up for those in need. In the private sector this style is typically used for two reasons. The first is obvious: a leader believes this is the most effective way to get high performance out of their team, especially performance that can be sustained over a long time. The second common reason to apply it is when the leader is not in a position to use more hands-on approaches, such as bureaucratic or transactional. The situation may be too complex or too fluid, or it may be a topic they don't fully understand, so they must rely on the followers for some clarity.

5.1.4 How this leadership style builds trust in people

This leadership style clearly prioritises ethics, a very low power distance between leader and follower, and building strong relationships. It does not just build a strong relationship between the leader and each follower, but a sense of community between the whole team. All these things build trust. The process of applying this approach also develops the leader's emotional intelligence so that they can appreciate people's concerns better. It is easy to say that a leader should be a good listener, but, for a variety of reasons, many people don't say what they are truly thinking. Many followers know from experience that the messenger of bad news 'can be shot', so bad news is often not communicated to the leader. Many people want to display positivity at work even if they are worried about something, so a leader with good emotional intelligence can read between the lines and understand the underlying issues.

Equally importantly, there is no part of this approach, at least in theory, that reduces trust either directly or indirectly. The biggest threat to trust when applying this approach is that if there is no wise and experienced leader making most of the decisions and shaping the strategy, the team may become disjointed or go in the wrong direction. It is natural for a team member to want more freedom and independence, but not having a leader single-mindedly driving the project can cause problems. A second risk to trust is that while it is true that we often get frustrated by our leader, in most cases they are not the least trusted colleague we have. Therefore, if the power is in the leader's hands, we have more trust in them than if it is spread around to many team members, including the one we trust the least. This is a slightly nuanced point, but it is often true that while we may not be entirely thrilled with our leader, we have some trust in them, and at the very least they are a 'known quantity' and we know what to expect. Even if we do not trust our leader, we may still distrust them less than another team member. The well-known saying 'better the devil you know' often applies here.

When trust is built by this leadership style, it is more sustainable, as the principles and process of applying it are beneficial. The most resilient and sustainable trust is when real bonds and loyalty are created. When followers feel security they show loyalty. The servant leader not only builds trust, but they have some 'credit in the bank'. When followers have some goodwill in their leader, they will not question every decision but will show some faith and togetherness.

Key concept: The servant leader believes it is more effective to support, remove obstacles, and give their followers some autonomy in what they do. They are not weak or subservient and can be as ambitious as any other leader. They can still have control over the team, but this is achieved with moral authority and soft power, as opposed to hard power.

Leadership tip: Applying this style can make people feel empowered and encourage them to collaborate more openly because they are all treated fairly without favouritism. They are also not pitted against each other to meet individual targets in an overly pressurised environment.

Trust-building tip: This leadership style prioritises ethics, integrity, a very low power distance between the leader and the follower, and building strong relationships and a sense of community between the whole team. When trust is built by this leadership style it is more sustainable and resilient, as the principles of this style and the process followed to apply it are beneficial.

5.2 The strengths and weaknesses of servant leadership

Leadership is not about being in charge. Leadership is about taking care of those in your charge.
— Simon Sinek, leadership author

5.2.1 Strengths and opportunities

5.2.1.1 The strengths of servant leadership from the follower's perspective

There are many strengths to this approach, but two stand out from the rest. First, it is very appealing to people, and second, its different elements are very synergistic to each other. It is not hard to appreciate why people respond well to this approach. Who wouldn't want a leader that always offers their time to actively listen to them? Who wouldn't want a leader that is supportive in both emotional and practical ways? If we reflect on Maslow's hierarchy of needs (Maslow, 1943), this approach can support all of the typical categories of human needs. Followers are usually particularly pleased about getting involved in all aspects of the work, including decision making and conceptualising together what the big picture beyond the day-to-day operations will be. It is not just about having an influence on the final decision, but it is also about everyone involved appreciating all the challenges involved. In our workplace, we often have a negative knee-jerk reaction to a decision from senior management, but when we reflect a little more and try to come up with a better solution, we start to appreciate that while the choice made may not be ideal, it was the best option available at the time.

The sense of security followers feel from the time servant leaders invest in them, and the practical and moral support they give them, builds resilient and sustainable trust within the team. When the leader is more honest and authentic in their communication, this becomes the norm in the group. The sense of community includes the leaders and the followers, and there is less of an institutional class system. The more support a leader can provide by removing barriers, the more the followers can focus on their role and have fewer distractions. Organisations tend to amplify what the leader puts into them. If it is negativity and favouritism, this gets amplified by the rest of the staff and the organisation quickly becomes toxic.

I have unfortunately experienced terrible leadership first-hand many times. In a hotly contested field, the worst leadership I have seen is a leader that is incapable of doing even the most basic management, such as organising what people are supposed to do. The quality of their team is inevitably dreadful, and the only solution their small mental capacity can come up with is that the employees are not good enough. The servant leader accepts people with their limitations but still expects the effort to be at the right level. This means this leader develops their people and does not resort to playing musical chairs on the Titanic. Typically, the worse the leader is, the more intolerant they are to imperfect employees. The old French proverb 'a bad workman blames his tools comes to mind'.

The strengths of servant leadership for Generation Z and Alpha employees

This leadership approach is a very natural fit for followers from Generation Z and Alpha and meets all their expectations. It can make them feel more appreciated at work and helps them achieve the work-life balance they want. Being socially responsible and receiving what can be called purpose-driven leadership is rightly very appealing to them. These generations want to celebrate successes more regularly, and this approach clearly commits a lot of time to showing appreciation and recognition. Flexibility is not guaranteed in this approach and not every servant leader will offer it, but they are more likely to see the value in offering flexibility in comparison to more authoritarian top-down approaches.

5.2.1.2 The strengths of servant leadership from the leader's perspective

This approach broadens the team's problem-solving capabilities, meaning less of that responsibility falls on the leader. One of the hidden costs of concentrating power in more authoritarian styles is that more of the problem solving falls on the leader. By fostering open communication, the leader learns what is happening faster and the risk of losing touch with what is happening is lower. The increased quantity and quality of communication improves the cohesion in the team, reducing the need for the leader to deal with the negative fallout of feuds. By having less conflict and more motivated followers, the leader also feels more fulfilled working with them. The positivity and good vibes inside the organisation inevitably improve the external 'brand' image and reputation. In the age of social media, what happens inside an organisation does not stay within the walls of the organisation for very long.

Key concept: The servant leader creates a positive environment in the team with mutual respect, honesty, and accountability. There is less of a class system and less power distance.

Leadership tip: Followers appreciate getting involved in all aspects of the work, including the decision-making process and conceptualising the big picture beyond the day-to-day operations together.

Trust-building tip: The sense of security followers feel from the time servant leaders invest in them, and the practical and moral support they give them, builds resilient and sustainable trust within the team.

5.2.2 Weaknesses and challenges

5.2.2.1 The weaknesses of servant leadership from the follower's perspective
This approach sounds excellent in theory, but while it is possible to apply it successfully, there are often some typical weaknesses. We all want to be involved in the decision making, but this is only one of many conflicting priorities we have. We also want a clear plan and to not waste time at work due to confusion and unnecessary meetings. The overemphasis on collaboration and collectively making decisions can create confusion and frustration. This leadership style can inadvertently create ambiguity in the roles and no clear direction. While everyone being happy at work is an honourable aspiration to have, it can make decisions harder to make. Additionally, if someone in a team looks for compassion and for people to put their feelings first too often, it can lead to compassion fatigue.

With the leader getting more involved in the day-to-day operations and supporting different followers in different ways depending on what each one asks for, there is a risk of drifting into favouritism. If a leader is determined to show favouritism they will probably be able to do this whatever leadership approach is used, but here there is a risk of unintentionally drifting into it. Does the pushier follower truly need more support, or are they just more demanding?

This approach has synergies between all its principles and priorities, but it does not always align with the environment around it, nor does it always fit with traditional hierarchies of an organisation. Hierarchies need authority and control, which is not always easy to marry with servant leadership. Additionally, if the organisation has an incompatible, weak, or dysfunctional culture, it will be hard to implement this approach. Servant leaders may be a suitable choice to gradually improve a culture, but this will not be easy and takes time.

When I worked in Germany, my personal experience was that the leadership was as far from servant leadership as is possible, but because of the clarity in what everyone's role was – and everyone 'staying in their lane' and not interfering in each other's work – the overall feeling was one of contentment and calm.

The weaknesses of servant leadership for Generation Z and Alpha employees
There are no weaknesses inherent in this approach that would specifically disappoint people from these generations. The risks of disappointing them come from any unintended consequences of this approach, such as time-consuming meetings, a lack of clear roles, and people pulling in different directions.

5.2.2.2 The weaknesses of servant leadership from the leader's perspective

Can backfire if not applied effectively
This leadership approach may come naturally to people with a generally more hu-mane outlook on life and whose character traits include empathy, but it can neverthe-less be tricky. The autocratic leadership approach, where the leader decides and then applies pressure on followers to get things done, may not be the most heart-warming approach, but it is straightforward and clearly works in many situations. The servant leader needs to do quite a few things at the same time, which will overwhelm many. A less experienced servant leader, or one trying to get things done through periods of great uncertainty, may feel that it is too challenging. It is challenging to not only take many different steps, but to also predict how everyone will react to those steps. Set-ting boundaries becomes harder without the power distance. Having boundaries can give a leader some protection and not leave them constantly exposed. Without bound-aries, they may come across as indecisive or too passive. As a servant leader tries to strike the right balance on issues such as delegating while still being in the loop, they may come across as inconsistent. As we said, starting off by giving the followers a lot of freedom and then taking it away will probably be received even worse than work-ing under an authoritarian leader.

This is human nature and completely natural. Most of us have been in situations where we are disappointed because, in some way, we are in a worse situation than we were a few weeks ago, even though overall we are still in a good position that we should be happy with. Up to a point, we measure our happiness as an absolute – for example, can I afford to pay my bills? – and, to some extent, we measure it in relative terms. A servant leader that gives less freedom and support may feel more oppressive and unhelpful than someone who was authoritarian all along.

The absolute versus relative aspect is one part of it; the other is that people want to know what to expect. When I first worked in Germany, I was told in December what module I would be teaching in September of the next year. This wasn't part of an informal discussion, but formal communication. I thought this was absolutely fan-tastic as I was able to organise my time, read a book, and prepare the module. It is an obvious point and definitely not rocket science, but sometimes we need to be re-minded that these simple but important things are worth fighting for.

Time-consuming to implement
This approach is typically time consuming. If we go through the list of things this leader needs to do, it is quite long. Not only there is a long list of things that need to be done, but some are done in a very time-consuming way. For example, the decision-making process takes longer than other approaches. All these responsibilities may have the result that the leader puts the followers' wellbeing above their own and gets burned out. There are many times when a leader that does not use the servant leader-

ship style can avoid suffering by moving it onto the followers. In servant leadership, the followers can potentially shift the suffering onto the leader.

When a leader is involved hands-on and more immersed in what is happening day to day, they can achieve many things, but they are also more exposed and vulnerable. The more involved a leader becomes, the more they can be blamed for the outcome, and in a sense the less accountable the staff are. For example, when I finished my army officer training, I was having a meeting with the head of the unit before taking command of some soldiers. To set the scene for what to expect, he told us that the soldiers were waiting for us to arrive, as the responsibility would shift from them to us. As long as there is no officer involved in everything they do, they hold the responsibility. However, once the official leader is there, the responsibility shifts to them. There is the more romantic side to leadership that involves what we aspire to create, and there is the more pragmatic side of who will be blamed if something goes wrong.

Key concept: The servant leader needs to strike a delicate balance, so they come across as helpful without losing their authority.

Leadership tip: The followers need to be given freedom and autonomy, but not to the point of the team becoming disjointed. As with most leadership styles, it is risky to be too dogmatic in its application. Even the most committed servant leader may have to 'park' this approach from time to time.

Trust-building tip: Freedom and autonomy build trust but so do stable and predictable processes. The effective leader knows how to analyse the situation and take the necessary actions to ensure that people feel sufficiently free, but within a suitable structure.

5.3 Servant leadership's impact on AI adoption and trust

The best way to find yourself is to lose yourself in the service of others. — Mahatma Gandhi, leader of the Indian independence movement

5.3.1 How this leadership style can support AI

Effective allocation of resources to digital transformation and AI

Innovation with AI is far more about allocating resources effectively than being creative and inventive. This means transactional leadership is a good fit in some ways, such as its regular targets and monitoring, but servant leadership is also a good fit for managing resources. If we go a little deeper into servant leadership than just the meaning of the name in English, we will see that stewardship of resources is central to this approach. So, while it is not a very centralised top-down approach, servant leaders don't just care about the people, but also the organisation's resources. It is central to this approach to use these resources wisely. It is not a centralised authoritarian style, but the leader still makes the final decision to make resources available.

Resources are central when adapting the business model to be more centred on AI to fully utilise its characteristics. The logic of simpler times in the past was that if there were fewer resources, a less ambitious approach should be taken, but if there were more resources, something more ambitious could be done. It is not that straightforward with AI as there isn't a direct relationship between the resources put in and what you get out. Utilising AI can be about pouring resources into research and development, or it can be about bringing resources together in a clever way. The capabilities of AI are often more dependent on the quantity and quality of the data, rather than the sophistication of the technology itself.

Resources do not perfectly dictate ambition with AI. For example, a company might choose to use software as a service from the cloud if they want to scale very quickly and grow significantly in size. Alternatively, they may prefer to keep more in-house so they have more control over updates and customisations. The prevailing wisdom is that doing more in-house is more expensive, but in reality, it is often less expensive but more time consuming. We need to be on top of what resources we have and what resources we have access to, but this is not a simple case of choosing the expensive option if we have the resources and the cheap option if we do not. The process of applying servant leadership, with its focus on collaboration and team-building activities, increases the likelihood of successful implementation.

Driving change in the organisation and in the people themselves

In addition to creating a conducive team dynamic, this approach also puts individuals in the right mindset to get the most out of AI. By encouraging personal development, people are put in the mindset to see the potential benefits of change and not be too fearful of it. By prioritising wellbeing, followers have the confidence to take some risks and overcome obstacles. Many people's instinct is to fear change, but when they develop their ability to learn and adapt, they can be more willing to move forward. While the servant approach prepares people for change, it does not typically attempt to crush all resistance and any healthy scepticism. Some healthy reservations about change should not be crushed, and given the limited top-down nature of this approach, this is unlikely to happen.

Sustainable results from digital transformation and AI

When making significant renovations to a house, builders can actually drive a digger into the house and park it in what was once the living room, using the digger's bucket to break down walls. While driving fundamental change to how an organisation operates can be challenging, it is not always the hardest part. Especially in the times we live in, making the case for using more AI is not always difficult. There is often plenty of evidence to illustrate its financial value that can be used to convince people, and there is often a receptive audience. Unlike the situation with the builders driving a digger into the living room while the family that usually lives there is temporarily staying somewhere else, the employees remain in the organisation throughout digital transformation. Strong communication and collaboration are always useful, but they are absolutely critical when business models are being changed. The change should not be used by one group to increase their power and authority to the detriment of others. Often, senior management or one division of the organisation see change of this magnitude as an opportunity to increase their influence, but this should not happen. A servant leader has the right skills and the right methods to make the new AI-centred model sustainable and beneficial to everyone. When we say sustainable change with AI, we are not referring to its green credentials, but that the new AI-centred organisation will be successful and not require fundamental changes again.

5.3.2 How this leadership style builds trust in AI

In general, servant leadership principles such as integrity and ethics build trust. While the overall humane philosophy and many of the priorities of this approach contribute to this, it also has some characteristics that are particularly useful in digital transformation towards an AI-centred organisation.

Resilient and adaptable at times of change

When we think about digital transformation towards an AI-centred organisation, we need to appreciate that it is not just a case of many structures and processes changing. We need to appreciate that this change, and the challenges and uncertainty it brings, puts more pressure on the team. The team that successfully navigates this process and maintains its confidence and trust is a resilient and adaptable one. When we think of strength, we may think of something hard and inflexible such as iron, but often more flexible materials can be more resilient as they can adapt to the force they are hit with. The flexible material does not need to feel the full force of the blow. Something similar applies to servant leadership where soft power can often be stronger than hard power. All the characteristics of servant leadership come together to make it resilient and adaptable at times of change. The leader is in the loop, keeping up to date with what is happening. The leader needs to persuade the followers of the value of their ideas and the followers need to persuade the leader. When a team needs to think about how they can make their case as strongly as possible, and everyone challenges each other's arguments, this process leads to regular recalibration of the plan, helping to overcome problems quickly. Implementing technology is a mix of long-term planning and regular tweaks, so the process of implementing servant leadership benefits it. Most people appreciate that there needs to be a long-term plan, but many people do not appreciate that, however good that plan is, endless regular tweaks are needed. This cannot be avoided by having an excellent plan because of the very high rate of change across technology, but also the economy and many other aspects of our lives today. Issues such as the lower processing power required by a new AI algorithm, or the lower cost of new processors, can influence strategic decisions.

People that follow what tech companies do regularly will see that even the companies that lead on technology make adjustments and pivot all the time. Sometimes the change is needed to overcome a challenge, other times to make more of an opportunity, and at other times to outmanoeuvre a competitor. Some of these changes can be quite surprising, catching even those quite close to the company by surprise. One large tech company that specialises in generative AI software used to rely on a big tech company, which was also a major shareholder, for its technology infrastructure. Most people assumed these two tech companies were completely intertwined. Suddenly, the AI company dropped them in favour of making a joint venture with an investment bank. It is quite unexpected for a deal worth tens of billions of euro to completely blindside people close to it, but that is the dynamic nature of AI. Not only did people not expect it, but many could also not understand it. Was it simply to get investment for their own infrastructure so they free up their own resources for other things? Was it because they did not want to give the large tech company that was providing them with infrastructure too much power? It is hard to tell, but what is certain is that there was a very serious reason to take such a decisive step that ruffled some feathers.

Stable leadership behaviour at times of change

At this time of constant change, servant leadership – with its strength in resilience and robustness, but also healing – will constantly build and repair trust. Implementing new processes and technologies takes time, and the people involved need to feel that they will be trusted to complete the process. Servant leadership does not prioritise stability in the operations, and it is open to changing processes. While this approach is open to changes in the organisation's operations, the behaviour of this leader is consistent and they reliably follow through in the commitments they make. This can strike a good balance between change and having some consistency and reliability. This balance will support trust and put it at less risk. The last thing an organisation needs during digital transformation is a breakdown in trust and an increase in turnover. By reducing the risk in all the other aspects of work, people will be more willing to take on the new risks from digital transformation and AI.

Avoids focusing too much on targets to the detriment of people's lives

There are many modern practices that put a strain on trust and can be demotivating. In addition to those already mentioned, overly focusing on targets can 'eat away' at trust and motivation over time. While approaches such as transactional leadership offer clarity, putting targets over relationships and people can gradually erode trust.

AI does not create or necessitate overly focusing on targets, but it can take this practice to the next level with more targets and more monitoring. Obviously, this should be avoided, but it is likely that it will happen to some degree whether we want it or not. The humane principles of this leadership style counterbalance the increasing role of machines. An organisation with AI at its core can also have people at its core.

5.3.3 The business models that work well with this leadership

Does not need to match the organisation's principles

Many people associate servant leadership with selflessness and assume this approach is only suitable for charities, non-profits, and mission-driven organisations that prioritise ethical goals. This is once again an example of assuming the name of a leadership approach entirely encapsulates its principles, which is not the case. The reality is servant leadership can fit most business models. The leader applying this style can still drive an organisation forward, just like other approaches, but they do this by getting the most out of people and situations rather than barking orders.

The leadership approach does not always have to have the same principles as the organisation where it is being applied. Having the synergies between the two can help as it can send a coherent signal internally and externally, but it is not entirely necessary. You can have an autocratic leader of a charity or a servant leader of a hedge fund that is happy to take half the profits of their clients as fees, as many do. While it is not limited to one type of organisation, it does have additional synergies with more customer-centric organisations, such as education, hospitality, and healthcare.

Can be used with all six business models optimised for AI

In relation to utilising AI, there are business models that will help organisations already active in an area to fully utilise AI, and there are business models that enable organisations to move into new areas to utilise the opportunities created by AI (Zarifis & Cheng, 2023, 2025). The six business models proven to be ideal for a world with AI at its centre are: (1) focus on one part of the value chain and disaggregate, (2) absorb AI into existing model, (3) incumbent expanding beyond current model to fully utilise the opportunities of AI and access new data, (4) startup disruptor focused on one sector, built from the start to be highly automated, (5) disruptor focused on tech adding a new service such as insurance, and (6) disruptor that is not necessarily tech-focused with an extensive user or fanbase. A servant leader can benefit all these organisations in using AI more effectively.

The fourth strategy – a startup disruptor focused on one sector and built from the start to be highly automated – is often used to take advantage of a new technology or change in regulation. Typically they already have a clear plan and want to implement it quickly. This is in no way a rule, but this is what typically happens. This business model is usually created because a more effective one is identified, so there is a clear plan from the beginning. This is not to say servant leadership would not be beneficial in any way, but typically the goal of these organisations is to move faster than the existing companies in a sector, and faster than any other new disruptors. When the startup utilising the fourth business model is in this situation and wants to focus on implementation, the servant leadership approach would not be the most natural fit if applied on its own.

This approach can be used for all six approaches and is a natural fit for the typical implementations of five of them, but it fits the third one particularly well. It could be argued that it is the most suitable leadership style for the third business model – an incumbent expanding beyond current model to fully utilise the opportunities of AI and access new data. In this model, the organisation wants to keep what it already does and expand to offering new services. In such a scenario, a servant leader building consensus and developing solutions everyone is comfortable with is ideal. The transformational leadership approach is also a natural fit here. It is not a coincidence that two of the three most popular leadership styles are a good fit for the situation many organisations find themselves in today.

Key concept: Servant leadership's soft power can often be stronger than hard power. All the characteristics of servant leadership come together to make it resilient and adaptable at times of change. The leader is in the loop, keeping up to date with the digital transformation.

Leadership tip: This approach is not just about helping everyone. The servant leader has the stewardship of the organisation's resources and must use them wisely to reposition the business for a future where AI plays a more decisive role. Most organisations will only get one chance to get this right, so using the resources wisely will be decisive.

Trust-building tip: During digital transformation, creating a team that is resilient and adaptable at times of change builds trust within the team and gives them confidence that they can be successful. The servant leader is engaged in the process making tweaks to the long-term plan where necessary to resolve the team's concerns and keep everyone on board.

5.4 The popularity of servant leadership in the future

Ego can't sleep. It micro-manages. It disempowers. It reduces our capability. It excels in control
— Robert K. Greenleaf, founder of modern servant leadership

5.4.1 The trends in the popularity of this approach

Popular, but not always suitable

The popularity of the servant leadership approach is very high with followers, but its actual use is limited by what the leaders themselves want and what the context dictates. There are leaders that do not want to be helpful, and they get a sadistic pleasure out of using and abusing people. The word 'sadistic' might seem a little strong to some, but more experienced professionals would have probably come across at least one boss that meets that description. However, most leaders do not set out to be negative but are forced into it by the pressures they face, such as limited resources and time. In a partly globalised world, for many of us the competition is fierce, and this puts pressure on everyone. Often, this competition leads to a race to the bottom in terms of how staff are treated. If the leader faces serious limitations, they cannot fully implement servant leadership. They can still listen, encourage collaboration, build consensus, and so on, but support will be limited. If there are constraints and there is limited support with time and money for people's personal development, it is not truly servant leadership. Therefore, it is the practical challenges in applying this style that are holding it back from being used more widely, not its popularity.

Increased awareness of this style

Despite the practical challenges in utilising it, its popularity is increasing because more leaders are learning about this approach, either in formal education or in their free time. Someone studying in a business school, for example doing an MBA twenty years ago, would have not been encouraged so much to use servant and also transformational leadership. More traditional management with a focus on monitoring and controlling was the priority back then. It is also easier for a servant leader to be effective if the follower recognises that they are applying that style and not simply trying to be the follower's friend. I once had a line manager that applied this approach very thoroughly. As I recognised that he was applying a leadership style and not being subserviate to me, I respected his position and did not push my luck. He was always willing to listen to my problems, but I did not confuse this with friendship and take liberties or offload too many problems on him.

Lastly, the technological landscape we are moving towards needs empowered employees that can innovate and are willing to take the risk to do so. All the issues discussed strongly indicate that servant leadership will become increasingly popular where it can be applied.

5.4.2 How does servant leadership compare to other leadership styles

Servant leadership is often grouped with other purpose-, meaning-, or vision-driven leadership approaches, such as charismatic and transformational. It is seen as fundamentally different in its approach to the more top-down approaches, such as authoritarian and transactional. It is, however, quite unique in its approach and distinct from the other purpose-based approaches. Having support as its primary focus gives it this different character. Even if we compare it to democratic leadership – which is also ethical and gives followers autonomy in a similar way to servant leadership – the democratic leader does not prioritise supporting them like the servant leader does.

Some people see authentic leadership and coaching as separate approaches to servant leadership, which has some logic to it, but an effective servant leader encompasses both authentic leadership and coaching. The distinction is made by some because authentic and coaching are narrower, more focused approaches that do not necessarily cover all the aspects of servant leadership. However, servant leadership is broader and encompasses them both. Someone can be an authentic leader or apply coaching without being a servant leader, but a servant leader encompasses the other two approaches.

Servant leadership has clear strengths and limitations. It is very attractive, but even its strongest proponent will not argue that it fits all the situations we can find ourselves in. My personal anecdotal evidence suggests that it is often either combined with another approach, typically transactional, or there is someone else in the organisation that essentially plays the role of the 'bad cop' or 'the enforcer'. This 'good cop, bad cop' approach is so prevalent because it works. In the army, the head of the base is more of a figurehead, focusing on collaborations outside the base, while the second in command deals with the day-to-day operations and keeping people in line. The head of the base avoids the daily friction with personnel to maintain belief in their leadership, and the second in command does whatever it takes to get the job done, even if this involves upsetting some people. Many countries have this approach, with a monarch or president who needs to be appreciated by everyone, and a prime minister that has to make the tough decisions, like raising taxes and enforcing the rule of law. The strengths and weaknesses of this approach on its own, and when it is combined with transactional and transformational styles, are summarised in Table 5.1.

Key concept: Employees increasingly demand servant leadership, leaders are becoming more extensively educated in how to apply it, organisations are increasingly being structured to support it, and the new AI-focused business models benefit from it.

Leadership tip: Servant leadership has clear benefits, but it is not always the best approach to apply on its own. If a leader wants to always be the nice guy and fully apply servant leadership, they need someone else to be the enforcer and take the unpopular but necessary actions.

Table 5.1: Servant leadership's strengths and weaknesses in supporting AI and trust.

	Strengths in supporting AI	Weaknesses in supporting AI	Strengths in supporting trust	Weaknesses in supporting trust
Servant leadership	Effective allocation of resources to digital transformation and AI, driving change in the organisation and in the people themselves, sustainable results from digital transformation and AI.	May cause a disjointed approach, time consuming to implement and may slow process of digital transformation down, may create a false hope in people that the change will fully satisfy their demands.	Genuinely caring and supportive, builds community, makes team resilient and adaptable at times of change, stable leadership behaviour at times of change, avoids focusing on targets to the detriment of employee's lives.	May cause drift into favouritism, can backfire if not applied effectively, can make leader appear weak.
Primarily transactional leadership with some servant leadership	More support for experts working on technologies the leader does not fully understand. Avoids overly focusing on targets that are unlikely to be perfect and comprehensive. Encourages free thinking and creativity.	–	Illustrates an overarching inspirational, caring, and ethical vision of the organisation.	–
Primarily servant leadership with some transformational leadership	More emphasis on change and motivation can encourage digital transformation.	May lose some structure.	Promotes overarching vision of the value of innovation.	May increase uncertainty.

Trust-building tip: The principles of servant leadership have many differences to the principles of transactional leadership. The first leadership style is seen as purpose-driven and more caring, while the second is seen as more pragmatic and practical. However, in both approaches, the leader is involved, very hands-on, and is in the loop with the day-to-day operations. This common ground is one of the reasons these two leadership approaches go together so well.

5.5 Summary

If you want to govern the people, you must place yourself below them. If you want to lead the people, you must learn how to follow them. — Laozi, ancient Chinese philosopher and founder of Taoism

5.5.1 The enduring value of the servant leadership approach

A servant leader is not subservient or weak, but supportive. Their support is focused on achieving the goal of the team; it is not just about generally being nice to followers. Being a servant leader does not mean you let the followers give you orders. The difference to more authoritarian styles is not necessarily in the leader's position in the hierarchy or their status: a servant leader can have absolute authority, as in the other approaches. The difference is that the servant leader believes it is more effective to support, remove obstacles, and give their followers some autonomy.

Less caring and less ethical approaches, such as authoritarian leadership, are effective and may be necessary in some cases, but we should try to achieve our goals without putting more pressure on people than what is necessary. Being more ethical and kind can achieve sustainable results and avoid employee burnout. Therefore, where this more caring approach can be used, it should be. Furthermore, by understanding the mechanics of why this approach works, we can apply it to contexts that a less skilful servant leader would not be able to.

This more humane approach is deeply appreciated by most people at a time when pursuing narrow targets set by senior management has dominated the workplace. A leader following this approach provides support and leads by example. Applying this approach means being selfless, caring, empathetic, an active listener, and committed to the team members' work-related self-development. Mentoring and coaching are part of this approach. If more authority is delegated to the followers, it is especially important that they are as capable as possible in AI and other emerging technologies, and that they have the mindset of lifelong learning.

Not only are more employees increasingly demanding servant leadership, but leaders are becoming more extensively educated in how to apply it, while organisations are increasingly being structured to support it, with the new AI-focused business models benefiting from it. A leadership style that was seen in the past as a novelty, quite quirky, and counterintuitive is now firmly in the mainstream.

5.5.2 Is the servant leadership approach the best for AI and trust?

This approach can ensure the effective allocation of resources to digital transformation and AI. Moving to an organisation with AI at its centre is more about allocating resources effectively and less about being inventive. Servant leadership can be effective at managing resources. Stewardship of resources is central to this approach. It is important to remember that while it is not a very centralised top-down approach, servant leaders don't just care about the people but also the resources.

This style has synergies by driving change in the organisation and in the people themselves. In addition to creating a conducive team dynamic, this approach puts individuals in the right mindset to get the most out of AI. People that are encouraged to develop themselves as professionals will be more confident about change. By prioritising wellbeing, followers have the confidence to take some risks and overcome obstacles.

By applying servant leadership, sustainable results from digital transformation and AI can be achieved. AI is so powerful and has so much potential, that convincing people of the need for a decisive change is not usually the hardest part. The biggest challenge is achieving sustainable results that achieve the goals without causing problems. The change should not be used by an individual or group to shift the power balance in their favour. A servant leader has the right skills and the right methods to make the new AI-centred model sustainable and beneficial to everyone. Sustainable change means that the new AI-centred organisation will be successful with their new model and will not be required to fundamentally change again.

Building trust in AI
This approach has trust at its core, so it is in a good position to build trust in AI in several ways. Firstly, by creating a team that is resilient and adaptable at times of change, there is more trust and confidence. The team that successfully navigates this process and maintains its confidence and trust is a resilient and adaptable one.

Secondly, it provides stable leadership behaviour at times of change. At this time of constant change, servant leadership – with its strength in resilience, robustness, and healing of past 'wounds' that broke trust – will constantly build and repair trust.

Thirdly, this approach avoids focusing too much on targets to the detriment of employee's lives. Obsessing over targets for long periods of time reduces trust. While approaches such as transactional leadership offer clarity, putting targets over the relationships with people can gradually erode trust. The humane principles of this style should lead to an organisation with AI at its centre and people at its core. More AI does not necessitate less humanity. It is not the AI that reduces the humanity in an organisation, it is greedy and selfish leaders using AI to pursue their selfish goals that reduces the humanity. We do not need to act and think in the same way as machines – or have no feelings like machines – to successfully work with them.

5.5.3 Choosing the right leadership style and priorities at each stage of a project

The best version of the project stages for a leader of people and AI is one with six stages. This includes the typical five first stages of forming, storming, norming, performing, and adjourning, and adds a sixth stage of post-project collaboration (Zarifis & Cheng, 2024; Zarifis, 2024). Servant leadership can be applied at all of the six typical stages of a project. As it is even hard for a leader that is hands-on to understand every aspect of AI, this approach will empower the various experts to move forward. The servant leader can use the six stages to structure their digital transformation and hold a meeting to touch base and evaluate progress at each stage. Even if a leader uses this approach that promotes meetings to develop a consensus, this is more useful at the start in the stages forming and storming, and less necessary later.

Key concept: A servant leader is not subservient or weak. Their support is focused on achieving the goal of the team; it is not just about generally being nice to people. These leaders believe it is more effective to support, remove obstacles, and give their followers some autonomy in what they do.

Leadership tip: By applying servant leadership there can be an effective allocation of resources during digital transformation towards an organisation with AI at its centre. While it is not a very centralised top-down approach, servant leaders don't just care about the people, but also the resources. Resources are utilised to drive change in the organisation, and in the people themselves.

Trust-building tip: This approach can create a team that is resilient and adaptable at times of change. It provides stable leadership behaviour and avoids focusing too much on targets to the detriment of employee's lives. The humane principles of this style should lead to an organisation with AI at its centre that also has people at its core.

Best blended leadership approaches using this style: (a) Primarily transactional leadership with some servant leadership where necessary. Transactional and servant styles are both hands-on, so they have some common ground in terms of how they are applied. Transactional leadership can help focus a team and mitigate the weaknesses of servant leadership. (b) Primarily servant leadership, with some transformational leadership. In many ways servant leadership supports change, but it can also slow change down. For example, building consensus can take time. Transformational leadership can encourage more dynamism but will increase the risk of losing the necessary structure in the team.

5.6 Exercises

Exercise 5.1

The value of servant leadership to legal professionals
Scenario: You work in the technology department of a solicitors' firm (a British term for what others call a law firm). The lawyers focus mostly on advising clients on tax issues and do not regularly go to court to represent them. The clients are mostly multinational companies that want input on their strategy and how to structure their op-

erations effectively, but these companies also need advice on the many unexpected problems that emerge from time to time. The leadership style of the solicitors' firm is typically delegation, with lawyers operating very independently. They get a standard wage, but bonuses based on performance make up the largest part of their income.

Some of the younger lawyers that started in the last two or three years argue that AI should be used far more extensively, particularly as they are primarily advising clients and not representing them in court. These younger lawyers also believe that they would appreciate the servant leadership approach more. Because of these views of the younger lawyers, the partners of the firm are considering whether AI should be utilised more extensively and how support can be provided to the lawyers on this. They are not sure if the servant leadership approach would be a good fit for their organisation but they can see how the emerging technological landscape may require it in some shape or form so that they can keep up with the developments in AI.

Questions

1) Prepare a plan for how AI could be used in this organisation. The plan should cover what services will be provided and how. Should licences to existing services be provided, or should generative AI solutions be hosted in-house? What are the implications for client data with the solution you propose?

2) Prepare a SWOT (strengths, weaknesses, opportunities, and threats) analysis of using servant leadership in this context. How can some of the weaknesses and threats be mitigated? You can make links to the previous answer where necessary. Would you combine the servant style with other leadership approaches?

3) If you were to implement more AI and servant leadership in this organisation, what are five ways you would build trust? Are the implications for trust different because they are involved in providing legal advice?

4) Briefly outline what the priorities of the digital transformation would be at each of the six typical stages of a project.

5) Briefly discuss if any of the six business models for organisations to fully utilise the new opportunities created by AI are suitable (Zarifis & Cheng, 2023, 2025). The six business models proven to be ideal for an AI-centred organisation are: (1) Focus on one part of the value chain and disaggregate, (2) absorb AI into the existing model, (3) an incumbent expanding beyond current model to fully utilise the opportunities of AI and access new data, (4) startup disruptor focused on one sector, built from the start to be highly automated, (5) disruptor focused on tech adding a new service such as insurance, and (6) disruptor that is not necessarily tech-

focused with an extensive user or fanbase. Can a servant leader benefit the business models you identified as suitable for the solicitors' firm?

6) Given the increasing importance of technology in the legal profession, do you think that professionals such as technology experts that are not lawyers but work in a solicitors' firm should be promoted to partners in the firm? Is it better to remain with the current norm of all the partners being lawyers? What would be the benefits and drawbacks of applying this?

Exercise 5.2

How a servant leader adapts to changes in the technology landscape
Scenario: Your company provides accounting, auditing, and various consultancy services. It typically applies autocratic leadership. They gathered a team together to develop a detailed plan on how to go through digital transformation and wish to move towards the third business model for fully utilising AI (an incumbent expanding beyond current model to fully utilise the opportunities of AI and access new data [Zarifis & Cheng, 2023, 2025]). As part of this plan, they want to use AI services mostly because they believe the costs of running AI on their systems are too high. While the costs of the software seem manageable, the hardware costs seem prohibitive. The need for very powerful processors and all the other associated costs that come with them, such as more cooling, are too high to host in-house. This is unfortunate, as the sensitive client data they have needs to be kept within the EU due to GDPR.

However, the open-source generative AI models from China offer high performance and require far less powerful processors. It appears that the plan this small group of people made is not the best way forward, which is causing some frustration and loss of trust. Some colleagues are explicitly pushing back, arguing for better control of clients' data. Your line manager is concerned that competitors with more flexible management structures will be more agile and outflank them. He is concerned that the top-down autocratic approach is not the best for digital transformation with AI because the technology moves quickly.

For convenience in answering the questions, the six business models proven to be ideal for an AI-centred world are provided here once more (Zarifis & Cheng, 2023, 2025): (1) focus on one part of the value chain and disaggregate, (2) absorb AI into existing model, (3) incumbent expanding beyond current model to fully utilise the opportunities of AI and access new data, (4) startup disruptor focused on one sector, built from the start to be highly automated, (5) disruptor focused on tech adding a new service such as insurance, and (6) disruptor that is not necessarily tech-focused with an extensive user or fanbase.

Questions

1) To help your line manager make the case to the board to move towards servant leadership, write a report on how servant leadership is better suited for navigating the fast-moving technological landscape in the age of AI.

2) Write a short report on how open-source AI – which is as capable as or even more capable than closed-source versions, and can run on less powerful processors – changes the AI landscape and makes running these systems and keeping the data in-house possible.

3) If the company moves to using servant leadership and running their AI systems locally, how will this impact the trust of clients, regulators, and employees? How can servant leadership build trust in this situation?

Space for your notes

References

Greenleaf, R. K. (1970). *The servant as leader*. Robert K. Greenleaf Publishing Center.

Hesse, H. (1933). *Journey to the East* (H. Rosner, Trans.). [Original work published 1932]. Fischer Verlag.

Maslow, A. H. (1943). A theory of human motivation. *Psychological Review, 50*(4), 370–396.

Zarifis, A., & Cheng, X. (2023). AI is transforming insurance with five emerging business models. In J. Wang (Ed.), Encyclopedia of Data Science and Machine Learning (pp. 2086–2100). IGI Global Scientific Publishing. https://doi.org/10.4018/978-1-7998-9220-5.ch124

Zarifis, A., & Cheng, X. (2024). A model reducing researchers' challenges in projects: Build trust first for better mental health. *Cogent Business & Management, 11*(1), 1–13. https://doi.org/10.1080/23311975.2024.2350786

Zarifis, A. (2024, September 23). Building trust to support researchers' mental health. *Times Higher Education*. https://www.timeshighereducation.com/campus/building-trust-support-researchers-mental-health

Zarifis, A., & Cheng, X. (2025). The new centralised and decentralised Fintech technologies, and business models, transforming finance. In A. Zarifis & X. Cheng (Eds.), *Fintech and the emerging ecosystems: Exploring centralised and decentralised financial technologies*. Springer Nature. https://link.springer.com/book/9783031834011

Chapter 6
Transformational leadership and its role in using AI with trust

6.1 Introduction

A leader is a dealer in hope. — Napoleon Bonaparte, former French military leader and emperor

Digital transformation with AI is throwing everything up in the air and nobody knows exactly where things will fall. We may not need crisis management yet, but there is an element of crisis management in what needs to be done. The soul searching and reflection is not just on the organisational level, but also on a personal level. Some of the tasks we used to do that gave our life meaning, some small victories, will not be part of our lives anymore. There are many new technologies in the world that never become part of our daily lives and do not affect us so much. Our leader is the one driving the change and bringing these technologies into our lives. As they are taking some things away from us that gave us some purpose, the leader needs to give us a new purpose. This is where transformational leadership really works well with digital transformation. If you are going to take a part of someone's life away, you need to give them something in return. We might not be talking about something as dramatic as taking someone's house away from them, but there are many little tasks we do every day that give us some self-worth and make us feel useful. We cannot fill every day with big victories, so we need these smaller victories, in a similar way to a computer game such as Nintendo's Super Mario that gives the player many small tasks to give them a sense of achievement between the bigger tasks, like beating the main villain, Bowser. There is a British proverb that says if you look after the pennies, the pounds will look after themselves, and the same applies to motivation and having a purpose. Someone might believe that only big issues, such as getting a good wage, matter, but on some level, consciously or subconsciously, the small tasks we used to do that are now automated also matter. One of the tasks I had in the past was scheduling classes and allocating academics. It was tedious, but I got satisfaction out of doing what was an important task. When it was automated, I had to find something else to replace it. A transformational leader can fill the large and small voids left in people's lives by AI and automation.

As with the other main leadership styles, this approach has probably been used for as long as there have been humans, but at some point in recent times, someone named them and framed them more specifically. For transformational leadership, this was in 1970 when it was contrasted to transactional leadership (Burns, 1978). So, in its most well-known modern framing, it has been argued that a leader can be transactional, focusing on the exchange of value, or transformational, focusing on being a

https://doi.org/10.1515/9783111630137-006

role model and setting an example, providing motivation, driving change, creating a vision, offering intellectual stimulation, and providing some personalised support. As we know, there are more than two leadership styles, but contrasting these two is a very useful way to look at it. We can think of where we want to be on this spectrum. Do we want to focus more on specific exchanges of value, or do we want to focus more on motivating?

Many leaders, however, choose to use transformational leadership exclusively. There are situations where motivating, inspiring, and providing some individualised consideration to get colleagues on board with change is the priority. Often, these issues are more important than the traditional management priorities of monitoring and controlling. It may be that followers can handle the details themselves; it may be that there is another manager handling the details. It might be the case that some encouragement is needed to achieve some goals. There are many different situations where this approach is effective, but it fits best to situations where there is change. This might be an organisation such as an insurer that is changing their business model, and once they have done that they will go back to more stable operations, or it might be an organisation that is constantly innovating. When we think about an organisation that is constantly innovating, we may think of an aerospace company such as Airbus, or a tech company such as SAP, but many other organisations, such as the online bank Revolut, also innovate constantly with technology. As technology is such a big part of many organisations, they also operate in a similar way to innovative tech companies. Organisational structures, professional roles, and leadership styles are, in many cases, shifting towards those typical of technology-focused and fast-innovating companies, such as those in aerospace. This is not to suggest that it is now all about motivating staff and selling them big visions of changing the world. There is still a place for specific time-bound targets in transformational leadership, but as with servant leadership, they are not the main focus. This is a subtle but important difference. A transactional leader focuses on short-term targets, while a transformational or servant leader has a broader focus.

This is one of the leadership styles that is very exciting both for the leader themselves and their followers – at least when it works. It can be straightforward to apply in some situations, such as when there is a clear need for change and everyone is eager for someone dynamic to make that change, but it is harder in other situations, such as when there is no need or no ability for change. Would Napoleon Bonaparte get the same traction in France today? The answer is probably no, as that is not the kind of leadership that is needed today. If there is no ability for real significant change to an organisation, there may still be some opportunities to change the culture, the working conditions, and so on, but this approach really fires on all cylinders when there is a real disruption, such as digital transformation with AI.

This approach has really strong synergies when we are talking about changing an organisation in a very fundamental way, replacing some roles with AI and creating new ones, starting new partnerships, accessing different clients than before, and so on. When the level of disruption is very high, and a purely transactional leader would struggle to keep the control that approach needs to be successful, we need a transformational leader to make everyone love the change they used to fear. The reason this style is so effective in this context is that we need confidence and emotional engagement to overcome our fear. In some stressful situations, the only two possible reactions are 'fight' or 'flight'. 'Flight' in the context of digital transformation can be interpreted as several things, such as avoiding making the iterative changes that are probably necessary or avoiding making one really significant change, such as pivoting the whole organisation to offer different services. 'Fight' in this context would be charging forward despite knowing that there will be challenges and knowing that things will probably get worse before they get better. We need confidence, courage, and faith in the plan, even when things are not going well. If the team start questioning the plan as soon as some things inevitably go wrong, the digital transformation will probably not work.

At difficult times we do not need a team that is moderately interested in breaking the whole organisation down to build it up again better. We need colleagues that are obsessed – those that have the drive to solve the big problems and also get all the details right. A servant leader may build consensus and remove some obstacles, but will that approach put some 'fire in their belly'? An emotional surge is needed, and this is why this approach is so valuable for digital transformation. If we are going to take risks to take a bigger step forward than our competitors, we need to really want it. If the transformation to an AI-centred organisation attempts to maximise return, then the return can be something very significant, such as putting our major competitor out of business, but the cost of failure might be putting ourselves out of business.

I once knew some fintech entrepreneurs that were setting up a crypto exchange. I used to go to their offices and have a coffee and discuss possible collaborations. Because they wanted extensive advertising across various mediums, they had to book it many months in advance. This was a really large marketing campaign that would get everyone talking and create a buzz around the brand. When the advertising kicked in, they did not have the crypto exchange up and running yet. People could drive down a motorway and there would be around ten billboards in a row advertising their online crypto exchange, but nobody could use it. That was the end of that fintech company. Very ambitious but ultimately it failed. Could they have handled it better? Probably, but when an innovator wants to take a big step with technology the risks are there. Their leader certainly matched the mould of a transformational leader. Maybe the problem was not that he was overambitious, but that he failed to motivate everyone in the organisation sufficiently. Alternatively, maybe he sufficiently motivated the middle managers, but they did not sufficiently motivate their teams. Even with the benefit of hindsight, it is not always easy to decide what the best leadership approach would have been. The process of trying to be a great leader can be in itself inspiring for the person putting themselves through that process, while at other times it can be quite humbling as we cannot understand why something happened.

6.1.1 Personality traits and skills

Inspire with the plan for change

It is easy to oversimplify things and assume a transformational leader is a charismatic leader that is focused on change. Certainly, charisma can be a helpful trait to have for a transformational leader, but the inspiration should come primarily from the long-term goals and the plan for change. It should be more about creating an inspiring plan or finding what is inspiring about the plan. Workers want to be intellectually stimulated, and there are few things more intellectually stimulating than planning and implementing a dramatically different future. Not everyone gets excited about the same things, of course, but for many of us, a dramatically different and better future is very intellectually stimulating as it forces us to question everything and see it with fresh eyes. Finding how to intellectually stimulate followers is not always easy. It requires intelligence, understanding the business and the technology, but also understanding individuals and what their biggest dreams and fears are.

Influence by being a role model

Beyond crafting and communicating a motivating plan, the leader should behave as a role model. Often, being a role model is more powerful than telling someone to do something. Unfortunately, the other side of that coin is that a leader's weaknesses can also be very influential. I once had a senior officer in the army that was trying to tell us in a delicate way that if he was, on some occasion, forced to bend the rules, it did not mean the rest of us could bend the rules all the time. Most of us can completely understand where he was coming from, but it does not send the right message to bend rules and then tell others not to do the same. There are many reasons why being a role model is so powerful, such as the leader coming across as more genuine, but a less obvious and equally important one is that the follower makes their own choice to replicate behaviours of their leader. It's human nature to not always want to follow orders. The degree to which a person has a rebellious nature is very different from one generation to another, one culture to another, and from one individual to another, but most of us have at least the potential deep inside us to be rebellious. To some degree, it is human nature for us to want to draw our own conclusions about things and have as much independence as possible. Followers being given instructions can sometimes feel it is a form of oppression, while a person deciding for themselves is a form of expression.

Along with creating an overarching goal, having influence through being a role model is one of the reasons why this approach is so popular with younger generations, particularly Generation Z. The more a person sees work as something to fulfil them rather than a necessity to survive, the more likely they are to express themselves than follow orders.

Empowering and emotionally engaged

A transformational leader encourages innovation in the organisation and personal development. These are two of the many synergies that make this approach so powerful. The other typical priorities of this approach also have synergies. These include empowering followers by giving them autonomy and confidence. The empowering can involve delegating, but this delegating is not done in a way that makes the leader less involved with what is happening day-to-day. The leader still tries to be involved in the day-to-day activities and tries to build strong relationships with mutual respect.

There is one school of thought that suggests a leader does not need to be particularly smart but should simply take the right steps, while another believes that if the leader is the smartest person in the building, they will be successful. The truth is somewhere in the middle, and being stronger on the leadership process or in raw intellect can compensate for weaknesses in each other. For some leadership styles, however, certain specific things are really important, if not a requirement. A transformational leader needs to be able to connect with people easily on an emotional level. Someone isn't a well-rounded transformational leader if they are perceived as distant and in their own world. I once worked under a professor that had many strengths: he was smart, organised, professional, and gave very clear instructions. However, I did not enjoy working for him or feel motivated, as he did not come across as emotionally engaged in our interactions. This is not about being uncharismatic or neurodiverse; it is about fully sharing the moment with someone. It is about showing recognition of what the other person is doing. Someone can be as uncharismatic and socially awkward as possible but be completely engaged and fully sharing the moment with the person they are speaking to.

Other leadership styles, such as transactional and autocratic, do not prioritise being emotionally engaged, but transformational and servant leadership do. It might not be a coincidence that the two most popular styles from the follower's perspective prioritise emotionally engaged leaders. As technology moves us towards personal isolation and less socialising – and therefore less emotional engagement from our friends – we need more emotional engagement from our leader.

All these actions – such as being visionary, intellectually stimulating, and empowering people, as well as being emotionally engaged and empathetic – culminate in creating a culture of enthusiasm, commitment, and strong morale.

6.1.2 What does an effective team using this leadership style look like?

There is a maxim, mostly used politics, that states, 'personnel is policy'. The point this maxim makes is that the best way for a government to implement policy is by putting people that believe in that policy in key positions. For example, if a government wanted to increase green environmental initiatives, they would not try to do that through the existing managers in key positions, but by replacing them with others that have a track record of being passionate about environmental initiatives. The benefit of this approach is that you do not need an overly detailed plan and things will start moving in the preferred direction very quickly. This strategy can also be applied to digital transformation. If you want a transformation, put a transformational leader in charge.

Transformational leadership creates a culture where everyone is accountable, has strong emotional bonds, collaborates enthusiastically, celebrates successes together, and trusts each other to a high degree. We must not be naive and believe that the collaboration and trust is absolute with this approach. This approach cannot create some kind of hippy utopia with people holding hands and singing *All You Need Is Love* by the Beatles without a care in the world. It does not necessarily always create the ideal mindset and the ideal team, but it moves everything in the right direction. When everyone in a team moves a little more in the right direction, the cumulative benefit can be quite large.

6.1.3 Transformational leadership examples

This leadership approach does not necessarily need to involve technology, but most of the obvious examples involve utilising new or existing technology to make drastic progress in an organisation's processes and people's mindsets. The best examples of this approach illustrate how a leader changed what people inside and outside the organisation believed was possible. Anita Roddick, who created The Body Shop and made consumers understand the power they had when they bought ethically, is an example from outside technology-driven businesses, but let's look at an example focused on technology.

Hasso Plattner, one of the founders of SAP, is a prime example of how much change a leader can drive when they have both a vision and technical knowledge. It is an example of how, while technology is indeed at the centre of the transformation, many other things need to also be in place. In addition to technology, a clear strategy, strong culture, and confidence are needed. Beyond creating a successful tech company – arguably the only European 'big tech' – he also invests in the towns where the company has large offices. By investing in universities, charities, and sport teams, he does not only build up the company, but also the places where the employees live. This kind of total transformational leadership – this 360-degree progress across employees' personal and professional lives – is not usually possible, but it is what we should aspire to. This German big tech company that he created is not just another successful German company. It is different because it broke the mould of what a successful company from Germany could be, as software was not one of their traditional exports. Beyond the ones that are household names, there are many different kinds of successful German companies, but nevertheless, building a global tech company was a completely new approach.

6.1.4 How this leadership style builds trust in people

There are some leadership styles that do not prioritise building trust in various ways and rely on only a few methods to achieve it. An example is transactional leadership, where reliably delivering an agreed reward is the primary method to build trust. Transformational leadership is similar to servant leadership in the sense that the whole approach builds trust. These leaders try to always be authentic and transparent. Instead of authority-based relationships, trust-based relationships are created. This is not just a nice thing to have in this approach, it is entirely necessary as this leader wants to create dramatic change. The larger and more widespread the change is, the more additional risk is being created. Having a leadership approach that has many synergies in building trust is necessary to counterbalance all this additional risk. Many of the actions of this leader build relationships and confidence in digital transformation.

Some believe that if a leader is too friendly and emotionally engaged with the team, it can backfire and weaken trust. Many believe if the leader and the follower are too close, the boundaries and authority of the leader will not be respected. This is a real risk; nevertheless, we may argue with friends and temporarily weaken our trust in each other, but once the disagreement has been resolved, we gain confidence that our relationship can withstand similar challenges in the future.

Key concept: Broadly speaking, a leader can be transactional, focusing on the exchange of value, or transformational, focusing on being a role model, providing motivation, driving change, creating a vision, offering intellectual stimulation, being emotionally engaged, and providing personalised support.

Leadership tip: A transformational leader needs to be able to connect with people easily on an emotional level. Someone isn't a well-rounded transformational leader if they are perceived as distant and in their own world. This is not about being charismatic or not – it is about fully sharing the moment with someone. It is about empathising with them and recognising what they are doing.

Trust-building tip: The larger and more widespread the change is, the more additional risk is being created. Having a leadership approach that has many synergies in building trust is necessary to counterbalance all this additional risk. Many of the actions of this leader build relationships and confidence in the digital transformation.

6.2 The strengths and weaknesses of transformational leadership

The role of a leader is not to come up with all the great ideas. The role of a leader is to create an environment in which great ideas can happen. — Simon Sinek, leadership author

6.2.1 Strengths and opportunities

6.2.1.1 The strengths of transformational leadership from the follower's perspective

While this approach is not the simplest to understand or implement, it is not a coincidence that there is a very strong consensus on what a transformational leader should do, and what the benefits are for the followers. While there are some different interpretations of what this approach encompasses, the relatively high level of consensus is testament to the clarity of the purpose of this approach, and the synergies of all the actions. Many of us find that this approach usually gives workers a high level of job satisfaction and improves their wellbeing both inside and outside of their work, as one influences the other.

The overarching benefit of this approach from the follower's perspective is that it is often successful in getting everyone in the team on the same side. This togetherness 'bakes in' resilience and adaptability. This is an oversimplification of course, but this is essentially the common thread through many of the actions of a transformation leader. This sounds like common sense, but while there is no leadership approach that is against having everyone in the team on the same side, other leadership styles do not prioritise it. If we contrast it with transactional leadership again, the transactional leader focuses on rewarding certain actions, not building the team. Transactional leadership is very effective and practical, but the advantage of transformational leadership is especially clear at times of turmoil, where we cannot plan and structure everything. At times of turmoil, uncertainty, and risk, what we really need is a team with strong bonds that will fight through whatever is thrown at them. If the team face a challenge that needs to be resolved urgently with some self-sacrifice, such as working overtime, we want colleagues that will get it done and be confident that they will be rewarded, rather than someone that will not be willing to go beyond the agreed transaction. Resilience and adaptability are the end result of building emotional bonds and friendships.

People can have disagreements and clash for a variety of reasons, such as different personalities or conflicting interests. Beyond these typical triggers of conflict, the dynamic in the team can encourage or discourage conflict. The priorities of this approach, such as creating a shared sense of purpose, focuses people's minds on goals that will benefit everyone rather than focusing on personal agendas that can lead to conflict. In addition to the collective goals, encouraging personal growth gives everyone a personal benefit. Supporting personal growth does not just involve providing financial support, it is also the time the leader invests in this. A leader that is used to supporting the personal development of their team will probably have some useful advice and guidance on what is available to each team member.

If an employee is given opportunities for personal development, they feel they are in a stronger position if the whole project fails and they lose their job. This is a good thing because it reduces anxiety. Too much anxiety makes many of us react negatively or aggressively, as we may feel we have been backed into a corner. This is one of the main weaknesses of approaches that focus on piling on the pressure to get results. If someone's leadership style is constantly pile on pressure, at some point this will cause problems. When the problems will come and what they will be is hard to predict, but the built-up pressure will have to be released in some way.

When I was teaching at the University of Liverpool, they paid for me to prepare and take a teaching qualification. It was in the university's interest for those teaching to get this accreditation, but nevertheless, I felt that they cared about my personal development, which was a very good feeling. It is a very different feeling to receiving the wage which is payment for your labour. A leader showing that they care gives everyone a sense of security and reduces the likelihood of conflict.

If implemented successfully, this approach creates a positive culture of mutual respect where the follower feels valued and has clarity in what their role is.

The strengths of transformational leadership for Generation Z and Alpha employees

This approach, along with servant leadership, is the most natural fit for the characteristics of Generation Z and Alpha. Compared to the transformational approach, servant leadership emphasises the ethical aspect of work more, which will resonate strongly with many from these generations. However, transformational leadership's focus on purpose and having a meaningful impact will make it even more appealing. For these generations, having a purpose is central to making them fulfilled and committed. Rightly or wrongly, some organisations feel pressured to have positions and make statements on a variety of issues beyond their business. The jury is out if this is a good approach as it can alienate as many as it pleases, but the fact that it happens illustrates how organisations feel they need to speak out on issues such as the environment, human rights and various other things.

While giving a purpose is often the most important thing for these generations, there are also other issues that they value more than others. As they were born digital, they are tech-savvy and instinctively try to find technological solutions to problems. They didn't live through the pre-internet age, so they do not miss it. Older workers, including myself, sometimes fear technology and fear that we may be losing control, but younger employees seem to instinctively want to find the quickest and easiest way to get things done by utilising technology as far as possible. This means that they will not only be receptive to a message of digital transformation, but they can be very supportive in driving it. A transformational leader – possibly also utilising a servant leadership approach – is best suited to engage them, allowing them to contribute their knowledge and enthusiasm. Digital transformation can benefit from these generations feeling empowered to make decisions.

6.2.1.2 The strengths of transformational leadership from the leader's perspective

While it is not entirely true that this approach only fits contexts where there is dramatic change, it is a very strong fit for those situations. If you are in a complex situation where you either do not want to continue with business as usual or this is no longer an option, this approach is ideal to encourage adaptability and creativity in the team.

Even for someone that is very intelligent, knows their topic well, and engages with people effortlessly, this is still a challenging approach to apply. However, by building strong bonds and strong relationships, this then makes many situations easier, especially at times of dramatic disruption. Many would argue that transactional leadership is easier to implement during more stable times when the business model and processes are not changing. However, is it easy for a transactional leader to take a team thorough digital transformation? Is it easy to have the necessary understanding and control even at turbulent times? If we are going through digital transformation, it is often easier for the leader to choose the right business model to aim for through digital transformation, build a motivated team, and hope the team get us over the line. If we want to build the team and hope they get us over the line, then transformational leadership is more suitable than transactional.

Beyond helping the organisation achieve its immediate goals, this leadership approach is often the most rewarding for the leader. The positive feedback loop of emotions and learning from each other is far more rewarding than what is often the case in the workplace, where there is suspicion of each other's motives and sniping at people. People need people, and if we get some rewarding socialising at work, it will be a more sustainable way to lead and help to avoid burnout and stress-related health problems. Implementing transformational leadership to a high standard over long periods of time is challenging, but the rewards of getting it right make it worth trying.

Key concept: The overarching benefit of this approach from the follower's perspective is that it is often successful in getting everyone in the team on the same side. Many find that this approach gives employees a high level of job satisfaction and improves their wellbeing, both inside and outside of their work.

Leadership tip: Generation Z and Alpha were born digital, so they are tech-savvy and instinctively try to find technological solutions to problems. They didn't live through the pre-internet age, so they do not miss it or have the reservations about technology that older generations can have. This means that they will not only be receptive to a message of digital transformation, but they can be very supportive in driving it.

Trust-building tip: At times of turmoil, uncertainty, and risk, what we really need is a team with strong bonds that will fight through whatever is thrown at them. If the team face a challenge that needs to be resolved urgently with some self-sacrifice, we want colleagues that will get it done. Resilience and adaptability are the end result of building emotional bonds and friendships.

6.2.2 Weaknesses and challenges

6.2.2.1 The weaknesses of transformational leadership from the follower's perspective

Not all aspects of transformational leadership will necessarily appeal to all followers, but most aspects of it do. While this approach makes a big effort to keep everyone happy, it is very demanding due to the change being implemented. While this approach is less restrictive for the followers than autocratic or transactional approaches, it doesn't offer them the same level of freedom and autonomy as laissez-faire or servant leadership. The heavy emphasis on the broader vision means we are essentially putting all our eggs in one basket. Even for issues that you would hope there would be consensus, such as reducing pollution, there is not always agreement. Unfortunately, not everyone is willing to make the effort to save the planet. If there is no consensus for these broad important issues, we can appreciate that building consensus on many things is not always easy. Not everyone wants to reduce pollution, and certainly not everyone is motivated by Elon Musk's vision to go to Mars. Additionally, building consensus is not necessarily a good thing if some valid concerns get abandoned. Before the 2008 financial crash, a broad consensus had been built on some dangerous strategies, with those disagreeing either leaving the organisations or keeping quiet. Therefore, the heavy reliance of this approach on the vision can often be a weakness.

Other leadership approaches primarily encourage action through something they can reliably deliver. Methods like authoritarian or transactional leadership rely on tools such as authority and rewards to encourage action. If the authority exists, it will usually have a reliable effect, and as long as rewards can be offered, they too will produce results. The transactional approach can easily increase the rewards if necessary. If, for example, we cannot find someone to work on big data for us, a transactional leader can increase the wage. Of course, a transformational leader can also increase the wage, but as this is not the primary way to motivate people, it may not work as well. For example, if a person is inspired by the overarching vision of helping stray dogs, they may not be inspired by going to Mars, and offering a little more money will not make them want to go.

Another potential weakness is that, as the transformational leader is at the centre and has extensive influence over all aspects of the organisation, they could manipulate situations – and even the whole team – for their own personal interests. Compared to European companies, US firms traditionally pay higher wages to their senior managers and CEOs relative to the average wage within the company. In other words, a company from the USA may give their CEO a wage that is ten times the average wage of the organisation, while a European company may give them five times the average wage. Rewarding the senior managers at the top and giving them a lot of sweeping authority to make decisions often leads to a strong dynamic organisation that can outflank competitors, but this is not always the case. As many European companies found when attempting to copy the US model, giving senior managers at the top too much power can, in some cases, lead them to pursue their own agendas for personal benefit. There have been clear examples of this, with some even ending up in court. Therefore, while there are benefits to digital transformation from having a strong leader, it can, and often has, backfired.

The weaknesses of transformational leadership for Generation Z and Alpha employees

Transformational leadership along with servant leadership, is a very good fit for Generation Z and younger generations. The biggest risk is if it is not implemented effectively, problems will start to emerge. However, there are some typical issues that may be especially frustrating for workers of these generations. Generation Z value having an overarching purpose and regular feedback. While transformational leadership is all about the long-term vision and broader purpose, the lack of short-term targets being achieved may make followers feel disappointed and disconnected. A transformational leader is engaged, but if there are limited short-term targets, the feedback will not be about achieving goals and giving praise for that. Transactional leadership is the worst fit for these generations overall, but it is actually better for this issue. With transactional leadership, there are short-term milestones with an immediate impact and reward. Even for those that want to go to Mars, some small victories before completing the journey would be rewarding.

6.2.2.2 The weaknesses of transformational leadership from the leader's perspective

One potential weakness is that as the transformational leader gets more involved, they may make more serious mistakes. Even worse, they may be manipulated or drift into favouritism. This is the risk of being more involved – a risk that servant leadership also has. The more involved in the day-to-day activities the leader is, the more mistakes they can make. If a leader just limits themselves to some typical small talk and only asks for what is agreed in the employees' contracts, there is far less risk of making serious mistakes. When the mistakes build up, they can cumulatively erode credibility.

While many of us appreciate that a leader is just a normal person that is playing their role, it helps if the followers believe there is something a little special about them and that they are charismatic. Transformational leadership replaces the 'shield' of keeping some distance that the autocratic leader has, with the 'shield' of having a great long-term vision. This works up to a point, but it is dependent on the followers being excited about the vision, and maintaining that excitement as well. This is one of the tricky issues in leadership where a leader needs to use their judgment. Do they want to sacrifice their 'shield' to be close to followers and appear more human, or do they keep some distance and maintain an aura of authority? This dilemma is even trickier for a transformational leader, as they rely on their charisma to sell their vision. Taking all this into account, we can see how the positive feedback loop created when the transformational leader is pulling it off can quickly turn into a negative feedback loop. On the plus side, they may have built strong relationships in the good times to help them through the bad times.

Finally, as with servant leadership, when the leader makes a big effort to be involved and show true leadership all the time, this can be tiring and lead to burnout. The emotional and mental energy required is very high. Additionally, when a leader is more involved, the day-to-day disagreements, conflicts, and rivalries can make it difficult to stay positive and to project that positivity. If a leader cannot project positivity any more, they are no longer a well-rounded transformational leader. It is harder to show charisma, embody something different, and bring something new to a group if we become one with them.

At a university I worked at in the past, the senior managers were not around us all the time, but when they were with us, they were dressed very smartly, stood very straight, and networked and made small talk to a standard that even a member of the British royal family would be impressed by. Could they keep this up if they were around us all the time? Would the charm fade? Very possibly.

Key concept: Transformational leadership makes a big effort to keep everyone happy, but it is very demanding due to the change being implemented and the effort needed from the leader. While this approach is not as restrictive for the followers as autocratic or even transactional approaches, it does not give followers as much freedom and autonomy as laissez-faire or servant approaches. The heavy emphasis on the broader vision means we are essentially putting all our eggs in one basket.

Leadership tip: Many employees, particularly from younger generations, value having an overarching purpose and regular feedback. While transformational leadership is all about the long-term vision and broader purpose, the lack of short-term targets being achieved may make followers feel disappointed and disconnected. A transformational leader needs to find a way to give followers small victories along the way towards the grander purpose.

Trust-building tip: While many of us appreciate that a leader is just a normal person that is playing their role, it helps if the followers believe there is something a little special about them. Transformational leadership replaces the 'shield' of keeping some distance that the autocratic leader has, with the 'shield' of having a great long-term vision. The 'shield' of the long-term vision needs to protect the leader, so the followers do not start to see their flaws and mistakes and start to distrust them.

6.3 Transformational leadership's impact on AI adoption and trust

To lead people, walk beside them. As for the best leaders, the people do not notice their existence.
— Laozi, ancient Chinese philosopher and founder of Taoism

6.3.1 How this leadership style can support AI

This leadership approach can build up an organisation's AI capabilities in two ways. Firstly, it encourages change, and secondly, it prepares everyone for the far-reaching implications of dramatic change. Someone needs to trigger the change, and then everyone needs to keep their faith in the implementation until it becomes a success.

Making a strong case for more AI and encouraging change
We all have a limited bandwidth, habits, and entrenched beliefs. These habits and entrenched beliefs may have merit, but they need to evolve to encompass digital transformation. The evidence supporting the value of digital transformation and putting AI at the centre of the organisation is openly available in many reports and studies. One example of this is the way thousands of Chinese companies incorporated DeepSeek. There is, however, a lot of conflicting information and many concerns, including, for example, the environmental impact of the higher processing needs and the potential loss of jobs.

The transformational leader may consult with stakeholders inside and outside of the organisation to develop a plan and a new business model to aim for. The leader does not have to be the sole parent of the new business model. However, once the new business model that fully utilises AI has been collectively identified, the transformational leader is the one that is going to act in a similar way to a salesperson to champion this cause. They need to prepare a clear narrative that will be absorbed by the followers and the limited bandwidth that all humans have. The negative assumptions about AI should be challenged. The narrative can also show employees how change will be an opportunity for personal development for them so they do not assume change will lead to them losing their job. The people involved need to believe there will still be a place for them in the future so they do not lose their sense of belonging and camaraderie. The team need to feel empowered to act and believe they will feel a sense of achievement and pride by completing the goals of digital transformation. These two steps – collectively identifying the new AI-focused business model and building consensus around it – are the two steps that enable 'lift off'. Transformational leadership is the approach best suited for this, at least on paper.

Preparing a team for the far-reaching implications of digital transformation
Getting the most out of AI requires strong collaboration both within the organisation and with various external stakeholders. This approach can build the necessary relationships and common understanding to create this strong and resilient collaboration with a culture of problem solving. The positivity and strong trusting relationships will reduce the stress in the difficult times.

The truth is, there is clear evidence of the need to use AI more extensively; it is not a big challenge to prove this. However, the process of using it more extensively is often a step into the unknown with many risks and uncertainties. The current global environment, with competing visions for the future and almost daily changes to regulations, trade agreements, and tariffs, can disrupt even the most well-thought-out plans for digital transformation. When most of the world was aiming for globalisation, the priority for organisations was to be efficient. Strategies such as just-in-time manufacturing prioritise efficiency over resilience. With many competing visions of how to move forward in business and trade, resilience becomes a bigger consideration. For example, what happens if the software we use is banned for 'national security reasons', or if tariffs on hardware from a certain country jump by twenty-five percent? This influences the choices of business model and technology used. It also means the employees need to be more resilient. It takes many different things to make employees productive, but one of the most important is to be able to stay focused on the goal of the digital transformation and making the new business model a success. If the transformational leader can keep the team's confidence in the new model, they can turn the uncertainties they come across into new opportunities. The organisations that effectively implement an AI-focused business model will get some certainty from it. Those that fail to make the transition will remain in uncertainty for longer and anxiety will keep building.

6.3.2 How this leadership style builds trust in AI

Builds trust in every aspect of the operation which is then transferred to trust in AI
This approach is built around confidence and trust. As discussed, this is very important so that followers overcome the fear of the risks that come from change. Other approaches rely on one or two methods to build trust, but the more holistic approach creates trust in all directions. If we are a transactional leader making an agreement to exchange value, we are mainly building trust in the agreement. There will be some residual trust spreading across other areas, but this is mostly a very targeted trust building. In the transformational approach, it is more like a 360-degree trust: followers trust the leader, the plan, and themselves. When the leader and the plan are in the direction of using AI more, there is trust transference to AI, so the AI is also trusted. It is easier to have trust transference from one thing, such as the leader to the

AI implementation, if there is a lot of trust. It may seem strange to some of us that trust drifts from one thing to another. For some of us, it may seem more logical that trust is specific to one issue and cannot simply drift to another, however, this drifting does happen. If someone has trust in one part of what the organisation does, to some degree this can drift to other areas.

It does not mean a transformational leader should not build trust specifically for AI and simply hope the trust built in the past will just drift over to cover AI as if it was blown by the wind. Trust still needs to be built in AI specifically, but we will be in a stronger position because, firstly, we will have some trust transference as discussed, and, secondly, the trust-building mechanisms the leader uses have been proven to work. These are some of the most important reasons why this approach is an excellent fit for digital transformation. We need trustworthy AI – in other words, AI that deserves to be trusted – and we need colleagues to trust it so that we get the most out of it. There is no way of bypassing the need to trust AI. Even if it is a compulsory system using AI, it will not be used as much, or as wholeheartedly, if there is limited trust (Zarifis & Fu, 2023; Zarifis & Cheng, 2024).

If a company that typically applies autocratic leadership wants to become an AI-centred organisation, and the leader realises they need to build trust in AI, they will have to rely on mechanisms they may not be experienced or skilled at using to establish that trust. The transformational leader not only uses the best approach to build trust in AI, but also has the skills to do so as they practise building trust all the time.

A transformational leader tries to consistently deliver on promises, as most leadership styles do, but they take some steps others don't and they also put more emphasis on some steps than others. Some of these additional steps do not make a huge difference for trust on their own, but all together the aggregated effect can make the difference between having enough trust to move forward with AI or having pushback. One of the additional steps that builds trust compared to most leadership approaches is how this leader shows their human side. As we are all human, this may seem to some a strange point to make, but many leaders, either instinctively or by following a traditional approach such as the authoritarian style, prefer to keep some distance and not show their more human side. If we show our human side, we are more vulnerable, and some troublemakers might find something to use against us. At the same time, as we are more transparent, people may trust us and engage more. People need people. This is especially true in the age of AI. A human working with autonomous AI for a few hours doesn't then want to meet their leader who also acts like a machine because they are following the script of an 'autocratic' leader.

The humanness of the leadership approach compensates for the loss of humanness due to AI

A positive consequence of the transformational leadership approach, along with some other more people-centric approaches, is that it compensates to some degree for the loss of humanness through the use of AI. Many of us consider Elon Musk to be a transformational leader. He is not the perfect embodiment of transformational leadership, but one lesson we can draw from his leadership style is that he gives his organisations character. He is not only a figurehead; he is more than that: he makes the organisations he leads more human. As we said, a leader showing their human side also makes them vulnerable, and we also see this with Elon Musk, as not everyone agrees with the many different things he says.

Other typical behaviours that are emphasised by this approach that benefit trust are: acting with integrity, honesty, and transparency; showing genuine interest and care for followers' feelings and wellbeing; and regularly showing recognition and appreciation. This is certainly not the only approach where the leader shows recognition and appreciation, but this is done more regularly and in a warmer and more emotionally engaged way.

6.3.3 The business models that work well with this leadership

The leader of digital transformation must identify the most suitable AI-focused business model and then keep the team focused on moving towards that model despite the uncertainty and challenges. If the transformational leader can keep the team's confidence in the new model, they can turn the uncertainties they come across into new opportunities. The organisation that effectively implements an AI-focused business model will get some certainty from the model and gain an advantage over those that struggle to make the transition.

The six business models proven to be ideal for a world with AI at its centre are: (1) incumbent focusing on one part of the value chain and disaggregating, (2) incumbent absorbing AI into their existing model, (3) incumbent expanding beyond their current model to fully utilise the opportunities of AI and access new data, (4) startup disruptor focused on one sector, built from the start to be highly automated, (5) disruptor focused on tech adding a new service such as insurance, and (6) disruptor that is not necessarily tech-focused with an extensive user or fanbase (Zarifis & Cheng, 2023, 2025).

Transformational leadership is suitable for all six AI-focused business models. As this approach is not always the easiest to implement, and it can backfire when used clumsily, it might be worth only using it where it is needed most. This approach is needed most where the change and disruption are largest. Furthermore, change is fuel for a transformational leader. They will have a better chance of success, and the followers will be more receptive, if the change is drastic.

From the six business models, three are for organisations that are already operating in a sector, and three are for organisations that are moving into a sector that is new to them. There are two models that are typically more disruptive: the third model – an incumbent expanding beyond current model to fully utilise the opportunities of AI and access new data – can often involve extensive disruption and would be suitable for this leadership style; and the fourth – a startup disruptor focused on one sector, built from the start to be highly automated – would also benefit from this approach. In the fourth, as it is a startup, all the employees will be new and there will be minimal or no organisational culture. A transformational leader can create a shared sense of purpose among all these new colleagues.

Key concept: Transformational leadership supports digital transformation with AI in two ways. Firstly, it encourages change. As all of us have a limited bandwidth and there is conflicting information on AI; this leader selects an AI-focused business model and builds consensus around it. Secondly, by creating a resilient team, they are better prepared for the far-reaching implications of digital transformation.

Leadership tip: A positive consequence of the transformational leadership approach, along with some other more people-centric approaches, is that it compensates to some degree for the loss of humanness due to the use of AI. A leader showing their human side is more transparent, so followers engage and trust them more. People need people. This is especially true in the age of AI.

Trust-building tip: Unlike other approaches that rely on one or two methods to build trust, transformational leadership builds trust in multiple synergistic ways and creates a more holistic trust in all directions. Followers trust the leader, the plan, and themselves. When the leader and the plan are in the direction of using AI more, there is trust transference to AI. It is easier to have trust transference if there is a lot of trust to begin with.

6.4 The popularity of transformational leadership in the future

Be the change that you wish to see in the world. — Mahatma Gandhi, leader of the Indian independence movement

6.4.1 The trends in the popularity of this approach

This approach resonates with most of us, especially those from younger generations, and it is a good fit for the typical challenges organisations face. It is an approach that can resonate with colleagues and encourage them to perform better. Many studies, across different countries and different types of organisations, support its effectiveness. In uncertain times, most organisations face the constant challenge of adopting new technologies better than their rivals. We went from a period where there was consensus – at least in western business schools – on the merits of globalisation and limited regulation, to an age where very few serious analysts would even claim to be able to predict the future. There are competing visions of isolationism, globalisation, or simply making a series of deals without an overarching vision. There are also competing visions on the role of regulation and if it is worth sacrificing some growth to protect citizens and the economy. These issues have serious consequences. The life expectancy in the USA is reported to be five to six years lower than Europe, yet there is pressure on Europe to adopt its policies.

Why are we discussing these issues when we are interested in leadership and AI? We are discussing them because we need to appreciate that, while we need to pursue some stability by choosing a suitable business model (Zarifis & Cheng, 2023, 2025), AI brings a layer of technological and organisational uncertainty, in addition to an increasingly uncertain context. Leadership approaches that used to be popular with short projects are now popular for all of an organisation's operations. Often, the typical management approach of monitoring and controlling is hard to apply in turbulent times and may simply waste time with little benefit, so a leader needs to find another way to add value.

As with servant leadership, the popularity of transformational leadership is growing among leaders, followers, and institutions that have some influence in what is adopted, such as business schools and business consultancies.

6.4.2 How does transformational leadership compare to other leadership styles

Transformational leadership is in the category of more human-focused and authentic approaches, but it is also in the group of approaches that are suitable for turbulent and changeable environments. Some could argue that there is a gradual shift in popularity from methods that are easy for a leader to apply, such as autocratic leadership, but not enjoyable for most followers, to methods that are harder for the leader to apply but more enjoyable for followers. This discussion applies mostly to knowledge workers that have some bargaining power and not to those less fortunate who have no bargaining power and must accept anything an autocratic leader puts them through. Transformational and servant leadership styles are unfortunately not reaching employees that work in warehouses or make fast-food deliveries.

Because transformational leadership is tricky to implement consistently over long periods of time in different contexts, a more practical approach, such as transactional leadership, can be combined. This can also bring a better balance between the long-term vision and the immediate execution. The more practical transactional approach, with its short-term targets, will also be more useful for giving autonomous AI agents instructions. While all popular leadership styles can be applied either ethically or unethically, autocratic leadership, despite its practicality, can lead to unethical behaviour in a way that transactional leadership usually does not. Transactional leadership is not particularly human-focused, but as it relies on a series of agreements on exchange of value, it is not inclined to drift into unethical behaviour. The agreement a transactional leader makes includes a well-defined reward for the follower. Therefore, the more inspiring but harder to implement transformational approach can be combined with the far more practical transactional approach. Many of those that would identify as transformational leaders would acknowledge that while they always aspire to be transformational, they are often transactional.

Bringing in some of the principles of servant leadership can beneficial and may help in certain situations, but it does not solve the fundamental weakness of transformational leadership – its difficulty to implement. It can be argued that the second biggest drawback of transformational leadership is that it does not fit every context, so servant leadership can be utilised in the contexts where transformation is either not suitable or not possible. Both approaches are supportive to followers, but the servant leadership approach typically puts more of the burden of critical thinking on the followers. This can be beneficial if the followers are very capable. Nevertheless, transformational leadership combined with servant leadership does not make as compelling a case as transformational with transactional leadership.

It is necessary to know the main leadership approaches and when they are helpful, but they also must be applied in a way that sends a reasonably coherent message. If the message is not coherent, trust will be destroyed. Switching between two human-focused approaches – transformational and servant – should not be too much of an unexpected bump in the road for followers. When transformational is combined with transactional, it is better if this is done on a consistent basis. In other words, it is better if followers understand that their leader is combining transformational and transactional, rather than if one of these approaches suddenly appears out of nowhere. For example, if followers are convinced they are working for a caring, environmentally friendly organisation, but they then discover the organisation is not living up to those standards and their leader offers them more money, they may not respond positively. It would have been better if the message from the start had been that the company is environmentally conscious where possible, but that employees are not expected to be motivated by that. Instead, they are expected to be motivated by the rewards they are given. Far less romantic, but most of us appreciate knowing where we stand.

If a leader has identified the AI-focused business model they want to move towards (Zarifis & Cheng, 2023, 2025), then transactional with transformational styles are the ideal approach. If a leader cannot identify the most suitable new business model to aim for because there is too much uncertainty inside and outside of the organisation, then the transactional and servant approaches may be the most suitable. These are the recommendations based on what has happened in many cases of digital transformation, but ultimately it is the leader at the coalface that must use their judgement to decide. The strengths and weaknesses of this approach on its own, and when it is combined with transactional and servant styles, are summarised in Table 6.1.

Key concept: Because transformational leadership is tricky to implement consistently over long periods of time in different contexts, a more practical approach, such as transactional leadership, can be combined. Bringing in some of the principles of servant leadership is also beneficial and may help in certain situations, but it does not

Table 6.1: Transformational leadership's strengths and weaknesses in supporting AI and trust.

	Strengths in supporting AI	Weaknesses in supporting AI	Strengths in supporting trust	Weaknesses in supporting trust
Transformational leadership	Makes a strong case for more AI and encouraging change. Better prepared for the far-reaching implications of digital transformation.	Less emphasis in short-term goals and rewards, may demotivate, and cause a loss of a clear sense of direction. Concentrating power on the leader may lead to selfish actions. Heavy emphasis on an overarching vision that may not inspire everyone.	Builds trust in every aspect of the operations that is then transferred to trusting AI. The humanness of the leadership approach compensates for the loss of humanness due to AI.	The difficulty in implementing the approach may lead to failures that reduce trust. Less emphasis on regular feedback may create a feeling of a lack of transparency.
Primarily transactional leadership with some transformational leadership	Achieves a balance between motivating long-term goals and short-term goals.	May lose some structure compared to transactional on its own.	Promotes overarching vision in the value of innovation but also regularly delivers short-term rewards.	May increase uncertainty compared to transactional on its own.
Primarily transformational leadership with some servant leadership	More support for experts working on technologies the leader does not fully understand. Avoids overly focusing on targets that are unlikely to be perfect and comprehensive. Encourages free thinking and creativity.	Less concentration of power on the leader.	Emphasises an overarching inspirational, caring, and ethical vision of the organisation. Easier to implement as the leader can switch to the approach better suited for each context. This may reduce failures and reduce the damage to trust from them.	Compared to transformational on its own, the combination may reduce the belief that the leader has a clear plan.

solve the fundamental weakness of transformational leadership – its difficulty to implement.

Leadership tip: Transformational leadership does not fit every context, so even leaders that identify as transformational often apply transactional or servant leadership in those instances. Nevertheless, the combination of transformational and servant leadership makes a less compelling case in comparison to the combination of transformational and transactional leadership.

Trust-building tip: When leadership styles are combined, they must be applied in a way that sends a coherent message, otherwise trust will be destroyed. Switching between two human-focused approaches, such as transformational and servant leadership, should not be too much of an unexpected bump in the road for followers. When transformational is combined with transactional leadership, it is better if this is done on a consistent basis.

6.5 Summary

> *The wise leader does not intervene unnecessarily. The leader's presence is felt, but often the group runs itself.* — Laozi, ancient Chinese philosopher and founder of Taoism

6.5.1 The enduring value of the transformational leadership approach

A transformational leader is not simply a charismatic and inspirational leader that is focused on change. For a transformational leader the inspiration should come primarily from the long-term plan for change and the new business model selected. To create a modern organisation that fully utilises technology, an AI-focused business model should be identified (Zarifis & Cheng, 2023, 2025). There are few things in life more intellectually stimulating and inspiring than planning and implementing a dramatically different future.

In addition to the plan, a transformational leader empowers followers, encourages innovation within the organisation, and supports personal development. The synergies between the priorities of this approach are what make it so powerful. For all this to work successfully, a transformational leader needs to be able to easily connect with people on an emotional level. Someone isn't a well-rounded transformational leader if they are perceived as distant and disinterested. Regardless of the character of the leader, they should be able to fully share a moment with someone. It is about empathising with someone and showing recognition of what the other person is doing. Other leadership styles, such as transactional and autocratic, do not prioritise being emotionally engaged, but transformational and servant leadership do. It may not be a coincidence that the two most popular styles from a follower's perspective prioritise emotionally engaged leaders.

6.5.2 Is the transformational leadership approach the best for AI and trust?

Some leadership styles do not prioritise building trust in several ways and only have a few methods to achieve it. An example is transactional leadership, where reliably delivering an agreed reward is the primary way of building trust. Transformational leadership is similar to servant leadership in the sense that the whole approach builds trust. Transformational leadership builds trust in multiple synergistic ways and creates a more holistic trust in all directions. Everyone involved trusts the leader, the plan, and themselves. When the leader and the plan are in the direction of using AI more, there is trust transference to AI. It is easier to have trust transference if there is a lot of trust to begin with.

Transformational leadership supports digital transformation with AI in two ways. Firstly, it encourages change. As we all have a limited bandwidth and there is conflicting information on AI, this leader selects an AI-focused business model and builds consensus around it. Secondly, by creating a resilient team, they are better prepared for the far-reaching implications of digital transformation. Strong collaboration within the organisation and with various external stakeholders can help implement the change efficiently. Digital transformation has many challenges, and they are not just technical. If the team lose their sense of purpose, this will be a very difficult challenge to overcome.

A beneficial consequence of the transformational leadership approach and other people-centric approaches is that they compensate for the loss of humanness due to the use of AI. A leader showing their human side is more transparent, so everyone involved engages and trusts them more. People need people. This is especially true in the age of AI.

6.5.3 Choosing the right leadership style and priorities at each stage of a project

The benefits of transformational leadership are significant, but as it can be difficult to implement in some situations, the leader needs to think selectively about when to utilise it. For example, this might not be the best approach if the leader does not know what the long-term plan for AI is and has no other plan for a powerful improvement to use as fuel for transformational leadership. A transformational leader will lose their credibility if they are not making significant improvements to their organisation. If the situation really needs an operations manager to monitor and control stable processes, then the transformational approach will need to be 'parked' for now.

Transformational leadership is tricky to implement consistently over long periods of time in different contexts, so it is beneficial to combine it with a more practical approach, such as transactional leadership. Transactional leadership can be less inspiring, but its short-term goals deliver reliable results for all stakeholders. Bringing some of the principles of servant leadership into transformational leadership can be beneficial and may help in certain situations, but it does not solve the fundamental weakness of transformational leadership that it can be tricky to implement.

Even leaders that identify as transformational apply transactional or servant leadership where those two are a more natural fit. However, for digital transformation with AI where change needs to be encouraged, transformational leadership combined with servant leadership does not make a compelling case compared to the combination of transformational with transactional leadership. Switching between the two human-focused approaches of transformational and servant should not be too much of an unexpected change in style from the follower's perspective. However, when the transformational style is combined with transactional, it is better if this is done from the beginning. Too much inconsistency in the leader's behaviour destroys trust. When these two are combined consistently across all the stages of a project, they create an ideal balance between the inspiring long-term big picture and handling the shorter-term challenges in an organised way. In some situations, more transformational leadership is needed at the start to light the spark of 'revolution', and more transactional leadership is needed for the stages in the middle and the end to ensure that the work is completed efficiently. This is a very common pattern, but it will not be the best for every situation.

Key concept: A transformational leader is not simply a charismatic and inspirational leader that is focused on change. The inspiration should come primarily from the long-term plan for change and the new business model selected (Zarifis & Cheng, 2023, 2025). In addition to the plan, a transformational leader empowers followers, encourages innovation in the organisation, and supports personal development.

Leadership tip: If a leader has identified the AI-focused business model they want to move towards, then transactional with transformational styles are the ideal approach. If a leader cannot identify the most suitable new business model to aim for because there is too much uncertainty inside and outside of the organisation, then the transactional and servant approaches may be the most suitable.

Trust-building tip: A transformational leader builds strong resilient trust with its ethical, caring, individualised, and human approach. When this leader promotes a plan to move to a business model that fully utilises AI, there is trust transference to the new plan. It is easier for the leader to utilise trust transference if there is a lot of trust to begin with.

6.6 Exercises

Exercise 6.1

Combining transformational leadership with transactional leadership
Scenario: You work for a European business-to-business (B2B) company that makes various electronic and mechanical parts for other companies to put into their applian-

ces. Many of the employees are engineers, which influences the prevailing culture. The organisation is very bureaucratic and there is a process and a form that needs to be filled in for everything. It is a very successful company, but it is starting to lose market share in some of the areas it operates to smaller, more agile companies from across the world that are applying AI in innovative ways. These smaller companies are not only utilising AI in their operations, but are quicker to provide electronics to companies creating new products, such as robots that utilise AI.

The company used to rely on its quality and strong relationships with its clients, but this does not seem to be enough any more. They are worried that they will continue to lose market share unless they make a change to how they operate and the leadership style applied.

The company has studied their new, more nimble competitors and found that they usually have an inspirational founder or founders that apply a leadership style that is closest to transformational leadership. Senior management does not believe transformational leadership will be a good fit for their organisation. They believe it will be too much of a culture shock and that the engineers and the other staff prefer the more structured bureaucratic approach. Senior management believe a combination of transformational leadership with transactional leadership might have a better chance of being accepted by the employees. They see it as a reasonable compromise to get some of the benefits of transformational leadership, without having too much of a culture shock.

Questions

1) For this specific company, what would be the general advantages and disadvantages of combining these two leadership styles (transformational with transactional leadership)?

2) Which elements of each style would you prefer to utilise? Would you select different ones for different stages of a project?

3) For this specific company, what would be the general advantages and disadvantages of combining these two leadership styles for AI and building trust in AI?

Exercise 6.2

Combining transformational leadership with servant leadership
Scenario: You work for a startup that is building large data centres as the processing needed by many organisations using AI are increasing. While different forms of AI have different processing needs and some newer models have lower processing needs, overall the processing requirements are higher.

The business model is to build data centres in the premises of the startup and provide processing as a service directly to some businesses, but also pool resources with other data centres. There is also discussion of doing some crypto mining when there is excess capacity, although this is still at the early stage of discussions. As mining Bitcoin requires specialised graphics cards, they might mine newer meme coins where the returns are potentially higher. For all this to work, several partnerships and long-term collaborations will have to be put in place.

Questions

1) As setting up a startup offering data centre processing services requires many new systems, processes, roles, and partners, the founder of the company thinks we should use transformational leadership. What would be the main benefits of transformational leadership in this context?

2) Given the very high complexity of setting up this business, including many technical issues, combining transformational leadership with servant leadership may make it stronger and easier to implement over the long term. What would be the main benefits of combining transformational leadership with servant leadership in this context?

Space for your notes

References

Burns, J. M. (1978). *Leadership*. Open Road.

Zarifis, A., & Fu, S. (2023). Re-evaluating trust and privacy concern when purchasing a mobile app: Re-calibrating for the increasing role of artificial intelligence. *Digital*, 3(4), 286–299. https://doi.org/10.3390/digital3040018

Zarifis, A., & Cheng, X. (2023). The five emerging business models of Fintech for AI adoption, growth, and building trust. In A. Zarifis, D. Ktoridou, L. Efthymiou, & X. Cheng (Eds.), *Business digital transformation: Selected cases from industry leaders* (pp. 73–97). Palgrave Macmillan. https://doi.org/10.1007/978-3-031-33665-2_4

Zarifis, A., & Cheng, X. (2024). How to build trust in answers given by Generative AI for specific, and vague, financial questions. *Journal of Electronic Business & Digital Economics*, 3(3), 236–250. https://doi.org/10.1108/JEBDE-11-2023-0028

Zarifis, A., & Cheng, X. (2025). The new centralised and decentralised Fintech technologies, and business models, transforming finance. In A. Zarifis & X. Cheng (Eds.), *Fintech and the emerging ecosystems: Exploring centralised and decentralised financial technologies*. Springer Nature. https://link.springer.com/book/9783031834011

Section C: **Leadership that builds trust in the age of generative AI**

Chapter 7
What a leader must know about applying generative AI

7.1 Introduction

It's actually quite difficult to build a really good generative AI application – you need a good model, but you also need to have the right guardrails, the right fluency of message, and you have to have the right UI. — Andy Jassy, Amazon CEO

It is often easy to make a case to senior management to automate a process with technology. Fewer staff means less costs, and the organisation's operations can be scaled more easily. It is easy to be selfish, but a leader must make the effort to understand how a new technology shaping our digital landscape will affect all stakeholders. The instinct some troublemakers have to impose their will to boost their ego must be resisted. Understanding how a change in technology affects all stakeholders can be difficult because it is not always the most obvious logical answer.

Furthermore, most services are a mix of technology and something else, and it is not always clear whether it is the technology that plays the decisive role. For example, do most of those that invest in Bitcoin do so because of the technology it uses? For Bitcoin, many do indeed use it because they appreciate the decentralised technology. If we look at another cryptocurrency such as meme coins, however, the role of the technology seems smaller and may not be the most decisive factor.

The same applies for the many different versions of AI. Many of us do not judge them purely as technologies. Autonomous AI agents use large language models, but they can also plan several steps ahead to complete a task, they have a memory of their past experiences, and they can choose what specialised tools to use for each task. Their influence transcends narrowly defined tasks and raises many questions.

Some general models about innovation, and some specific models about how users trust AI and other technologies, can help us. The model of diffusion of innovation illustrates how a new innovation usually goes through some typical stages. The technology adoption model (TAM) and its updated versions explain how people adopt technology by building on psychology and sociology. There are also specialised models on trust in AI and other technologies that have some similarities to the TAM. Relying on what is proven to work, and adapting it to a given context, should enable generative AI to 'flower' and reach its full potential, as illustrated in Figure 7.1.

Once we understand how the stakeholders adopt and trust technology, we can take the necessary steps to make them see AI and other technologies more positively. These issues are obviously important for large projects where very different services are offered, such as central bank digital currencies (CBDC), but these issues are still

https://doi.org/10.1515/9783111630137-007

worth considering when making smaller changes, such as changing how a user is authenticated online.

The point reiterated several times here is that, as we get experience applying these models of how humans' beliefs in technology are shaped, they start to become second nature to us. We need to understand AI, the most transformative technology of our generation, if not in human history, and these models will also help us understand new technologies that emerge in the future.

Some argue that theories on the use of technology are less helpful and that they have had success without them. One of the benefits of these theories is that they have been proven over many years, in many parts of the world, so they can help us get sustainable success over a long period of time. If we are pushing against one of the consumer's beliefs, we may have success for some other reason, but it may be harder and may not be sustainable. For example, many consumers may not like the way their personal information is used by company A, but since it's the only company offering that service, they put up with it. Almost inevitably, company B emerges and offers consumers better protection for their personal data, and they start to take market share. Ignoring some of the stakeholders' beliefs isn't a problem, until it is. Consumers can quickly switch to company B and so can investors. It is the leaders in company A that should take stakeholders' beliefs on technology into account from the start to pre-empt the problem.

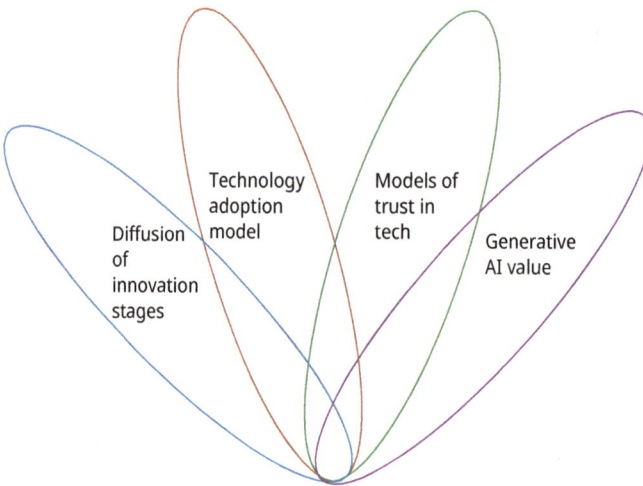

Technology
adoption
model

Models of
trust in
tech

Diffusion
of
innovation
stages

Generative
AI value

Figure 7.1: The overlapping knowledge a leader must have for generative AI to 'flower' to its full potential.

Leaders that understand technology better can create a strategic advantage. It is not a coincidence that so many of the self-made richest billionaires in the world have a technology background. Beyond our organisation, we must understand how AI changes our sector, our competitors, and society. Using several models to understand different stakeholders' perspectives is necessary for this.

Key concept: Apply proven models of human behaviour with technology for long-term sustainable success.

Leadership tip: Understanding all the stakeholders' beliefs on a technology and their motivations can be used to build a more effective strategy.

7.1.1 Show courage and take necessary risks to innovate, but not recklessly

If someone becomes a leader because they are confident and to some degree aggressive – characteristics often associated with an alpha male – this can also lead to recklessness and a destruction of trust. Courage should be shown once a good plan is developed. Being decisive just to build the brand of a decisive leader and assert authority is not a sustainable approach. The option not to act should always be on the table. One of the biggest tragedies of humanity is when bad leaders undo the good work done by those before them.

Use proven theories and experience to frame every situation well

Many consider intelligence to be some kind of gift that some of us have and others don't. The truth is, if we reflect on a situation, know some proven theories, and also have experience, we can frame a situation accurately and then act in a more informed way. This is a simple point, but too many leaders jump to make a spontaneous decision without going through some thought process. This can sometimes take only a few minutes, and we don't necessarily need to write anything down. Traditionally, a manager would use a SWOT (strengths, weaknesses, opportunities, and threats) analysis to frame an issue – an excellent start, but it is not usually enough. A clear benefits case for the AI initiative is necessary. Decide what truly belongs in that frame, and what should be left out. When it is clear in our mind, we will be able to make better decisions and communicate effectively.

The rest of this chapter will cover the stages of the diffusion of innovation (7.2), TAM (7.3), the models of trust in technology (7.4), the opportunities and challenges of using generative AI (7.5) and finally the summary. The theories presented in the rest of this chapter will help the leader frame a situation and make a decision regardless of what leadership approach they apply.

Leadership tip: Take some time to reflect and frame the issue you are looking at. Identify what should be included, and what should be left out. Go through the cycle of framing, consulting, reframing, and acting.

Key concept: An effective leader must bring simplicity and clarity to the team and the systems used.

7.2 The stages of diffusion of innovation and the typical challenges at each stage

When we venture in that unfamiliar sea, we trust blindly in those who guide us, believing that they know more than we do. — Paulo Coelho, author of *The Witch of Portobello*

The main point of the diffusion of innovation is that a new innovation usually goes through some typical stages. As with the other theories and models we are looking at here, it is not always true, but it helps us shape our strategy. In a sense, we need to try to overlay all these models to understand what we need to do to lead effectively with AI. For example, in Figure 7.2 showing the diffusion of innovation, it is not too hard to overlay where the high and low risk will be and where most of the work on trust should happen. As all managers do, we need to deal with the immediate, pressing challenges but also have the foresight to pre-empt the typical challenges further down the road. There may be a sense of excitement in feeling that what we are doing has never been done before, but it is more rewarding to stand on the shoulders on giants.

If we were talking about leadership some decades ago when change was more gradual, the timing of a leader's move was less challenging. We could simply follow what our peers did and, as long as we were not too slow, that was usually enough. An example is European carmakers copying the just-in-time process from Japan. They took some time to copy it and implement it effectively, but the delay was not fatal. Nowadays, customers will not wait a few years for us to catch up with our competitors or correct a strategic mistake. For example, comparison websites across travel, insurance, and other services make competition brutal. To some degree, we are in a situation where the winner takes all. The first challenge in terms of the timing is to figure out where we really are now. This is actually a challenging question that even organisations that usually lead on innovation often get wrong.

In the diffusion of innovation there are usually the categories of innovators, early adopters, early majority, late majority, and laggards. This applies to individuals and organisations. For example, just as a consumer can be an early adopter of a technology such as a smartwatch, a government can be an early adopter of a CBDC. One of the central themes that pretty much anyone who has studied business will remember is the idea that an innovation must achieve a critical mass to be successful. For example, when it became clear that one of the first online virtual worlds, *Second Life*, would not reach critical mass, the interest in it from businesses evaporated. Most businesses decided that *Second Life* would not go beyond a niche adoption. The organisations that were 'innovators' started projects in *Second Life*, but there was certainly no early majority.

When we are thinking about leading with AI, we are interested in how individuals use it and how the organisation adopts it. We need to keep in mind both the formal and informal systems used. We should remember that workers use the formal

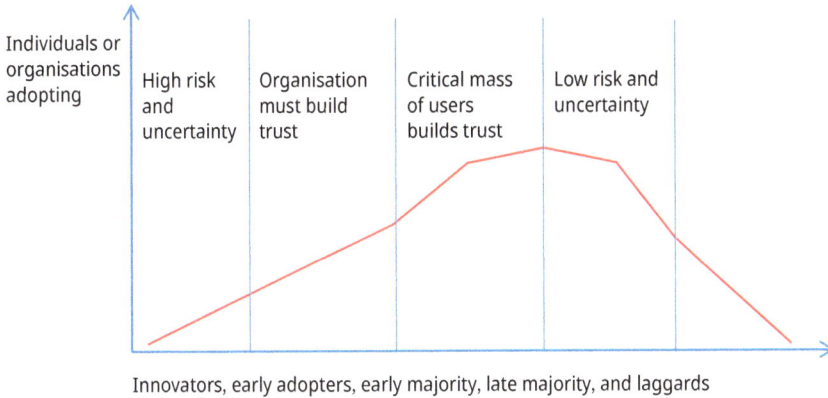

Figure 7.2: The diffusion of innovation and its influence on trust.

systems their organisation provides them, and other systems that they choose to use. This is an obvious point, but it is particularly critical in the diffusion of information systems, as a typical strategy is to offer them free at first so many of us get hooked and then start charging.

One of the nice things about this model is that it takes into account the communication channels and the social system. This makes it completer and more holistic. If we are trying to understand how change happens and we are neglecting one of the factors playing a role, we will not reach the right conclusion. The communication channels between adopters sharing information about the innovation are important. Often this is manipulated to create hype. An extreme example is meme coins, such as the popular Pepe Coin.

The social system includes broader influences such as mass media, social media, government, and other institutions. It also includes more personal influences, such as social relationships, and how receptive someone is to opinion leaders. Understanding who has it in their nature to want to innovate, and who will delay using a new innovation for as long as possible, can inform a leader's approach.

It is obvious that we need to get the innovators involved at the start when we launch a service utilising a new technology. We do not need the model to understand this, but the model makes it clear that it is equally important to take the next step and get the early adopters engaged. These two types of users are different and have different priorities. An innovator may not only be comfortable with the risk, they may enjoy it. They may be the type of person that will be attracted by the new features, even if they are not entirely practical or easy to use. The early innovators of Bitcoin are very typical examples of this. They learned how to use digital wallets and protect their 'keys'. The early and late majority, however, are typically expecting a more polished service with benefits that are explained to them clearly. If we think about the predominant message that attracted early adopters of Bitcoin, it was something along the lines of 'take ownership of your finances with a decentralised cryptocurrency that utilises a distributed ledger'. That is an attractive message to those that would fall under the category of technology 'innovators', but what percentage of the population are they? What was the price of Bitcoin when only that type of person was interested? The price was probably a few hundred euro. After some years, the predominant message now seems to be 'beat the inflation of traditional currencies with Bitcoin because there is a finite number of them'. This is clearly a simpler message that most, if not all, adults would understand. Therefore, it is not just about making it easier and less risky to use, but it is also about having a clearer message to target the early and late majority of the population. The clear, more transparent message is as important to building trust as the service and the technology that deliver it.

Another key insight of the diffusion of innovation model is that, unlike other models that focus on one period of an innovation's journey, this model covers the whole lifecycle. For example, TAM focuses on the adoption stage only. Therefore, it helps us have a strategy for the adoption of the innovation we are working on now, but it also helps us time our next innovation so that we can 'disrupt' ourselves at the right point before a competitor disrupts us. Typically, once the late majority have started adopting the technology we are offering, we need to start thinking about launching the next innovation. The exact time depends on many factors, but typically we do not want the one innovation to complete its cycle. We want to utilise the momentum of the first innovation to launch the second, similar to a four-by-one-hundred-metre swimming relay race.

While the diffusion of innovation is quite simple and intuitive, it can be the foundation for more sophisticated analysis and strategies. Good strategies are built on understanding basic human behaviour.

Key concept: When an innovation starts to get used, fewer of us are using it and there is more uncertainty and risk. Trust needs to be built at this stage by someone. A leader must decide if it is worth it to be an early adopter or wait a little. The timing is critical. Many of us understand that we can be too late to innovate, but we can also be too early.

7.3 The technology adoption model and the challenges at each stage

Trust is earned, respect is given, and loyalty is demonstrated. Betrayal of any one of those is to lose all three. — Ziad K. Abdelnour, author of *Economic Warfare*

TAM and the diffusion of innovation stages are two complementary theories that a leader should apply almost instinctively, like second nature. Unlike the diffusion of innovation that is more general and covers all innovations, TAM is more focused on information technology such as AI, virtual reality, and blockchain (Davis, 1989). It is one of the main theories in the area of human-computer interaction (HCI) and user interface design (UI).

The beauty of this model is that it frames and explains how people adopt technology by building on psychology and sociology. In a sense it starts from the most basic issues: a person's psychology and the sociological issues influencing the behaviour of the group they are in. This is beneficial because, while technologies change regularly, an individual's psychology and the sociology of the group they are in move more gradually. Of course, those that we refer to as Generation Z are different to baby boomers, but that change covers many decades of gradual evolution.

This model started by capturing a small number of the most important issues, but over time newer versions became more complicated and comprehensive. A leader must understand the fundamental, initial version first. If we want to go into more depth on this and look at the more complicated models, we can do that, but not every manager will want, or need, to go into that level of detail. The more complicated versions are also often more focused on one situation and may not apply to another. The norms, usefulness, and ease of use are three of the important factors that typically play a role.

This model can be adapted to fit a leader's particular situation. The leader does not necessarily have to collect and analyse data every time they want to use the logic of TAM to structure their thinking. This model can be used to frame our thoughts and think about where issues such as trust and privacy fit into our situation. Either with data or with our judgement if there is no data, we need to think about what issues will have a decisive influence and which will not. When we look at the takeover of Twitter by Elon Musk, it is clear to see that he identifies a smaller number of issues that play a decisive role, compared to what the previous leadership of Twitter believed. He chose to focus on fewer issues and could therefore reduce the workforce.

In its most basic form, the TAM includes: external variables (e.g. social influence), perceived usefulness (PU), perceived ease-of-use (PEOU), attitude towards technology, behavioural intention to use, and actual system use. If we are implementing an AI chatbot or using blockchain for open banking, some of the issues will be similar and some will be different, but this model is a useful starting point. If we continue with the example of blockchain for open banking, we need to consider the usefulness and ease of use for different stakeholders in this scenario. If a leader can answer these questions sufficiently, they are making an important step to creating a vision that will get everyone on board. Lastly, as with the other figures here, their visual nature helps a team be 'on the same page' when discussing the issues. The TAM model is illustrated in figure 7.3.

The logic TAM captures is very helpful; those are often the most important issues. One popular extension is the unified theory of acceptance and use of technology UTAUT2 (Venkatesh et al., 2003) presented in Figure 7.4. This model with more variables will capture some situations better, but the variables added can have a weaker or even negligible influence in some situations. The first three variables on the left are similar to TAM despite the wording being a little different. The first three – (1) perfor-

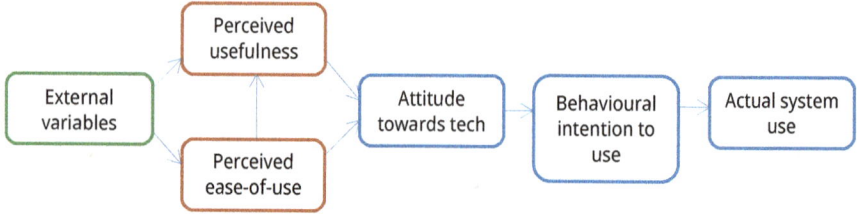

Figure 7.3: Basic technology adoption model (based on Davis, 1989).

mance expectancy, (2) effort expectancy, and (3) social influence – are the ones that will have a role in most situations. The four that are often added are: (4) facilitating conditions, (5) hedonic motivation, (6) price value, and (7) habit.

Facilitating conditions refer to the consumer's perception of whether the support and resources are in place for them to use the technology effectively. If the technology requires some resources and support, such as doing a simulation in a virtual world, facilitating conditions may be important. If the technology in question does not require any particular support or resources, then this may not play a significant role.

Hedonic motivation refers to the enjoyment we can get out of using a technology. This does not have to be about a technology that is exclusively about enjoyment, such as playing a game on a Sony PlayStation 5. Many work-related technologies also give us some pleasure, such as typing on a Lenovo ThinkPad keyboard.

Price value and habit are more straightforward; they are what someone would expect them to mean. Price value is the benefit we perceive to get compared to what we paid. Habit is a factor, as most of us have some momentum built into our habits and we need some time and convincing to change them.

An example of an additional variable that can be added to capture people's beliefs on technology is the content. Content refers to the quality of the material provided by the technology, including the text, images, sound, video, etc.

The moderators make this model more scientifically rigorous than the basic version of TAM. As we said, these models are based on the individual's psychology and the sociology of the group they are in, but there are some demographic characteristics that have been proven to play a role in many situations. A leader cannot be consumed by virtue signalling, which may be in fashion for some, but must remain grounded in reality. Some demographic characteristics such as age, gender, and income often play a role. The list can be far longer, sometimes including other demographic information such as education level and nationality. We call them moderators because they can influence many, or all, of the other factors.

These two models, TAM and UTAUT2, offer a technology-focused perspective on a person's relationship with a technology, but they also share clear parallels with the marketing perspective, which frames similar issues, such as consumer behaviour. There is significant overlap between HCI, UI, and consumer behaviour.

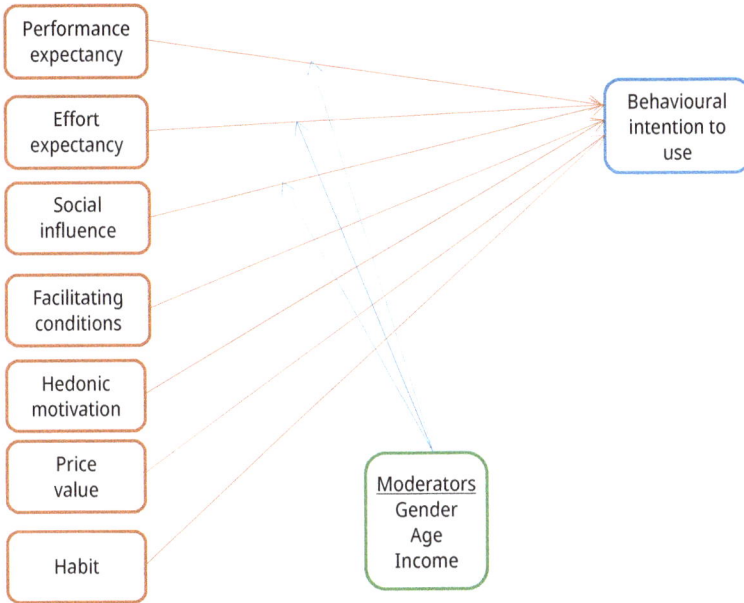

Figure 7.4: Unified theory of acceptance and use of technology 2 (UTAUT2) (based on Venkatesh et al., 2003).

Trust-building tip (reminder from Chapter 1): Gauge the level of vulnerability users of AI feel and take the steps necessary to reassure them and make them feel less vulnerable.

Key concept: There are many issues that may logically affect a person's behaviour with technology. Usually, however, a small subset of four to eight issues have a decisive role. Usually, ease of use and usefulness are two of them. For a given situation we need to find the rest.

Key concept: Demographics usually play an important role, particularly age, gender, income, education level and nationality.

Leadership tip: Make sure the organisation's processes and values that are encouraged are aligned with the issues that are definitely decisive in shaping people's choices.

7.4 Models of trust in technology

> *To persevere, trusting in what hopes he has, is courage in a man.* — Euripides, ancient Greek playwright

In addition to the general models of technology adoption and use, there are specialised models on how we trust a specific type of technology, such as AI or cryptocurrency. Some of the models presented here, such as the model of trust and privacy concerns associated with using insurance that explicitly utilises AI, are clearly based on TAM and UTAUT2, while others are less directly related. In all the models presented here, however, having the basic logic of how humans typically interact with technology is helpful for us. As discussed, when we perceive that using a technology will expose us to some kind of risk, we need to sufficiently trust the technology to use it. Building trust in the technology is not just a technical issue for the IT department, but is also an issue for the leader. The leader must ensure that sufficient trust is built through everything the organisation does. If the IT experts implement a secure solution for a bank but the bank makes risky investments, the business side will ruin the trust the technical side may have built. As many services are delivered by an ecosystem of organisations, it is not always clear what each organisation is responsible for and under which jurisdiction it is regulated.

For example, a popular online bank active in the UK did not have a full banking licence but stored consumers' money in other banks that did have such a licence. Another example is that when someone buys shares using the British bank Revolut, they are actually using a Berlin-based API provider called Upvest. This may change in the future, but it is the case at the time of writing. As this online bank is successful, it seems like an effective way to operate, but the risks stem from several different areas, and trust building must be established in multiple ways. Such complex businesses can be successful if they sufficiently understand the implications of their operational methods on risk and trust.

In addition to the complexity of operations that spread across several organisations, there is also the issue that, due to the speed of innovation, organisations often do not have the time they once had to build trust. While in the past offering a good service and being reliable would build trust through word of mouth, new organisations cannot only rely on this method. Ideally, a new organisation should build trust into all of its services in a way that both a current consumer and a potential new consumer can be convinced that it is trustworthy. Ideally, this trust should be built quickly and sustained throughout the consumer's interaction with the organisation.

The benefits to being trustworthy, however, are not limited to a consumer using an organisation's services or products. Research has found that if an organisation makes the effort to build trust, a consumer will reward them by behaving in a similar way to how a citizen of country does – supporting them and defending them (Su et al., 2025). On a partly philosophical point, we could argue that the consumer becomes part of the ecosystem and not simply someone external that a transaction is made with. Building trust and reducing privacy concerns in a sustainable way creates a positive feedback loop that benefits everyone.

It is clear that trust needs to be understood in relation to specific processes and technologies. These things are intertwined and cannot be separated, and some examples follow. These examples are from research published in reputable journals; they are not hypothetical examples. First, we will look at two detailed examples of using AI in finance and insurance and the implications this has for trust. While AI is at the centre of our attention, there is a lot of innovation happening with other technologies as well, so we will also look at two other examples of blockchain-based technologies, namely, cryptocurrencies and tokens.

7.4.1 Trust in using AI

As we have discussed, trust is more important when the risk is high. Sectors such as health and finance, or anything else where a large amount of money is at risk, are usually areas where we need to think about building trust. While trust is less important when the risk is low, when the risk is very high, some things are typically already in place to manage the risk and make us feel that we can trust the process.

For example, if someone buys an expensive house, the money does not directly normally change hands from the buyer to the seller, but there are estate agents and lawyers there to support the process and reduce the risk. (Whether estate agents and lawyers in England do indeed reduce the risk or increase it with their untrustworthy behaviour is another matter.) So, we need to build trust in high-risk scenarios where trust is not already being built sufficiently. Obviously, new technologies fall into this category, but new applications of existing technologies also fall into this category.

We will now turn our attention to two detailed examples of using AI in finance and insurance, and the implications this has for trust.

7.4.1.1 Illustrating trust in using AI with the example of insurance

The capabilities of AI are increasing dramatically, and it is disrupting health insurance In insurance, AI is used to detect fraudulent claims, and natural language processing is used by chatbots to interact with the consumer. In healthcare, AI is used to make a diagnosis and plan what the treatment should be. The consumer is benefiting from customised health insurance offers and the real-time adaptation of fees. Currently, the interface between the consumer purchasing health insurance and AI raises some barriers, such as insufficient trust and privacy concerns.

AI offers some unique capabilities, but most of the impact is as part of a wave of innovation that will optimise and create new products, services, business models, and business ecosystems. AI can be seen as the catalyst as it harnesses the full potential of hardware and software in a way that was not possible before. It can mask the complexity and provide value to the health insurance consumer. This increased role of AI, along with the ecosystem of technologies it utilises, influences the consumer's attitude.

The challenges to AI depend on the specific context and implementation, as well as the information system it is part of. One challenge is the implementation of AI that has negative impacts, for example on individuals' health (He et al., 2019). The risks caused by AI seem to come from either using its capabilities to do something harmful more effectively, or by AI making incorrect evaluations. In a fully automated system, mistakes will be implemented directly. If AI is working with humans, the humans may act based on the incorrect evaluation it made. As AI can be unpredictable and opaque, this raises some questions in terms of control and how to manage the risks. Society, governments, and other institutions, such as the European Union, are attempting to regulate and offer guidelines on how to move forward with AI in an ethical way, reducing the risks to the consumer (European Commission, 2019).

Consumers are not passive to the increasing role of AI. Many consumers have beliefs on what this technology should do. Furthermore, regulation is moving toward making it necessary for the use of AI to be explicitly revealed to the consumer (European Commission, 2019). The consumer will interpret some of the capabilities AI offers as enablers, and some as risks and concerns. For example, limited trust and personal information privacy concerns may be barriers. Therefore, the consumer is an important stakeholder, and their perspective should be understood and incorporated into future AI solutions in health insurance.

The change from related technologies and other trends in society, such as greener living, mean many of us want to see different principles and values from our insurers. Therefore, the new ethical, privacy, and trust challenges AI brings can be approached as part of a holistic re-evaluation of the relationship between a consumer and their health insurer. New business models may require a new ethical perspective. Ethics and regulation are evolving as the uses and business models of AI evolve. The new way of interacting with the consumer, the new interfaces, and even business models must consider the enablers and barriers to AI in health insurance from the consumer's perspective.

Two online scenarios: one with limited AI, one with extensive AI

The research presented here focuses on the barriers from the consumer's perspective when they are purchasing health insurance online. Recent research by Zarifis et al. (2021) identified two online scenarios: one with limited AI that is not in the interface, whose presence is not explicitly revealed to the consumer; and a second scenario where there is an AI interface and evaluation explicitly revealed to the consumer.

There is more risk when purchasing health insurance online because the consumer is taking a risk that the insurer will indeed cover them if they make a claim. The murder of the United Healthcare CEO in 2024 is an extreme example of the tension that can be created in this product realm.

Insurance companies and the information systems they use have developed sufficiently to build trust in scenarios involving limited AI that is not visible to the consumer. The increasing role of AI across the health insurance supply chain introduces new sources of distrust, stemming from the lack of human attributes at more stages of the supply chain. AI used in both the front end and back end can increase how unpredictable the result is.

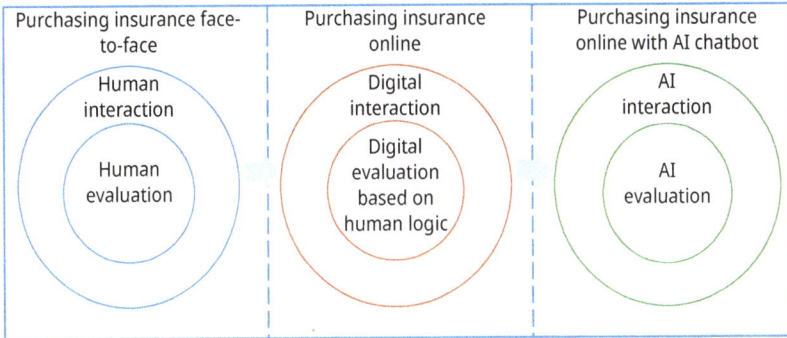

Figure 7.5: The purchasing process face-to-face, online, and online with AI.

As Figure 7.5 illustrates, the interaction of the consumer can be divided into three scenarios. Firstly, a traditional face-to-face interaction without utilising technology. Secondly, a digital interaction online that mainly utilises human logic and uses AI in a limited way that is not visible to the consumer. Lastly, the third scenario involves the consumer interacting purely with an AI interface and with the underlying logic and decision making also based on AI.

To better understand the scenario where the consumer purchases health insurance with an AI interface and logic, and the decision making involved, this new scenario needs to be contrasted with the typical existing scenario. In the existing scenario, there is limited AI visible in the interface and its presence is not explicitly revealed to the consumer. Therefore, as illustrated in the Figure 7.6, two scenarios are contrasted: one with limited AI, not explicitly revealed to the consumer, and one with an AI interface and evaluation explicitly revealed to the consumer.

For these scenarios to be tested, they are modelled as illustrated in the third and final Figure 7.7. This model is analysed twice – once for the first scenario and once for the second. The first two constructs are the enablers: firstly the additional ease of use offered by AI, and secondly the additional usefulness offered by AI. The second two constructs are the two barriers of trust and privacy concern. The final construct is the decision to purchase health insurance online.

The findings show that trust is lower when AI is used in the interactions and is visible to the consumer. Privacy concerns are also higher when the AI is visible, but the difference is smaller. The implications for practice are related to how the reduced trust and increased privacy concerns with visible AI are mitigated.

Mitigate the lower trust with explicit AI

The causes are reduced transparency and explainability. A statement at the start of the consumer journey about the role AI will play and how it works will increase transparency and reinforce trust. Secondly, the importance of trust increases as the per-

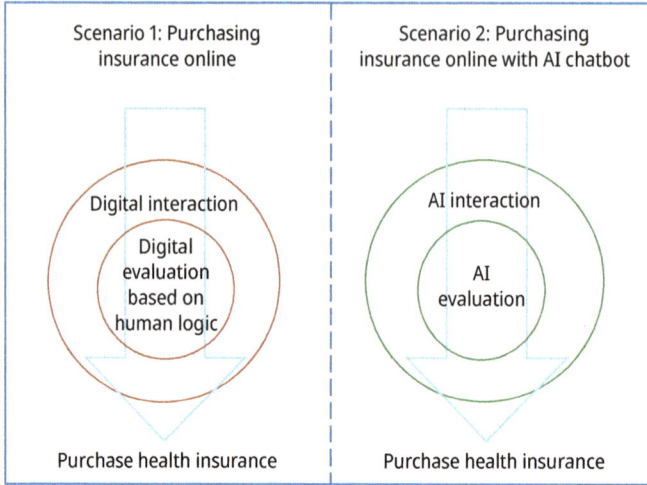

Figure 7.6: Purchasing insurance online with limited AI and extensive AI.

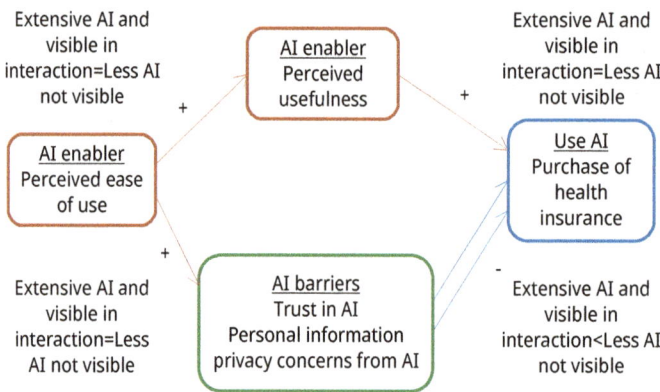

Figure 7.7: Trust and privacy concerns are barriers to using insurance that explicitly utilises AI.

ceived risk increases. Therefore, the risks should be reduced. Thirdly, it should be illustrated that the increased use of AI does not reduce the inherent humanness. For example, it can be shown how humans train AI and how it adopts human values.

Mitigate the higher privacy concerns with explicit AI
The consumer is concerned about how AI will utilise their financial, health, and other personal information. Health insurance providers offer privacy assurances and privacy seals, but these do not explicitly refer to the role of AI. Assurances can be provided about how AI will use, share, and securely store the information. These assurances can include some explanation of the role of AI and cover confidentiality,

secrecy, and anonymity. For example, while the consumer's information may be used to train machine learning, it can be made clear that it will be anonymised first. The consumer's perceived privacy risk can be mitigated by making the regulation that protects them clear.

Key concept: Understand the process the user goes through step by step, often referred to as the customer journey, and how the use of AI can cause uncertainty and risk.

Leadership tip: If a specific process is opaque because of the way AI is used, and this creates an increased sense of uncertainty and risk, trust must be built into another process to compensate for it. Ideally, trust should be established before the process that is perceived to be risky, not after.

7.4.1.2 Illustrating trust in generative AI with the example of simple and complex financial questions

Financial technology (fintech) is reshaping business models and the relationships between organisations and their consumers. Generative AI (GenAI) has significantly developed as a technology and has been adopted dramatically. However, it is not clear what the consumers' opinions are when using it for financial advice. Using this technology in this context involves risk, so trust is needed. Research by Zarifis and Cheng (2024) evaluated how to build trust in answers given by GenAI for specific, and vague, financial questions.

GenAI uses algorithms that can analyse data from many different sources and produce human-like output such as text, images, and sound. They are usually pre-trained so they can create something that seems original very quickly. These characteristics result in a technology that appears to be closer to human intelligence when offering financial insight. Popular examples include DeepSeek, Mistral AI, Baidu's Ernie Bot, Tencent's Hunyuan, ChatGPT, Dall-E 2, and Jasper AI.

GenAI has the typical risks that many information systems have, such as the accuracy of the data used, but it also brings some new risks, such as 'hallucinations'. GenAI hallucinations are when it provides completely wrong information that it fabricated. GenAI can also be manipulated to spread misinformation intentionally. Common challenges for information systems, such as data leakage, are more serious with GenAI. A widely held belief is that GenAI is still not accurate and reliable enough to be followed blindly and needs a human expert to make the final decision, using their own judgement and other information to have a more well-rounded perspective.

Regulation usually plays an important role in reducing the risk new technologies bring to consumers and the broader economy. Recent regulations such as those from the European Union are promising, but not yet fully tested. It will take some time for organisations to align to them and consumers to learn about them.

While the technology is making breakthroughs in its ability to offer better financial insight than other methods, there are still challenges from the user's perspective.

Firstly, there is a wide variety of different financial questions that are asked by the user. A user's financial questions may be specific, such as 'Does stock X give a higher dividend than stock Y?', or vague, such as 'How can my investments make me happier?'. Financial decisions often have far-reaching, long-term implications.

When someone starts to interact with a specific GenAI tool, it can be seen more as a longer-term relationship than just a single transaction. Interacting with GenAI can feel strange and unnatural to many users, with some even referring to it as creepy and frightening. It has been known since the 1970s that a partial human-like behaviour from a machine can make a person feel disturbed and unsettled. Despite these issues being known for some time, they are not the most important determinants with technologies that are less human-like. When the interaction with the technology has fewer human characteristics, ease of use and usefulness are typically the decisive issues influencing adoption behaviour.

Building sustainable trust in GenAI for financial decisions is not just needed to increase the rate of adoption, but it will also influence how much the advice received will be relied on. For example, higher trust will reduce the likelihood of several systems being used in parallel in financial decision making. It may also reduce indecision and second-guessing every move, which can be time consuming and inefficient.

The process of using generative AI to answer user's financial questions

As GenAI replicates human intelligence and the way we communicate, it also changes how some financial questions are posed to GenAI. Not all questions have to be narrow and specific, such as a car owner entering their car's details and asking for an insurance quote. Questions can be vague or be a combination of many questions made at once. For example, a user may describe their current job, what they earn, what their expenses are, and ask for investment advice. Figure 7.8 shows the stages a user can take when asking GenAI a financial question. A user will initially make a specific narrow question or a vague general question and receive an answer. After assessing the answer, a follow-up question can be made so it becomes more like a conversation.

This research identified four methods to build trust in GenAI in both of the scenarios (specific and vague financial questions) and one method that only works for vague questions (Zarifis and Cheng 2024). Humanness has a different effect on trust in the two scenarios. When a question is specific, humanness does not increase trust, while (1) when a question is vague, human-like GenAI increases trust. The four ways to build trust in both scenarios are: (2) human oversight and being in the loop, (3) transparency and control, (4) accuracy and usefulness, and lastly (5) ease of use and support. For the best results, all of the methods identified should be used together to build trust. These variables can provide the basis for guidelines to organisations in finance utilising GenAI. Figure 7.9 illustrates how four variables influence trust in one scenario, and five variables influence trust in the other.

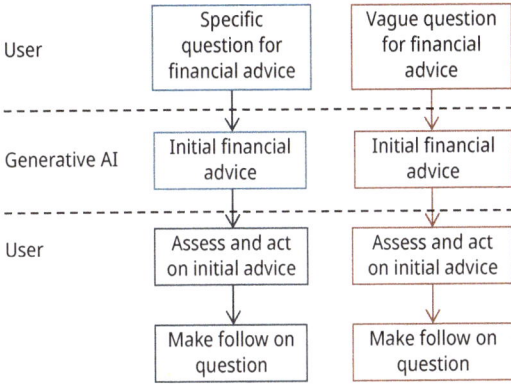

Figure 7.8: User journey when asking a financial question and receiving advice from generative AI.

This research supports the concept that if technology appears more human, this does not create a higher affinity and trust in all situations. If technology appears more human, this may reduce affinity and trust in the technology in some contexts. The five variables that can build trust will be explained in a little more detail.

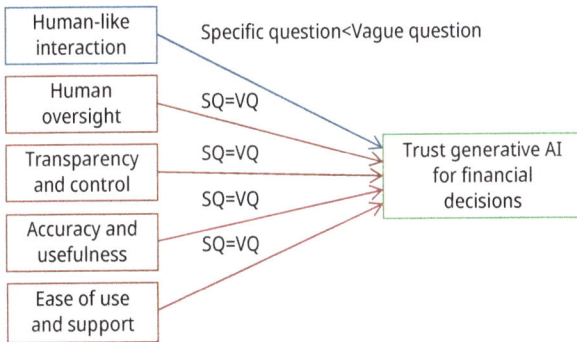

Figure 7.9: Initial research model expecting human-like interaction to be more important for vague question.

(1) Human-like interaction
If a question is specific, such as 'Does stock X usually give a higher dividend than stock Y?', a response from GenAI with a high humanness does not increase the user's trust. Humanness is not always appropriate. For a specific question, the response of GenAI should avoid human-like behaviour and emotion. When a user makes a vague question, such as 'How can my investments make me happier?', the user is more open to a response from GenAI with human-like behaviour and emotion. In response to a vague question, humanness does build trust.

(2) Human oversight and being in the loop
Asking GenAI to inform financial decisions involves some risks, and having some human oversight can build trust. This research finds that it is beneficial for trust to keep expert practitioners in the loop, have regular audits of performance, and conform to the norms and culture of the financial sector.

(3) Transparency and control
Transparency and control build trust in the financial advice from GenAI. There needs to be an explanation of how GenAI is used, clarity about the dataset the AI was trained on, and how data provided by the consumer are used. This supports the importance of explainable AI (XAI) in finance. However, given that several variables are needed to build trust, it also supports that XAI is not sufficient on its own.

(4) Accuracy and usefulness
In addition to some other typical issues such as transparency, the AI being useful and accurate in its primary purpose builds trust. The customisation of the answer to the specific user must be tailored well for it to be useful. This finding is in line with research on other technologies where the usefulness in relation to the primary purpose of the technology is important. Providing evidence that the answer is accurate will make it more likely that trust is built.

(5) Ease of use and support
Lastly, the analysis suggests that ease of use and support when using GenAI to answer financial questions build trust. Reliable support and error correction also build trust. This is typical when using technology.

The findings here suggest that more technology-based characteristics build trust in GenAI for financial decisions. While this research focuses on GenAI when responding to financial questions, most of these variables are expected to be relevant, to some degree, in similar contexts where there is financial risk.

Implications for business

The ways to build trust identified here can inform specific steps for existing implementations of GenAI. These steps are also guidelines to follow in the future to maintain and continue building trust. The more stakeholders that get involved in this the better. Several stakeholders can move towards addressing the five dimensions of building trust identified in a synergistic way. Figure 7.10 illustrates the two scenarios separately to make the one difference between them clearer.

Despite the ability of GenAI to learn and adapt to support various financial services, the most successful organisations will still be in the loop, utilising the unique knowledge of their experts to guide GenAI. Knowing when GenAI should respond to financial questions with a human-like response and emotion is important in building

GenAI answer to specific question   GenAI answer to vague question

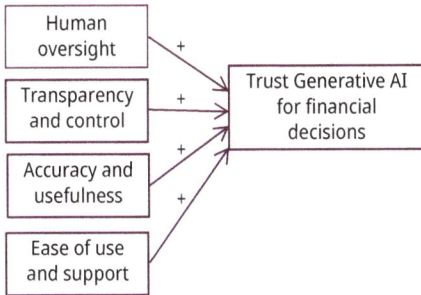

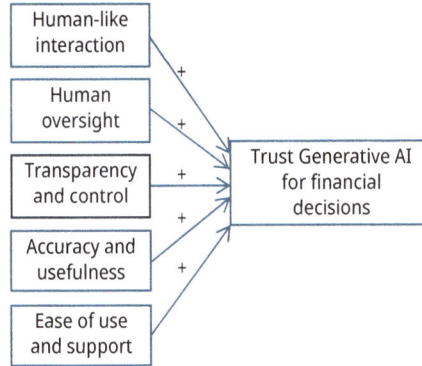

Figure 7.10: Model of building trust in advice given by generative AI when answering financial questions.

trust. A financial service can go through the list of typical questions a user asks and decide whether a human-like, emotional response is appropriate.

Trust must be built throughout the use of GenAI, but it is particularly important to build it when the financial advice received leads to unsuccessful investments. Financial advice, whether directly from a human, GenAI, or some other statistical analysis or data aggregation, will inevitably lead to unsuccessful decisions sometimes. It is important for the business providing the financial advice to be as clear as possible about why the GenAI did actually work reliably even if, for other reasons out of the company's control, there was a negative outcome.

If trust at some point is too high and unrealistic expectations are created, this may only increase disappointment at a later stage. 'Overtrust' may backfire. Therefore, the level of trust must be built on the solid foundations of its actual capabilities. Lastly, the findings here encourage providers of GenAI for financial decisions to have vigilance moving forward to understand and adapt to changes in technology, data, and regulation.

When providing GenAI for financial decisions, it must be clear what it is being used for. For example, analysing past financial performance to attempt to predict future performance is very different to analysing social media activity. The advice of GenAI needs to feel like a fully integrated part of the financial community, not just a system. The issues analysed here in relation to GenAI in finance should also apply, to some degree, in other scenarios where there is a high risk, such as health. Trust must be built sufficiently to overcome the perceived risk. The findings suggest that the consumer will not follow the 'pied piper' blindly, however alluring 'their song' of automation and efficiency is.

Key concept: Using GenAI for high-risk scenarios such as finance and health are different to using GenAI in low-risk scenarios such as predicting sales or recommending products. Building trust is a priority in high-risk scenarios.

Key concept: For a specific question, the response of GenAI should avoid human-like behaviour and emotion. When a user makes a vague question, the user is more open to a response from GenAI with human-like behaviour and emotion. In response to a vague question, humanness does build trust.

Trusting-building tip: There are five typical ways to build trust in GenAI for financial questions or other questions where there is risk: (1) When a question is vague, human-like Generative AI increases trust. The four ways to build trust for both specific and vague questions is: (2) human oversight and being in the loop, (3) transparency and control, (4) accuracy and usefulness, and lastly (5) ease of use and support.

7.4.2 Trust in other technologies beyond AI

Beyond AI there are several other transformative technologies. Cryptocurrencies and other blockchain-based technologies such as tokens are receiving a lot of attention for good and bad reasons. There is no denying that these technologies are often used for fraud, such as 'pump-and-dump' meme coins, but there are also serious implications of these technologies in both the private and public sectors. A leader may not be an expert in these technologies, but they need to understand them better than the average person.

We will also look at two other examples of blockchain-based technologies such as cryptocurrencies and tokens. Whether someone is a 'fan' of cryptocurrencies or not, their impact cannot be disputed, as millions of us invest billions in them. For example, imagine we are a project manager for a building development of several houses and we do not like, or trust, cryptocurrencies. A new client comes along willing to pay the list price for one of our houses, but they want to pay in Bitcoin. What do we do? Reject the buyer because we do not know how to handle that, and we are uncertain about the risks? As discussed, not only AI but also fintech cuts across industries and touches most of us.

We should not assume they are all essentially the same, as, for example, Bitcoin is very different from a meme coin. Even within meme coins, some, such as Pepe Coin and Dogecoin, may gain credibility due to those that back them, and might evolve into something serious and sustainable, while other meme coins are essentially clear pump-and-dump schemes.

Similarly, other blockchain-based tokens are not limited to the non-fungible token (NFT) implementation for art, and their use did not end when obviously overpriced digital art NFTs inevitably dropped in value. We will first examine the initial model of trust in cryptocurrencies globally, and then explore the process of purchasing a blockchain-based token, such as an NFT, and the trust required at each step.

7.4.2.1 Trust in cryptocurrencies model: The second extended model – CRYPTOTRUST 2

Despite many short-term fluctuations, cryptocurrencies' popularity is growing. Peer-reviewed research into trust in cryptocurrency payments started in 2014 (Zarifis et al., 2014, 2015). The model created then was based on proven theories from psychology, but a lot has changed over the years, both in the cryptocurrencies' technology and in how they are being used. More recent research by Zarifis and Fu (2024) re-evaluates and extends the first model of trust in cryptocurrencies and delivers the second extended model of consumer trust in cryptocurrencies, CRYPTOTRUST 2, as seen in Figure 7.11.

The first popular cryptocurrency, Bitcoin, was conceived in 2009, but it really started to be widely used from around 2016. More recently, a variety of cryptocurrencies and other cryptoassets, such as NFTs, have emerged. These technologies are not only stand-alone solutions. Whole ecosystems of decentralised finance (DeFi) have emerged. A whole parallel system to traditional finance is emerging. There is, however, some effort to merge these two parallel systems. Despite cryptocurrencies and other cryptoassets not being entirely embraced by traditional finance, there is an increasing overlap, with Bitcoin exchange-traded funds (ETFs) being a recent example.

Cryptocurrencies intrigue people from many different backgrounds, including economists and bankers. Despite the wide-ranging implications of this new form of currency, we must not forget that cryptocurrencies are, first and foremost, a technology. The technology that delivers them has evolved and matured over the years. In some cases, there have been forks, splitting Bitcoin into Bitcoin and Bitcoin Cash. In other cases, such as Ethereum, mining has been replaced by a proof-of-stake mechanism. With more choices between several cryptocurrencies, stablecoins, CBDCs, and other digital payments solutions, the consumer has more choice and is becoming more selective.

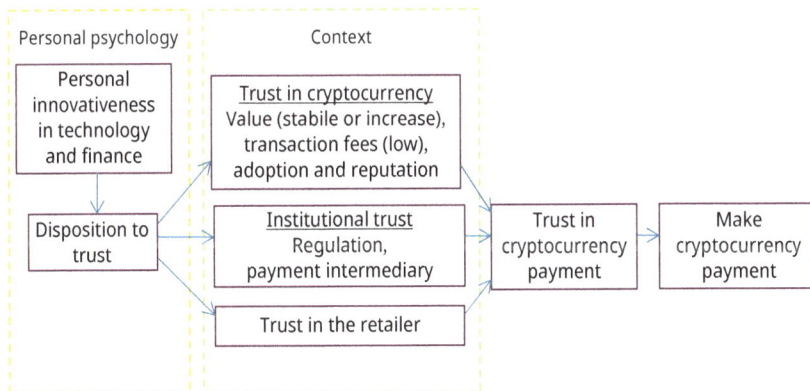

Figure 7.11: Trust in cryptocurrencies model (based on Zarifis et al., 2014; 2015; Zarifis & Fu, 2024).

Trust in cryptocurrency is a multifaceted issue. While some believe that consumers do not need to trust cryptocurrencies because they utilise blockchain, most of us recognise that trust is still necessary – just as we must trust any other technology we use that involves some risk. As cryptocurrencies are built on blockchain, some aspects operate without trust being necessary, but trust is still needed in certain parts of making a transaction and owning a cryptocurrency. While both Bitcoin and Ethereum use blockchain technology, which can increase security and support trust, several studies show that blockchain does not reduce risk sufficiently to take away the need for trust.

The many dramatic fluctuations in the price of cryptocurrencies is a valid reason for concern and criticism. Most cryptocurrencies, including Bitcoin and Ethereum, face volatility in their price. While stablecoins may have the potential to be more stable, they can also be volatile and collapse to a value close to zero – something that has not happened with Bitcoin. The variety and unpredictability of the sources of the volatility increase the uncertainty and risk, and therefore the need for trust.

The extended model of CRYPTOTRUST 2 includes twelve variables in seven groups. The first three variables of the model come from the individual's psychology: Personal innovativeness is divided into (1) personal innovativeness in technology and (2) personal innovativeness in finance. These two influence (3) personal disposition to trust.

There are then six variables that come from the specific context, and not the person's psychology. The first three are related to the cryptocurrency itself. These are, (4) the stability in the cryptocurrency value, (5) the transaction fees, and (6) reputation. Institutional trust is shaped by (7) regulation and (8) payment intermediaries that may be involved in fulfilling the transaction. The last contextual factor is (9) trust in the retailer. The six variables from the context influence (10) trust in the cryptocurrency payment which then, finally, influences (11) the likelihood of making the cryptocurrency payment.

Separating personal innovativeness to personal innovativeness in (1) technology and (2) finance is a useful distinction, as some consumers may have different levels of personal innovativeness for technology and finance. The analysis here supports that these are separate constructs.

This model improves our understanding of the role a cryptocurrency and related institutions play in building trust. The contextual factors of the cryptocurrency, regulators, intermediaries, and the retailer all play a role in building trust across the value chain. This supports the broader trend in appreciating the value of ecosystems as a whole, as opposed to the role of individual organisations. The processes of organisations collaborating are often too interrelated to separate out. The second contribution is that this research gives additional support to the role of trust in using cryptocurrencies to make transactions. This is important as cryptocurrencies and other blockchain-based technologies may have features that support trust, but they still need to be trusted.

The CRYPTOTRUST 2 model can inform technical and business decisions across the payment value chain, including the cryptocurrency, regulators, payment intermediaries, and the retailer receiving the payment.

This research shows that trust in cryptocurrencies has not changed fundamentally, but it has evolved. All the main actors in the value chain still play a role in building trust. There is more emphasis from the consumer on having a stable value and low transaction fees. This may be because consumers now have more experience with cryptocurrencies, and they are better informed. It may also be because there are more cryptocurrencies available, and other alternatives such as CBDCs, so consumers can review the many alternatives and try to identify the best one.

The regulation of cryptocurrencies has also come a long way in the past ten years, with some regions actively encouraging them, while others have banned them. While there is a belief among some in the cryptocurrency community that cryptocurrencies should not be regulated and stay separate from the traditional financial system, this research shows that regulation builds trust. Therefore, organisations involved in the cryptocurrency payment process, such as those involved in supporting the cryptocurrencies themselves and payment intermediaries, should engage with regulators and pursue effective regulation. Where effective and fair regulation can be achieved, it will enhance trust in using cryptocurrencies.

Those that back them are also very influential in elections, both with their vocal support for some candidates and also with their significant donations. What started as a movement against what was perceived to be the establishment, is merging with the establishment.

In the fast-moving and exciting – yet also unpredictable – world of cryptocurrencies, the CRYPTOTRUST 2 model offers leaders some clarity on how to effectively incorporate these technologies and build sustainable trust in them.

Key concept: The factors that affect trust in a cryptocurrency are the person's individual disposition to trust and some contextual factors, such as the stability in the cryptocurrency value, the transaction fees, reputation, regulation, payment intermediaries, and trust in the retailer.

Trust-building tip: Spend time to understand how people trust some key technologies beyond AI, such as cryptocurrencies. By contrasting how trust is built in other technologies we will also understand human behaviour and trust in AI better.

7.4.2.2 Purchasing a blockchain-based token such as an NFT and the trust needed at each step

There are several blockchain- and token-based solutions beyond cryptocurrencies. Tokenising assets can be used to prove that one person owns a physical or digital asset. Tokenised assets can also be used to share ownership between several investors. For example, hundreds of investors can own a fraction of a house and receive their share of the rent through smart contracts that get triggered automatically. One type of

blockchain-based token is an NFT. By understanding how NFTs work we can understand the main characteristics of all blockchain-based tokens (Zarifis & Castro, 2022).

An NFT uses data on a blockchain that cannot be changed after they have been
added. Therefore, while they share similar blockchain technology with cryptocurrencies, the functionality is different. NFTs' functionality allows them to prove ownership
of both intangible digital and tangible physical assets, along with the associated rights
of the owner. The most popular practical application of NFTs for digital assets is proving ownership of digital art, virtual items in computer games, and music.

As we spend more of our time online, the unique features of NFTs are becoming
increasingly appealing. Despite this increased popularity, there is a lack of clarity
over the final form this digital asset will take.

Many different types of people purchase NFTs, not just technology or crypto en-
thusiasts. The differences in the consumer's profile often mean someone without any
experience of purchasing a cryptoasset needs to figure out how to purchase them.
While most other digital assets are either a form of payment or investment, NFT purchases are often a one-off purchase of digital art. Consumers purchase NFTs for different reasons, such as the NFT's claim to uniqueness. This means an NFT purchase is
different to the purchase of a cryptocurrency.

In the context of an NFT, trust is the consumer's willingness to be vulnerable to
the seller for financial loss when purchasing an NFT. The risks that tokens such as
NFTs cause are hard to predict. While they have an almost unique ability to prove
that digital content is authentic, there are still several risks. The purchasing process
in particular needs to be clarified. There are several stages with their own distinct
risk, and it is possible that there is a cumulative effect on trust. Where there is risk,
trust is required.

When technology intermediates the relationship between the consumer and the
organisation providing them with a product or service, trust is necessary. Blockchain
technology may support trust, but there are aspects of the process a consumer goes
through that may create challenges to trust. The final application used by the consumer utilises a new technology that they are interacting with, supported by a new
infrastructure they do not see. The efforts of various regulators to reduce the risk involved for the online consumer in general, and for NFTs in particular, do not resolve
these issues entirely.

The risks include a criminal stealing the identity of a legitimate and reputable art-
ist and selling 'fake' NFTs, securities sold as NFTs by someone that is not licensed to
sell securities, wash trading' where a seller purchases their own NFTs to manipulate
the price, and an 'exit scam' or 'rag pull' where the seller takes payment and disappears without delivering on what was promised. Some early NFT issuers are attempting to mitigate this high risk and lack of transparency by issuing a virtual and physical version of the same thing so that the physical version, such as a pair of trainers,
gives legitimacy to the virtual version. Despite several early efforts from sellers and

regulators, the end consumer faces a lack of transparency and risk, which together create challenges to trust.

A model of the purchasing process of NFTs and the role of trust in this process is illustrated in Figure 7.12. The model shows that the purchasing process of NFTs has four stages, and each stage requires trust. We see here in Figure 7.12 the four stages in the purchasing process on the left, and the trust required in each of these stages along the centre. Finally, on the right we see that trust in all four stages leads to trust in an NFT purchase.

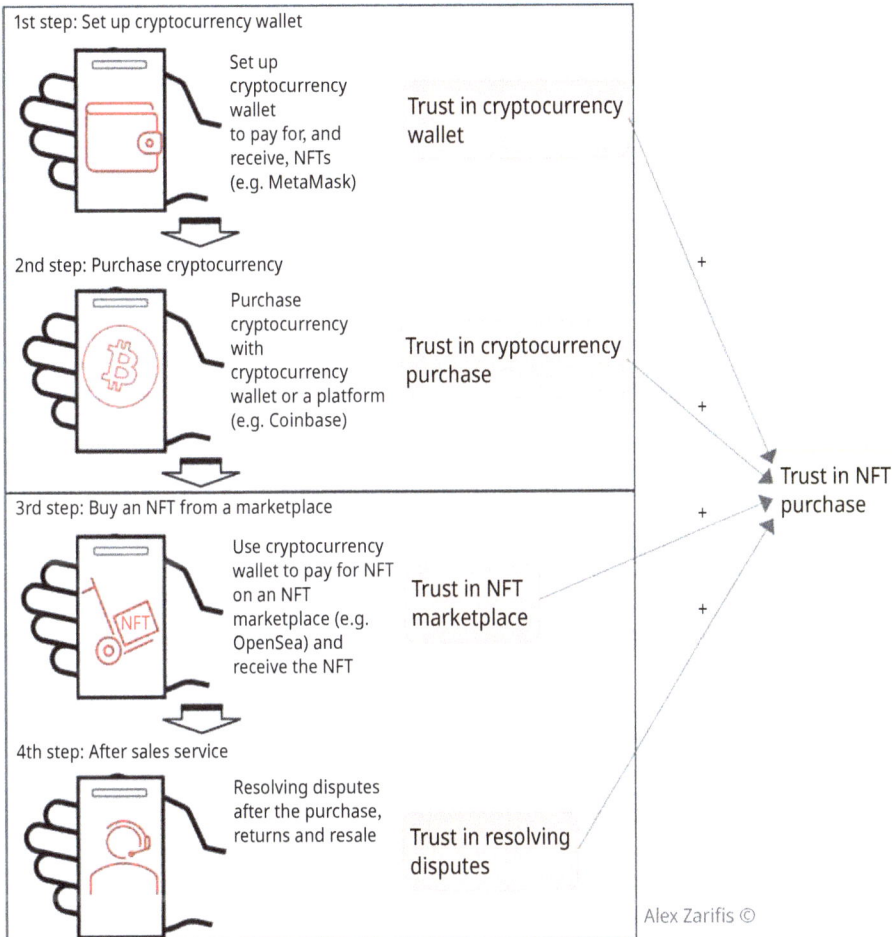

Figure 7.12: The process to purchase a blockchain-based token such as an NFT and the trust needed at each step (Zarifis & Castro, 2022).

The purchase of an NFT by a consumer should not be seen as one monolithic action, but rather four distinct stages of technology adoption (Zarifis & Castro, 2022), each with its risk and need for trust:

1) Set up a cryptocurrency wallet to pay for and receive NFTs (e.g. MetaMask)
2) Purchase cryptocurrency using the wallet or a platform (e.g. Coinbase)
3) Use the cryptocurrency wallet to pay for an NFT on an NFT marketplace (e.g. OpenSea)
4) Resolve disputes after the purchase, as well as returns and resale

Trust has a significant effect across the four stages of purchasing an NFT, but it is stronger in the first, third, and fourth stages. These stages are (1) trust in the cryptocurrency wallet, (3) trust in the NFT marketplace, and (4) trust in resolving disputes. Trust had a less significant effect in the second stage, (2) trust in the cryptocurrency purchase (Zarifis & Castro, 2022).

An organisation involved in one of the four stages of purchasing NFTs should be aware of the stages that come before and after them, and what trust concerns the consumer has. If there is a thorough understanding of trust across the four stages, some measures can be taken to improve it. If trust is weak in one stage, it can be reinforced in that stage, or if that is not possible, trust in the other stages can be increased to compensate for it. This is important as an organisation involved in one stage may not have influence over the other stages, so they may not be able to directly reinforce trust in those stages. Figure 7.12 sheds light on the NFT ecosystem, identifying several of the key players and their business models.

Given the importance of trust in every one of the four stages, there appear to be two effective strategies for a business: The first is to lead in one or two of the stages, similar to what is achieved by OpenSea, allowing other parts of the ecosystem to fulfil the other stages in an effective and seamless way. The other parts of the ecosystem are less likely to see such a company as a threat or a 'frenemy' and are more likely to collaborate wholeheartedly. The second strategy is to attempt to control all the stages, similar to what the Binance marketplace does. While building a broad, open ecosystem is a popular trend, so is its opposite: disintermediation. A company controlling all the stages will hope for 'trust transference' between them.

However, as the collapses of Terra (Luna) and FTX in 2022 have shown, a lack of trust can also transfer from one part of a business to another. The model with four stages in Figure 7.12 supports the value of understanding ecosystems rather than institutions. Regulators, lawmakers, and economists who are engaged in an ongoing effort to maximise the benefits of NFTs and mitigate the risks will benefit from focusing on the ecosystem rather than individual organisations. This is challenging as they face a cryptoassets ecosystem spread across national borders and jurisdictions.

Key concept: There are several blockchain- and token-based solutions beyond cryptocurrencies. They offer opportunities to create new business models by offering a secure way to prove ownership and store and exchange value.

Trust-building tip: When a consumer uses blockchain-based tokens, they typically go through several steps and engage with several organisations. A leader must understand where trust is built, where it is being weakened, and how there is trust transference across the stages of the process.

7.5 The opportunities and challenges of using generative AI

We cannot be a leader if we are a passenger in the implementation of AI and digital transformation. — Dr Alex Zarifis, academic

GenAI offers numerous opportunities and challenges that businesses, developers, and users must navigate to effectively harness its full potential. The starting point should be using this technology to solve problems for customers and staff, not because of the hype around it or a fear of missing out. If our technology providers, consultants, or even our IT department realise we want to throw money at GenAI simply so that we can say we are investing in it to send the right signals to investors, they will 'see us coming' and 'take us to the cleaners'. Once we are clear what problem we want to solve and for who, several key things discussed here need to be done.

In this section, we will first introduce the typical opportunities and challenges, before going into detail on some key issues we must consider when using this technology. These include the most important forms of GenAI and how it needs some constraints through guardrails, how the user interface of AI plays an important role, and the benefits of running GenAI locally rather than on the cloud. After discussing these important aspects of this technology we will turn our attention back to the role of the leader in implementing GenAI.

Opportunities offered by GenAI

We will look at some of the typical opportunities a business faces when applying GenAI before going onto the challenges. We all have some idea about the capabilities of GenAI, but we need to separate out the different benefits so that they are clearer in our mind.

Automation

GenAI can automate existing tasks, but it also offers the opportunity to carry out new automated tasks that were not possible before. Automating existing processes can create efficiencies and help an organisation scale. Current operations and supply chains can be enhanced. Automating new processes that could not be done before enables an organisation to build on their existing strength, but also expand into new areas. It is important to appreciate that automation is not just about efficiency; it opens exciting strategic opportunities. GenAI can automate customer service, especially the onboarding process, content creation, and data analysis, including risk analysis.

Offer insight and solve problems
Insight used to come mainly from an expert's knowledge, statistics, and static algorithms written by humans. GenAI, especially automated AI agents, can draw on larger volumes of data from more sources and offer valuable insights. The benefits are obvious for finance, but there are benefits for all aspects of business. This technology can also present the possible solutions in a variety of ways.

Use digital twins to analyse data and potential scenarios
A digital twin is a digital virtual representation of a system. They are widely used in engineering to predict when components will need service. They do not necessarily need AI to be created, as someone can manually enter several parameters for the virtual model to use, but AI increases their capabilities. While creating a digital twin is still not a trivial task, once a team has this ability, they can use it to play out different scenarios and inform their decision making in a far more sophisticated, expansive way. A well implemented digital twin in a business scenario will draw on diverse information, including regulation, economics, politics, and health risks. Digital twins applied to businesses have identified insights that were completely unexpected to leaders yet are very useful. In a fast-changing environment where not only tactics but also business models need to change regularly, this additional insight can make the difference between staying ahead of the competition and being outmanoeuvred.

Personalised services
The ability to personalise services received a huge boost, first with the internet, then with big data, and now it is getting another big boost with GenAI. While there are privacy concerns when a lot of data is collected on a person, there are also benefits. Many services can be personalised, such as insurance, product recommendations, and marketing campaigns. The consumer experience can be improved by summarising product reviews and having digital live streamers. Even the interaction on a website can be customised to better fit the user without them having to go through many menus to find the information they want. This ability also has a dark side, where organisations, such as online betting agents, take advantage of a person's addiction and lack of willpower.

Innovation
Unlike other technologies, GenAI can appear to be genuinely creative and artistic. While what happens inside the black box is more like mathematics, the end result can appear genuinely creative. It can provide content and inspiration. As there is often

less human interaction in our lives now, content is how an organisation can express their values and make the public engage.

Training staff

In the recent past, one of the capabilities that set leading organisations apart was the ability to provide high-quality training at the induction stage and whenever it was needed thereafter. Many organisations lacked the resources and had to make do with less frequent, lower-quality training. GenAI can potentially offer up-to-date, high-quality training. However, it is debatable if GenAI can be as engaging and motivating as a human, and if the experience will be as rewarding.

The challenges in utilising Generative AI

We will look at some of the typical challenges a business faces when applying GenAI and integrating it with existing systems and workflows. Some of these challenges can be resolved with a good plan, while others need to be mitigated on an ongoing basis.

Wrong decisions, misinformation, and ethical concerns

The price we pay for the capabilities of GenAI is that it is not always accurate. This problem is exacerbated by how convincingly it can present inaccurate or completely fabricated information. These are usually called 'AI hallucinations', which might not fully convey how serious this problem is. If a human provides fabricated information as accurate, they may face some penalty, and many have even lost their job. Famously, former British prime minister Boris Johnson lost his job at *The Times* newspaper over allegations he fabricated a quote from his godfather (Stubley, 2019). Some people trust technology so blindly that, when it is clearly false, we see it simply as a quirk. In some cases these fabricated untruths can be uncovered and corrected, and in others they cannot. Using GenAI with extensive automation means some mistakes will not be noticed. These issues create very serious ethical and moral concerns; safeguards are necessary.

Loss of skills, operational awareness, and knowledge from over-reliance on GenAI

It is tempting to get over-excited by GenAI and over-rely on it. If there is an over-reliance, skills will be lost and it will be difficult to get them back. Over-reliance can cause complacency and a loss of critical thinking skills. Without heavy human involvement in all the operations, an awareness of what is happening can be lost. The obvious answer is to have oversight, but the challenge is that it is harder to offer effective oversight on something we do not regularly do ourselves. It is a little like being a successful football coach without having played the game: it is not impossible, but it is harder. Some fans are even surprised when a coach like Jürgen Klopp is successful because, despite having played the game, he did not play at the highest level.

Trust and privacy

When a user has concerns about their personal information, this tends to negatively affect trust. Most of us would rather keep our personal information private, even if on some occasions we are forced to compromise in order to receive a service. The more sensitive the personal information, the less a user is willing to compromise.

Security

The radically different behaviour of GenAI causes several security concerns. The GenAI used by an organisation can create some security vulnerabilities. Additionally, GenAI in the hands of criminals can create more sophisticated and unpredictable attacks.

Implementation challenges due to the technical complexity

The implementation challenges include a lack of clarity on the future business model and strategy, limited relevant digital skills, resource constraints, and the constantly changing capabilities of GenAI. It is often difficult to understand AI algorithms and their computational requirements.

Fairness

When it is not clear how a decision is made and it is not auditable, questions are raised over fairness. Automation used to be based on human logic captured in static algorithms, but this is not the case with GenAI. Some implementations of GenAI are more like a black box and harder to audit than others. If the dataset used has been curated carefully and there is some kind of mitigation strategy, these issues are reduced.

Respecting intellectual property

GenAI is often trained on material from the internet without permission being taken. Additionally, it can inadvertently create content that resembles something copyrighted. There needs to be clarity and guidelines on the legal implications.

These challenges need to be addressed for the responsible and effective use of GenAI. The issues discussed in the following sections offer us some guidance on how to resolve these challenges.

7.5.1 Most important forms of generative AI

GenAI is not one stand-alone technology but an evolving field of AI with a variety of approaches and techniques. While some AI is designed to tackle a broad range of applications, many AI systems are created with mechanisms focused on specific types of challenges. Typical areas for GenAI to focus on are creating content in textual format, images, video, and music. The first decision a leader needs to make is whether the widely available AI is suitable or if something more specialised is necessary. The five main GenAI mechanisms are presented here.

Pre-trained transformer models

This form of GenAI is pre-trained on large datasets, but it can also be fine-tuned for specific tasks. They can understand text inputted to them such as questions and can give a reasonably coherent answer. While they can be useful for a variety of tasks, they are excellent in translating and summarising. The most common application is probably chatbots.

Generative adversarial networks (GANs)

This mechanism uses two neural networks: the first is the generator and the second is the discriminator. The generator creates new data, and the discriminator uses real data to try to decide if the data presented to it is authentic. This process gradually enables the generator to learn and improve its ability to produce realistic and convincing data. This approach is usually behind AI-generated art and can be used to create realistic images. It can also create fake but realistic data that can be used to train other machine learning models.

Variational autoencoders (VAEs)

These use an artificial neural network architecture for machine learning. An encoder compresses data into a lower-dimensional latent space, and a decoder reconstructs the data from this space. An over-simplistic explanation is to say that two encoders are training themselves. As this method combines autoencoders with probabilistic methods, some understanding of statistics will help someone appreciate the benefits of this method. VAEs are strong at image generation, anomaly detection, and data compression. It is used for natural language processing.

Recurrent neural networks (RNNs)

The mechanism used here is a deep neural network designed for processing sequential data. It can generate sequences of data that are contextually consistent. This method is effective at predicting the next word in a sentence and predicting future data points in a sequence. It can be used for meteorological predictions, speech recognition, language translation, and natural language processing. In the same way, it can also generate music that is decent.

Diffusion probabilistic models

These are latent variable generative models. The diffusion model has three parts: the forward process, the reverse process, and the sampling procedure. They gradually reduce noise through a series of transformation steps. An example is DALL-E, a diffusion-based image generator. In addition to images and audio, this method can model physical phenomena.

In conclusion, there are several popular categories of GenAI technologies. This is a fast-moving area with regular improvements and new ways to tweak the machine learning mechanisms. Each of the mechanisms being used has unique strengths and are better suited for different tasks. For GenAI to improve, it may need a different mechanism, but often the same mechanism with better data is the way to enhance performance.

A business leader will not be able to advance the technology of GenAI – even the CEO of one of the most well-known AI companies has allegedly lost touch with the day-to-day operations according to their staff. However, a business leader must be able to recognise the new opportunities a new development in an AI mechanism creates. A football coach may not fully understand how one of their players has the ability to see a pass to a teammate that others don't, but they know how to utilise that in their team and create a strategy to make the most of it. For example, the coach may tell their wingers to be more ambitious and make more early runs forward in the belief that the skilled passer of the ball will find them even from a great distance. Similarly, a business leader may know their AI can now be accurate with less data and therefore be more ambitious in how it is applied.

Leadership tip: A leader may not be able to fully understand the computer science and statistics behind the GenAI methods, but they must understand the benefits of current mechanisms and appreciate the significance of the new updates that are regularly emerging. A business leader will not be able to advance the technology of GenAI, but they must be able to recognise the new opportunities a new development in an AI mechanism creates.

7.5.2 *Generative AI needs some constraints through guardrails*

From the perspective of a technology provider, accuracy, unintended consequences, and misuse are two major considerations. From the perspective of most other organisations, accuracy and unintended consequences are the biggest considerations and must be addressed before turning to the risk of misuse. If they are not dealt with first, even honest, ethical people can get into trouble. Guardrails can help with all three of these, although in many cases if someone is determined to be mischievous, they will find a way. This may sound a little like an excuse along the lines of 'guns don't kill people, people do', but using the gun metaphor, the logic is similar to first making sure guns don't blow up in our hand before we worry about what criminals will do with them. For example, while harmful content such as false medical advice is a serious issue, it is not something most organisations will have to deal with, and those that do, such as pharmaceutical companies, are well equipped to do so.

Guardrails attempt to contain GenAI content and actions within accurate results and ethical guidelines, promoting positive use of the technology. Guardrails mitigate some, but not all, of the challenges of using AI. While some argue that guardrails are not necessary in the creative industries, many who saw the 2024 Jaguar advert that did not include any cars would argue that some kind of guardrails – not only for machines but also for humans – are necessary. Nevertheless, it could be argued that humans do not need guardrails because they have common sense and instincts, which AI can imitate but cannot possess. What follows is a short overview of some of the reasons why guardrails are necessary in most cases.

Increases accuracy

One of the main challenges discussed is the wrong decisions and misinformation that GenAI can cause, so one of the goals of guardrails is to ensure accuracy and reliability. While many that discuss AI often start with the ethics because that is arguably what is more interesting, when we are talking about a tool that must fulfil a task, we need to start from whether it is good at its reason for existence – its raison d'être. As GenAI can generate content that is incorrect or misleading, guardrails can take some steps such as cross-referencing reliable sources and data. This not only builds trust but stops fresh distrust being created.

Reduce risks of over-reliance

Guardrails cannot magically protect us from all the risks of over-reliance, but they can provide automated processes to engage humans where necessary. This will discourage many from accepting whenever AI does blindly. Humans can be encouraged to verify and critically assess AI-generated decisions and content.

Protecting privacy and supporting trust

Privacy and trust can be two different issues, but they often come hand in hand. Several issues related to AI can shape trust, but privacy concerns are usually at the front of the queue. This is because of how ever-present and invasive this technology can be. Guardrails can automate measures such as local processing, data minimisation, and anonymisation to reduce the risk of exposing personal information. Guardrails should ensure that AI behaves in a predictable and safe way and be as transparent as possible.

Support ethical behaviour

Guardrails can enforce principles such as transparency, accountability, and fairness. They can also try to stop the technology being used to harm humans. For example, if someone wants to 3D-print a gun, this could be stopped.

Legal and regulatory compliance

Keeping up with regulation is by no means a challenge specific to AI. Organisations in highly regulated sectors need support from specialised automated systems to be able to do this. For example, many companies need to adhere to EU data protection laws, such as GDPR, that are very different to the Wild West-style approach in some places. AI guardrails should also cover this issue. There are two schools of thought: one illustrated by Twitter before it was sold, saying we need large departments of specialists to ensure we are close to both regulation and the values of the community we are in; the second, illustrated by X, is that all this oversight should also be automated to achieve the best results. In addition to the typical regulations each industry has, in many cases there are regulatory and legal expectations in terms of security and reporting breaches.

In conclusion, guardrails can support the accurate, legal, trustworthy, and safe deployment of AI. Having these safeguards can address many of the challenges, but not all.

7.5.3 The user interface with AI plays an important role

The UI is usually important in information systems, and this is no different with AI. Many of the principles of UI design from other information systems also carry over to this technology. A medium or large tech company will have UI experts, but a leader must have an understanding of the key issues. The UI does not always have a strategic significance, but there are cases, such as the Revolut online only bank, where the UI was one of the strategic advantages from the start. A UI cannot always be easily copied if the technology and data making it possible is hard to replicate. When we talk about a leader having a clear vision this, incudes the UI.

In marketing they have a term 'touchpoints', meaning where a consumer comes into contact with an organisation. It is hardly revolutionary to think about these interactions, but the point is to focus on these as this is where the consumer experiences them and forms opinions about an organisation. An otherwise capable organisation with a bad UI is unlikely to succeed. An example of the importance of understanding specific touchpoints is that, in the early 2000s, many Mercedes car owners felt the quality had dipped. One point raised was that the car door no longer closed with the satisfying, reassuring sound that made it clear it had shut properly. An engineer at the time would probably argue the engineering of the car was not inferior and that the door making a certain sound was not important. However, that touchpoint, rightly or wrongly, was one of the ways a consumer experienced the engineering and drew their conclusions.

Some of the typical challenges for AI are also a consideration for the interface. These include transparency, privacy, and ethics. Other issues, such as user-centric design and aesthetics, are more central to the UI design.

User-centric design and appealing aesthetics

These are probably the first things most of us think of when we hear 'user interface' – and rightly so. The interface should be simple, easy to navigate, and provide feedback so the user knows that their inputs have been received. It should be easy to use for novices. Authentication should also be easy by being part of a wider platform or some other solution. As the technology adoption models discussed show, ease of use is always a consideration. The role of aesthetics goes beyond being simply visually pleasing; they can convey the character of an organisation. This point is particularly noticeable on websites of luxury brands. A consistent design language conveys a sense of professionalism. Offering customisations and visual appeal increases the level of engagement a user feels. Offering ways to give ratings and feedback will build a community around the organisation and stop someone who was disappointed from venting their frustrations elsewhere.

Fast responses

Load times and responses need to be fast. In the recent past, this used to be a challenge when a member of staff was searching their company database for some simple information such as a customer's contact details. Now, these basic searches are so fast they are perceived to be instant, but as GenAI is asked complex questions, it can take some time to respond. Often the initial response is not entirely satisfying, so getting to the final answer can take even longer. Resource management and scalability are necessary so that the performance is sufficient even when the level of use changes.

Transparency, control, ethics, privacy, and security

For someone using GenAI to feel they are in control of what is happening, many things need to be in place, starting with transparency. A related point to transparency is explainability. GenAI should be able to explain its decisions. When the user has this information, they should then be able to shape the behaviour of AI by adjusting some parameters. These parameters should also include the consent we give to our personal information being used. For most of us, this is by using some specific phrases in our interaction with GenAI. The user interface should also encourage ethical behaviour, with content moderation and prompts encouraging ethical use. Prompts have been used in social media to encourage ethical behaviour with some success. If someone writes a hurtful post, a prompt asks them if they are sure they want to send that. These prompts encourage ethical behaviour without limiting someone's freedom. The user still has the final say.

   In conclusion, creating an effective UI for GenAI requires a user-centred design and several other design principles, but also a solid strategy and technology supporting it.

7.5.4 Benefits of running GenAI locally and not on the cloud

One of the biggest changes in the past decade or so has been software moving from an organisation's server to the cloud. This was partly because internet speeds allowed for this, and partly because being able to scale and use more data was becoming more important. This approach has some weaknesses, such as concerns over whether we truly have sovereignty, privacy, and security over our data and operations. Assuming cloud services are secure is a little like not locking our house's front door and hoping our neighbour cares more about our security than we do and will keep an eye on it for us. We live in a world where, for an increasing number of us, money is everything, so we should not expect others to sacrifice one penny for our security. If money can be made by providing a backdoor, this will often happen.

Cloud computing is not going away, but with the rise in processing power of personal devices such as laptops and phones, the growing number of sensors they contain, and the increasing use of GenAI, more processing can be done locally.

The naive argument often used is that what organizations put on the cloud is not their core operations. This sounds more like the kind of lie we tell ourselves to feel better about cost cutting we know deep down will lead to problems down the line. Challenges to the use of AI identified, such as privacy and security, can be mitigated using a localised approach. However, the potential benefits go beyond enhanced security and privacy. As with many issues relating to technology, this approach offers opportunities to increase efficiency but also to innovate and create new business models. Some of the potential benefits are listed below.

Security, privacy, and data sovereignty

In many parts of the world, data sovereignty is a legal requirement and transferring data across borders is not straightforward. Regardless of legal requirements, in some scenarios we can build safer solutions without sacrificing performance. For some situations, such as analysing health data, it is better not to transmit all the information over the internet. An example is a solution I worked on with the Red Cross in Spain, where they provided some health monitoring equipment to the elderly. If an issue arose at home, the Red Cross would be automatically alerted. Not all the information collected by the various sensors needs to be transmitted over the internet. A signal only needs to be sent when the sensors and local processing of their data conclude that help is needed.

Reduced latency and offline functionality

When the processing happens locally, less data needs to be sent back and forth to the cloud. Even with the internet speeds we have today, local sensors may be collecting vast amounts of data that are better off analysed locally in some scenarios. Real-time analysis can be provided with a more seamless experience. While being able to use AI without the internet may still sound like a 'good-to-have' rather than a 'must-have', the more dependent we become on it for our work, the more we will want to be able to keep working even when we do not have access to the internet. An example where all of these issues play out is self-driving cars.

Being in control
Typically when the AI is running locally, we can decide what updates and customisations to make. While this takes extra time, the additional flexibility to adapt to the specific needs the organisation has is beneficial in many cases.

More economical
The biggest argument for an organisation to move their services to the cloud is that it is more economical. It might be surprising to some that now the argument to do more locally is that it is more economical. However, more experienced leaders will be well aware that we are in the age of the 'bate-and-switch' and 'enshittification'. Cloud usage fees and data transfer costs often go up. Furthermore, local processing uses less energy and can contribute to greener computing practices.

In summary, while running AI locally may not completely replace company servers and cloud hosting services, it can have some benefits. Some of these benefits, such as privacy and data sovereignty, address significant challenges AI faces. This makes running AI on local devises particularly appealing. Figure 7.13 shows how an LLM is hosted locally.

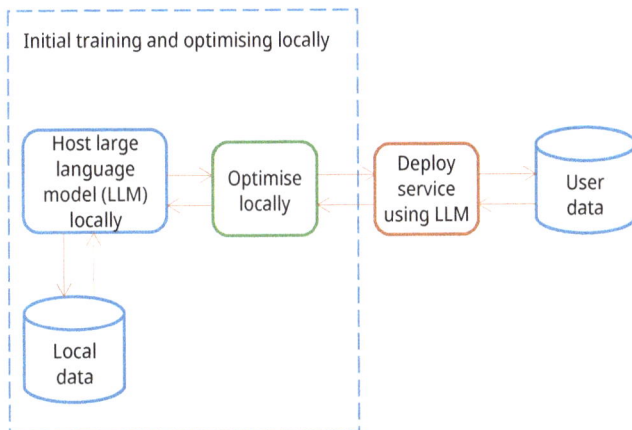

Figure 7.13: Hosting a large language model (LLM) locally.

7.5.5 The role of the leader in implementing generative AI
It is telling that even in a section focused on AI, the discussion has to link the technology to the process of digital transformation, business models, and strategy. We cannot be a leader if we are a passenger in the implementation of AI and digital transforma-

tion. A leader needs to weigh up various factors to ensure the best adoption process. Here are some key issues to consider.

Digital transformation process, final business model, and encouraging adoption

The starting point for our thought process does not need to be the same, but all the issues discussed here need to be covered. The starting point for the thought process can be noticing a new business model a similar organisation in another part of the world is using or identifying some use cases of GenAI to start with. Regardless of where the analysis of our options starts, we need to arrive at a point where there is strategic alignment and a sufficient return on investment. Even if new services are being added, every effort needs to be made to be more streamlined. There needs to be a plan for change management, but also a mentality of continuous improvement. The continuous improvement needs to cover all aspects of the business, but the consumer experience and getting the most out of AI must be priorities. While being data-driven, we need to also develop our knowledge and judgement. Being data-driven in a bad way can leave us open to being manipulated.

Optimal technology infrastructure and data management

The new AI solutions need to be seamlessly integrated with existing systems and workflows. The way AI is used should be scalable along with the rest of the infrastructure. High-quality data and not AI is often the competitive advantage, so this is a key battleground for a leader. The necessary agreements need to be made so that the required data can be accessed. A data governance framework is necessary to oversee data collection, storage, processing, and usage. The heavy reliance on technology means staff may need to be upskilled and new experts may need to be brought in.

Cybersecurity and risk management

I researched the risks to business from ransomware attacks and tried to make business leaders appreciate that cybersecurity is not just a technical issue but also a business issue, and that the risks are also financial, reputational, and legal (Zarifis & Cheng, 2018; Zarifis et al., 2022). It can even kill off a business. More business leaders are gradually appreciating this now. A risk management strategy is needed to identify, assess, and mitigate potential cybersecurity threats and the additional risks caused by GenAI.

Regulatory compliance

With AI and automation giving opportunities to scale and add more services, it is important to understand industry-specific regulations and broader data protection laws. For many small organisations, regulatory compliance involves following rules, but larger organisations can take a more proactive approach to interpreting and shaping regulation. Twitter was in a position before Elon Musk bought them where 'everyone and their dog' saw themselves as regulators of what was said there. Many are passionate about supporting free speech as long as it is one hundred percent in line with their views. Elon Musk turned the tables and by creating the Department of Government Efficiency (DOGE) and got power over many parts of the US government.

Ethics, privacy, and transparency

The best practices on ethics for every industry should be followed during both the development and deployment of AI. There needs to be transparency about how AI processes data. Care must be taken when using sensitive data. Robust data anonymisation and encryption practices are necessary. There need to be clear accountability for AI decisions, with no room for anyone to hide from their responsibilities. It needs to be clear who is responsible for monitoring AI outputs and addressing the issues that arise. As more and more of us interact with an organisation's AI, the harder it will get to hide mistakes and 'sweep them under the carpet'.

By addressing these issues, a leader can leverage GenAI to drive innovation while maintaining ethical standards.

Key concept: There are some typical challenges to applying AI, such as transparency and privacy concerns. Despite us moving into unchartered territories with this innovation to some degree, there are proven solutions for these challenges, such as implementing guardrails.

Leadership tip: The implementation of GenAI must not lead to a loss of accountability. We cannot be a true leader if we are a passenger in the implementation of AI. It must be clear who is responsible for every aspect of what AI does.

7.6 Summary

> *If you have been playing poker for half an hour and you do not know who the patsy is, you're the patsy.* — Warren Buffett, businessman and investor

There are many reasons why a leader must understand some key concepts of the most recent technology in order to get the most out of their team and AI. The casual observer will see the end result of a great leader's ability to get things done through others and technology, but they may miss the preparation that happened beforehand. For example, if we think of iconic leaders such as Napoleon Bonaparte, the casual observer may think he only had the charisma necessary to inspire soldiers. However, if we look at the start of his career, it was not his leadership charisma but his understanding of how to use technology (cannons and mortars) to achieve strategic objectives that set him apart. Soldiers, politicians, and citizens started to respect and admire him because of this knowledge that enabled him to get results. What many interpret as charisma is not the cause of a person's success, but the aura of authority of someone that has achieved success.

A leader that has prepared and has at least some insight to offer will also encourage a better engagement from all stakeholders in how to move forward and have more chance of directing discussions towards a clear decision. A passive, ill-informed 'leader' may not be generously given a solution and a clear plan on how to move forward by other stakeholders, instead remaining in a perpetual state of confusion and indecision.

There is no simple solution that fits every situation, but there is a lot of science behind the models of technology adoption discussed here. A leader should not feel overwhelmed by the complexity of the modern globalised world with its constant relentless innovation. Being clear on what problem they are attempting to solve and relying on proven models will be helpful. These models provide a strong foundation for leadership decisions:
- The stages of diffusion of innovation and the typical challenges at each stage (section 7.2).
- TAM and the challenges at each stage (section 7.3).
- Models of trust in technology (section 7.4)
- The opportunities and challenges of using GenAI (section 7.5)

By understanding the typical process workers in projects go through, the typical process new technology and innovation undergo, and the key issues when developing applications that utilise GenAI, the leader can develop a strategy and vision to get the most out of their team and AI. I researched virtual worlds and the metaverse the first time there was a lot of hype around them (Zarifis & Kokkinaki, 2015). Instead of trying to predict the future, I focused on clarifying what their relative advantage was for businesses compared to existing solutions. Similarly, a business leader, while not a technology expert, must be an expert in identifying what the relative advantage of a new technology is for business compared to existing solutions. This needs to be done as soon as possible. A business leader innovates effectively rather than 'placing a bet' on a technology and being bullish or bearish. If a leader is outmanoeuvred by their competitor's innovation, they end up being like the patsy in a poker game.

Many of us talk about the importance of a leader showing empathy, but when technology is involved, understanding what to show empathy about is not always so easy. An example is the challenges parents face in understanding the pressures social media put on their children. Many understand that there is an issue there, but what is it exactly? Is it bullying, lack of privacy, pressure to buy expensive products? The same applies to trust. AI can be applied in one scenario and increase trust by creating a more reliable service, while in an another, it can raise privacy concerns.

A leader needs to understand how technology changes relationships and business models to be able to act. A leader that has broad horizons and is constantly comparing different leadership styles, applications of technologies, business models, and contexts will be much stronger.

7.7 Exercises

Exercise 7.1

AI, globalisation, and regulation

AI makes scaling a business and moving into new markets easier. It is not an exaggeration to say that AI is moving us into a new stage of globalisation.

Questions

1) Taking into account what has been discussed here, do you think every country should have their own policies, regulations, and laws on the use of AI? If so, what are the key issues that should be covered?

2) If a company breaches a country's rules on AI, what should the punishment be? Should fines be proportional to the money made? Should they be banned from operating in the country? What would be a strong deterrent?

Exercise 7.2

The consumer's relationship with an organisation through technology

It is important to be able to evaluate the consumer's relationship with an organisation through technology. It is also important to be able to analyse the key choices an organisation can make to utilise technology to optimise their relationship with the consumer, both with their direct interaction and their broader operations.

Scenario: You have been hired by a startup that wants to design and offer a better digital wallet focussed on consumers that want to make purchases with cryptocurrencies. It may have facilities for investors, but the focus is on making purchases of products and services from regular offline and online stores.

Questions

1) Review existing digital wallets. Identify ten strengths and ten weaknesses. Also identify the three wallets with the best functionality and rank them. They might not be the most popular ones. Try to incorporate the material covered here where relevant.

2) For the new digital wallet you will design, what functionality would you want? Would you prioritise some features to create your niche? For example, security or ease of use?

Exercise 7.3

The opportunities of generative AI
Scenario: You work for a startup fintech company that wants to offer services through APIs to financial institutions such as banks, other payment providers, and insurers.

Question

Your manager asks you to research the developments in generative AI for the last six months, identify three new opportunities that have appeared, and present them to the team. The structure of the presentation should include: (1) explaining the new developments in generative AI, (2) the relative advantage provided by the new developments, (3) the financial service that can be provided, including how it would influence the business model of the fintech or its clients, and finally (4) what competitors are doing in this space.

Space for your notes

References

Davis, F. D. (1989). *Perceived usefulness, perceived ease of use, and user acceptance of information technology.* *MIS Quarterly, 13*(3), 319–340. https://doi.org/10.2307/249008

European Commission. (2019). *Ethics guidelines for trustworthy AI.* https://ec.europa.eu/digital

He, J., Baxter, S. L., Xu, J., Xu, J., Zhou, X., & Zhang, K. (2019). The practical implementation of artificial intelligence technologies in medicine. *Nature Medicine, 25*(1), 30–36. https://doi.org/10.1038/s41591-018-0307-0

Stubley, B. (2019, 25 May). Boris Johnson: The most infamous lies and untruths by the Conservative leadership candidate. *The Independent.* https://www.independent.co.uk/news/uk/politics/boris-johnson-lies-conservative-leader-candidate-list-times-banana-brexit-bus-a8929076.html

Venkatesh, V., Morris, M. G., Davis, G. B., & Davis, F. D. (2003). User acceptance of information technology: Toward a unified view. *MIS Quarterly, 27*(3), 425–478. https://doi.org/10.2307/30036540

Su, L., Cheng, X., & Zarifis, A. (2025). Passengers as defenders: Unveiling the role of customer-company identification in the trust–customer citizenship behaviour relationship within the ride-hailing context. *Tourism Management, 107,* 105086. https://doi.org/10.1016/j.tourman.2024.105086

Zarifis, A., & Castro, L. A. (2022). The NFT purchasing process and the challenges to trust at each stage. *Sustainability, 14*(24), 16482, 1–13. https://doi.org/10.3390/su142416482

Zarifis, A., & Cheng, X. (2018). The impact of extended global ransomware attacks on trust: How the attacker's competence and institutional trust influence the decision to pay. *Proceedings of the Americas Conference on Information Systems (AMCIS),* 2–11. https://aisel.aisnet.org/amcis2018/Security/Presentations/31/

Zarifis, A., & Cheng, X. (2024). How to build trust in answers given by Generative AI for specific, and vague, financial questions. *Journal of Electronic Business & Digital Economics, 3*(3), 236–250. https://doi.org/10.1108/JEBDE-11-2023-0028

Zarifis, A., Cheng, X., Dimitriou, S., & Efthymiou, L. (2015). Trust in digital currency enabled transactions model. *Proceedings of the Mediterranean Conference on Information Systems (MCIS),* 1–8. https://aisel.aisnet.org/mcis2015/3/

Zarifis, A., Cheng, X., Jayawickrama, U., & Corsi, S. (2022). Can global, extended and repeated ransomware attacks overcome the user's status quo bias and cause a switch of system? *International Journal of Information Systems in the Service Sector (IJISSS), 14*(1), 1–16. https://doi.org/10.4018/IJISSS.289219

Zarifis, A., Efthymiou, L., Cheng, X., & Demetriou, S. (2014). Consumer trust in digital currency enabled transactions. *Lecture Notes in Business Information Processing, 183,* 241–254. https://doi.org/10.1007/978-3-319-11460-6

Zarifis, A., & Fu, S. (2024). The second extended model of consumer trust in cryptocurrency payments, CRYPTOTRUST 2. *Frontiers in Blockchain, 7,* 1–11. https://doi.org/10.3389/fbloc.2024.1220031

Zarifis A., Kawalek P. & Azadegan A. (2021). Evaluating if trust and personal information privacy concerns are barriers to using health insurance that explicitly utilizes AI, *Journal of Internet Commerce, 20,* 66–83. https://doi.org/10.1080/15332861.2020.1832817

Zarifis, A., & Kokkinaki, A. (2015). The relative advantage of collaborative virtual environments and two-dimensional websites in multichannel retail. In W. Abramowicz (Ed.), *Business Information Systems. BIS 2015* (pp. 233–244). *Lecture Notes in Business Information Processing* (Vol. 208). Springer, Cham. https://doi.org/10.1007/978-3-319-19027-3_19

Chapter 8
Leading in digital transformation with six business models optimised for AI

8.1 Introduction

Men trust their ears less than their eyes. — Herodotus, ancient Greek historian and geographer

8.1.1 Using an AI-focused business model to lead in digital transformation

The point is made here several times that a modern leader must understand technology, particularly AI, so one would be forgiven for asking: Why not get someone with a computer science degree to be a leader? That is what most tech companies do, and many of them are doing very well. There are indeed many great leaders and entrepreneurs with computer science degrees, but they have the opposite challenge of having to learn the business side. Most people are more naturally inclined to the technical or business side. Whether we start with a more technical degree or a business degree, we have to educate ourselves to become comfortable with both. It is worth thinking about this simple question: What is more important in digital transformation – understanding the new technologies or understanding the current business of an organisation? The answer, of course, is that they are both necessary for success.

Based on a sound understanding of the technology and the stakeholders' beliefs on them, the typical way innovations diffuse – and some proven business models that make the most of AI – a leader can choose their destination and the shortest path there. There may be more than one right choice, but there are, most certainly, choices that are clearly wrong or extremely risky. For example, if we are a startup and we plan to go toe to toe with an established incumbent with more resources in the hope that we antagonise them enough so that they buy us out, that is a very high-risk strategy. It is equally possible that the incumbent will do everything they can to kill our business off to send a message to other startups. Finding a way to get an advantage is necessary.

It can be challenging to get the balance right when replacing some tasks humans do with AI. For some time, the most popular approach was to focus on augmenting a worker's role so that AI takes over some of their more repetitive and standardised tasks. This appeared to be getting the best of both worlds, but it often leads to a fragmentation of roles and tasks between the worker and AI that is counterproductive. Time is wasted and errors can be introduced when the task is handed over between the two. On a higher level of abstraction, new business models that were intended to be optimised for AI have in many cases underperformed compared to traditional models.

https://doi.org/10.1515/9783111630137-008

As discussed, it is important to first understand what the problem we want to solve with AI is, and for that to guide us. We may start from one problem (many digital transformations do), but eventually we need to think more strategically about how AI is changing our business model, and the business models of our existing and future competitors. Thankfully, there are proven business models we will discuss here.

When we try to understand a business model in depth, we need to understand some key aspects of what the organisation does. Traditionally when we looked at business models, we focused on cost structures, key partnerships, key activities, resources, income streams, customer relationships, channels such as offline or virtual worlds (Zarifis, 2019), value offerings, and customer groups. Today we must also focus on the key technology AI and how to build trust in how it is being used.

There are business models that will help organisations already active in an area fully utilise AI, and there are business models for organisations to use the new opportunities created by AI to move into new areas. As per Zarifis and Cheng (2023, 2025), the six business models proven to be ideal for an organisation with AI at its centre are: (1) focus on one part of the value chain and disaggregate, (2) absorb AI into existing model, (3) an incumbent expanding beyond their current model to fully utilise the opportunities of AI and access new data, (4) a startup disruptor focused on one sector, built from the start to be highly automated, (5) a disruptor focused on tech adding a new service such as insurance, and (6) a disruptor that is not necessarily tech-focused but has an extensive user or fanbase. This is the first look at business models optimised for AI and other disruptive technologies such as blockchain. We will go into these business models in greater depth later.

8.1.2 Are we a leader of just people, or a leader of people, innovation, and technology?

Project management, diffusion of innovation, and technology adoption are usually seen as three separate areas. In the past, if we were a manager, we were expected to be interested in project management, if we were involved in research and development or marketing, we would be interested in the diffusion of innovation, and if we were experts in information systems, we were focused on the process of technology adoption. This was when business changed more gradually, and a different person could worry about each of these things. At that time, a leader focused on managing their team and got advice from the IT department, consultants, or technology providers about how to use technology. The leader today is constantly playing catchup with technology, so they need to become good at doing this. We must be able to know when to move, how fast to move, and crucially, how far we want to go. We constantly face this question: There is an interesting new technology – should I update a process or pivot the whole business model? There is a spectrum from updating a process to pivoting the whole business model. This spectrum, along with some typical examples, is illustrated in figure 8.1.

AI and other technologies such as blockchain are increasing the level of automation and reducing the role humans have. This is the reality, and we are only at the beginning. While there is some truth in the point many make about AI enriching our professional lives and not replacing many of us, the trend is clear. Organisations need to keep adopting new technologies, but we cannot just assume everything new is better. We need to have good judgement of what we are replacing.

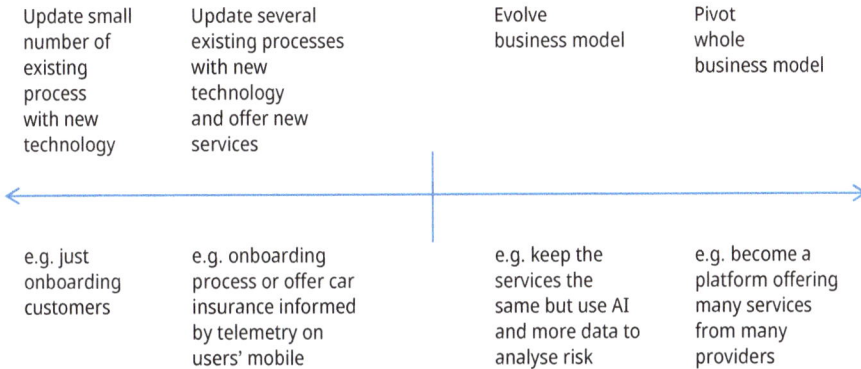

Update small number of existing process with new technology	Update several existing processes with new technology and offer new services		Evolve business model	Pivot whole business model
e.g. just onboarding customers	e.g. onboarding process or offer car insurance informed by telemetry on users' mobile		e.g. keep the services the same but use AI and more data to analyse risk	e.g. become a platform offering many services from many providers

Figure 8.1: The spectrum from updating a process to pivoting the whole business model.

While Elon Musk may not be the best example of how to build trust, he is an example of a leader that both leads people and innovates with technology. In his case, we could argue he believes that if someone leads in technology, the people will follow. The decisive change from Twitter to X suggests this. It was a very decisive pivot of a business model that did not seem to take into account many stakeholders, especially the staff of Twitter. We may need to be a form of oligopoly to be able to lead such a change, but what is certain is that leading with technology is increasingly necessary. If we face more competition than being one of a handful of social media companies, we will probably not survive so much destruction of trust.

Key concept: Know what to focus on at each stage and in each context, both for the team and for AI. Prioritise in the best way possible.

The rest of this chapter will focus on specific business models that have been proven to enable an organisation to fully utilise technology. First we will cover the six business models to thrive with AI (8.2), and then business models not focused on AI but other technologies such as blockchain (8.3). With all the strategies discussed, building trust needs to be planned and 'baked in' at the business model level. To bring our A(I) game, we need to build trust. Finally, there will be the summary and some exercises. The theories presented in the rest of this chapter will help the leader frame a situation and make a decision, regardless of what leadership approach they choose.

8.2 The six business models to thrive with AI

Trust only movement. Life happens at the level of events, not of words. Trust movement. — Alfred Adler, medical doctor and psychotherapist

In most sectors of the economy, the digital transformation driven by AI is, to some degree, predictable – such as increased automation – but also unpredictable: will it increase competition or concentrate power to a small number of oligopolies? While we cannot know all the answers before we start a journey, we can clarify enough points to give us a clear direction, so we know where we want to be in five years and try to get there in a straight line without too much zigzagging in different directions.

The idea of utilising a business model is not so much about forcing a structure onto others. It is more about understanding what works in terms of the technology, organisation, staff, and consumers, and implementing a solution that works for everyone. Staff and consumers have something to gain from AI, but also something to lose. AI increases the data and information held on both staff and consumers, so the already existing information asymmetry gets worse. As this asymmetry gets stronger, it is tempting for many organisations to offer increasingly worse conditions to staff and worse services to consumers. More and more information relating to how the decisions are made can be concealed, increasing the moral hazard.

A new sustainable business should go in the opposite direction, making sure staff and consumers are compensated for what they lose. A sustainable business model focused on AI should avoid increasing the information asymmetry and, if possible, offer lower prices or a better service, using AI to strengthen the consumer's knowledge on the services they are using.

A leader may not have a clear vision about what the business model should be right from the start, but at some point, they should. The sooner they arrive at this clear vision the better; looking at the six business models for organisations to thrive with AI will help. We might simply choose one of the models or combine them. Even if they are not ideal for our situation, they will at least help us in our thought process to arrive at the model we want. It is crucial to be able to think about the technologies in the context of our business. An amazing technology might not actually be compatible with what we are doing; a boring old technology implemented in a clever new way might actually be a better innovation.

The leader needs to educate, or at least signpost the team on what needs to be done. It is hard, if not impossible, to build trust without having a clear vision. It is natural for some of us to resent dramatically new ways of doing things. When something new comes along, something old dies. Many of us get attached to our current lives and our recent past and don't want to let go. A convincing vision of a better future will help with this.

In the past, technology moved slower, so adapting to its new capabilities had to happen less frequently – a leader could go through their whole career and retire with-

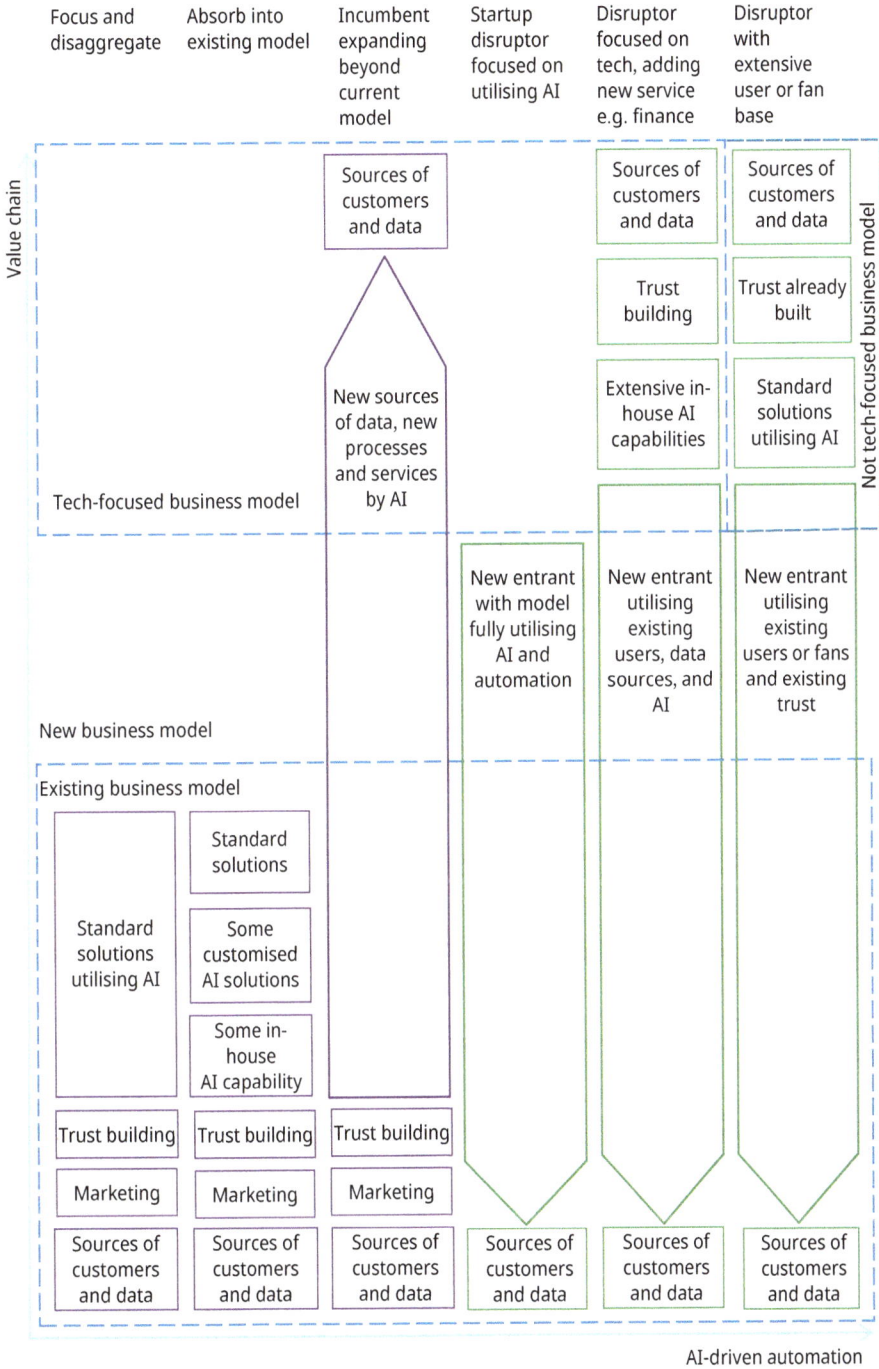

Figure 8.2: The six business models to utilise AI and build trust (previously presented in Chapter 1).

out needing to change their organisation's business model. Now, change is faster, and developing new strategies and processes is a key skill. Therefore, having a clear business model in mind has to be used along with the other theories discussed in this chapter, regardless of the leadership style preferred.

Figure 8.2 shows a model with six business models that are optimised for AI and blockchain. Previous research identified five optimised business models (Zarifis & Cheng, 2023). The models are (1) focus and disaggregate, (2) absorb into existing model, (3) incumbent expanding beyond current model, (4) startup disruptor focused on one sector, (5) disruptor focused on tech adding a new service such as insurance, and (6) disruptor with extensive user or fanbase. The first three models involve organisations that are already active in a sector, such as finance or retail. The last three models are new organisations using AI to move into a new area.

While the sixth model has similarities to the fourth and fifth, as it is an organisation coming from outside the sector, it also has some distinct features. The first key difference is that it has an existing user base with which trust has already been built. The second key difference is that it uses advanced but commoditised technology. So, unlike the fourth and fifth models, the key advantage does not come from the technology, but from the existing user base that already trusts the organisation. It is important to appreciate that sometimes the best way to innovate is with commoditised technology that can be applied quickly.

Now that the six business models' main priorities have been introduced, we will next look at each of them in more detail. It is important to understand all six business models, even if the one that will be used is already clear to us, as our competitors will be using the others.

Key concept: Despite the unrelenting pace of innovation, there are six proven business models to utilise AI and build trust that can serve as a starting point for an organisation going through digital transformation.

Leadership tip: When choosing one of the six business models, the leader needs to understand what the competitors will most likely be doing in the next four or five years. Implementing a business model takes some time, so many organisations will only get one chance at getting this right.

8.2.1 Focus and disaggregate, lead on one application of AI

In this model, the organisation implements a smaller part of the value chain, with the priority being to narrow the focus. Growth is achieved through complementarities with partners (Zott & Amit, 2017). There are several ways to implement this in terms of who does what for the rest of the value chain. The most popular approaches are to become part of an ecosystem of many independent organisations that collaborate in an integrated way. A second is to join a platform that takes care of a part of the value chain and makes the organisation's services easier to use by others. The third way is to merge with other companies in the sector.

The third way is to merge with other companies in the sector. This approach to focusing and disaggregating may be less obvious in some ways. The ideal scenario is that two or more organisations with complementary strengths come together so that they can provide a bigger breadth of services to consumers. For some, the third approach is less obvious, especially when there is so much enthusiasm for dynamic loosely knit ecosystems. Technologies such as blockchain can provide the infrastructure for loosely knit ecosystems, which could be a more efficient approach to collaborating. For this reason, taking the decision to deal with the challenges of AI with a merger may seem a little old school. The boards of directors of large organisations do, however, have many old-school managers. When an old-school manager sees turmoil and uncertainty ahead, their instinct is often to merge. It couldn't be a more basic human instinct: strength in numbers. It is, however, often a good approach. In China, they have super-apps that provide many services in parallel, so it is inevitable that things will go in that direction. We will have a combination of small companies that work together in a way that masks the complexity of what is happening to the consumer, and 'big beasts' that try to offer all the services. Often, a large company may be able to complete all of the value chain themselves, but they prefer to outsource part of it to a smaller company so they do not have the legal liability that comes with that task. As discussed, X is an example of an attempt to create a one-stop shop. There is a wave of mergers and acquisitions in the insurance and banking sector for these reasons. An example is the acquisition of Direct Line by Aviva. Both are strong British insurers, but Aviva also offers savings, investments, and retirement services. We could speculate that these moves are a recognition of two things: (a) AI's economy-bending automation means fewer companies are needed, and (b) we need to offer a breadth of services.

The principle behind the focus-and-disaggregate strategy is to find a way to operate that suits the size and competencies of the organisation. For example, if Europe will have far fewer insurers in the future, an insurer needs to either become larger or offer services to the larger insurers. If an insurer has a customer base and is strong in attracting new consumers, they may choose to focus on that and outsource most of the other processes. Other organisations in the value chain may be better positioned with stronger in-house AI capabilities and higher-quality data for AI to use. Becoming a smaller part of the value chain can be seen as an effective way to become part of a larger ecosystem. It is hard for a UK car insurer to provide car insurance in many countries, but it might be easier to provide image recognition or risk analysis across the world. Another example is that ride-hailing services, such as DiDi, need to insure passengers for one trip. This is a very small service, but it can be provided at a very large scale.

Growth through complementarities

When disaggregating and focusing on one part of the supply chain, it is important to achieve growth through complementarities with partners. Growth comes from attracting partners and utilising the available ecosystems better than others. Either by outsourcing or being part of an ecosystem, synergies need to be optimised. Increasingly, the most important synergies needed are around data. As discussed, it is often the data not the AI that is the main differentiator that gives a relevant advantage. Machine learning works better with extensive data. As this model does not involve expanding and accessing new sources of data directly, it may lead to an insufficient volume and breadth of data. An organisation needs to overcome the limited data they may have, otherwise they will have less ability to identify trends and train machine learning and large language models. A traditional bank or insurer that covers a large part of the value chain will be seen as a competitor by others, and they may be reluctant to share data. A focused and disaggregated bank or insurer may be seen more as a partner and data may be shared more willingly. When sharing data, it is important to be able to anonymise it and follow regulations such as the EU general data protection regulation (GDPR).

The role of AI in the disaggregate business model

There are several variations of this model, so the way AI is applied also varies. One approach is to use standardised off-the-shelf AI solutions with limited customisations. This is done, firstly, because they are considered sufficiently suitable for the job, and secondly, because the organisation is smaller, has fewer resources, and a smaller IT department. There are limitations to off-the-shelf solutions, but the benefit is that the updates, including security updates, are automatic. The uniqueness, or the relative advantage, does not necessarily have to come from the technology, even in the AI-centred world we are moving into. There is another variation of this business model where the technology is indeed central to what the organisation offers their ecosystem. This can be the machine learning itself, the data, or the whole automated process.

How to build trust with the focus-and-disaggregate business model

When faced with the economy-bending force of AI, choosing to focus and disaggregate is similar to the very common strategy of outsourcing. As with many strategies, it is very easy to make a strong case for the value of outsourcing, but implementing it is harder. Doing fewer things in-house creates challenges for quality, increasing the risk of problems and the need for trust. An organisation applying this strategy must clearly identify where risks emerge and who needs to build trust. This must not be left to chance. As building trust often involves some extra steps that can cost time and money, it needs to be made clear who in the ecosystem will pay for it.

If it is a merger then things are simpler, but it is worth reflecting on the trust-building capabilities of the organisations merging. There needs to be clarity on what trust-building capabilities each part of the new organisation has, going beyond the over-simplistic notion of how much consumers trust the brand. Marketing teams have a very valuable contribution to make to trust building, but it must not be entirely left to them. It must be addressed at every part of the value chain, whether it is within or outside the organisation. In the world of AI, in a sense, everything is different and everything is the same, as these issues already existed to some degree. For example, many companies have their own staff doing quality control checks on the premises of suppliers to ensure everything is done properly across the supply chain.

The leader must be at the centre of trust building across the value chain, making the necessary agreements and enforcing them. This, of course, is only possible if they understand the interplay of AI with the business model and the stakeholders. The leader should also ensure the principles and values of the organisation are upheld across the complex ecosystem and are still clear to all stakeholders.

Key concept: It is hard for most organisations to lead on AI across many parts of the value chain. With the focus-and-disaggregate business model, an organisation can lead in one AI application or process. By focusing on a smaller part of the value chain, the value added can be offered more broadly to many partners across the whole eco-systems.

Leadership tip: With the focus-and-disaggregate business model, the benefit comes from complementarities and creating synergies. A leader needs to be clear on what they have to offer and what they need in return.

Trust-building tip: Doing fewer things in-house brings challenges to quality. This increases the risks and the need for trust. An organisation applying this strategy must clearly identify where risks emerge and who needs to build trust.

8.2.2 Absorb AI into existing model, avoiding significant changes to it

The second model is the logical next option after the first. While the first model focuses on a smaller part of the value chain than before, the second model involves covering the same part of the value chain as before. On a high level of abstraction, the business model stays the same as before, and the process of digital transformation simply tries to find a more efficient and effective way to implement it. AI is used across the organisation's value chain but does not change the model. AI is forced to align with existing business goals and is integrated into existing services. As the model does not change, not all the new opportunities that emerge from AI are utilised. New sources of data are not accessed either.

There are football coaches that try to find the best system for the players they have, and there are football coaches that have a certain philosophy that they expect whichever players they have to adapt to. The same applies to businesses with similar advantages and disadvantages. There are benefits to constantly adapting to get the best out of the tools we have at our disposal, and there are benefits to having a clear identity so we, and others, know what we are about. Many organisations convey their values and try to connect with stakeholders based on those values instead of trying to cover every aspect of what they do. Having a clear, relatively stable identity helps with that. Many of us appreciate organisations that appear to have a consistency and authenticity, such as Barbour jackets, for example.

Within the limitations of the current business model, AI can still offer many benefits, such as enhanced data processing, optimising resource management, data-driven insights, predictive analytics, personalisation, and customer support always being available. AI can still support scaling and adaptability. The energy saved in not changing the business can be put into getting the most out of AI. Performance can be tracked, and continuous improvement implemented.

This approach may seem less innovative, and the organisation will most likely miss out on some of the new opportunities. However, when we look at the things that are retained and not sacrificed, the organisation is more independent and may be better positioned to innovate in the future. Other organisations may be allured by dynamic ecosystems, but what they often find is that once they give one 'piece of the pie' away, they are then forced to give another and another. They find that what was sold to them as a win-win only leaves them managing their own decline and prolonging their existence a little longer. Sometimes it is better to stand up to big tech and keep our sovereignty.

If AI is only used for efficiencies and not as an opportunity to change the business model, there will be no step change in growth from the strategy. Therefore, a strong competitive advantage is needed to achieve growth in this way and overcome the challenges to scaling.

The role of AI when avoiding significant changes to the existing model
Despite some lost opportunities, there are several benefits to this business model. The digital transformation can happen in a less dramatic way at a pace that suits the organisation. AI-driven automation may be implemented in some processes and services, but not at the enterprise level, keeping humans and non-AI software separate. While automation will still happen and some jobs may be lost, more employees will keep their positions and industry-specific knowledge will not be lost. As the organisation is not making its borders more porous to be part of an ecosystem, less data is given to partners. Because the organisation is, to some degree, adapting the technology to itself instead of adapting itself to the technology, it will not typically rely solely on off-the-shelf solutions. Some in-house customisations will be made; the IT department will need to be capable of doing this. Investments need to be made in data management and the right infrastructure to have the right technology stack, especially data analytics platforms, and machine learning tools.

How to build trust when avoiding significant changes to the existing model
When an organisation moves forward keeping as much in-house as possible, there are inherent advantages and disadvantages to building trust. At the same time, as is often the case, beyond the choice of business model, the quality of the implementation plays a decisive role.

One inherent advantage is that, as the processing is mostly done internally, consumers' personal information is kept private. The organisation does not face as big a challenge as it does with the other five alternative strategies in identifying new sources of risk. Furthermore, as the human experts and their skills are kept, they can identify risks and use their experience to deal with them. Keeping a large IT department with the ability to customise solutions gives a layer of protection, ensuring that if something goes wrong, it can be fixed quickly. The added risks of going through a disruptive digital transformation can be avoided. The simplicity of the model and the limited change are huge enablers to trust. In this model, trust is built in a similar way to how it was done before the digital transformation.

The in-house customisations of AI and its integration into existing systems, which will probably be needed so that new technology is adapted to the existing model, do create some risks that other models may avoid. The process of implementing these changes needs to be reliable to build trust both within and outside the organisation.

If we remember the stages in the diffusion of innovation, it is unlikely that an organisation adopting this strategy will be one of the leading innovators. Having this business model, therefore, will not have the burden of convincing all stakeholders of the benefits of a new innovation, as many other competitors would have already implemented that innovation. Similarly, if we remember the technology adoption models, most stakeholders, particularly consumers, would have already adopted similar technologies, making it easier for them to adopt these. Therefore, it is more a case of maintaining trust with stakeholders rather than having to build trust in something radically new.

Key concept: When avoiding significant changes to the existing model, the process of digital transformation simply tries to find more efficient and effective ways to implement it. AI is used across the organisation's value chain, but the model does not change.

Leadership tip: When avoiding significant changes to the existing model, an organisation can keep its identity and play to its strengths. A clear competitive advantage is necessary for an organisation to stand on its own two feet.

Trust-building tip: When not making significant changes to the business model, it is necessary to manage the risks from customising AI solutions to avoid trust destruction. A strength of this approach for trust building is to make the most of having a clear identity at a time when many others don't.

8.2.3 Incumbent expanding beyond current model to fully utilise AI

Just as the second model is the logical next alternative to the first, the third model is the logical next alterative to the second. Here we have an organisation that chooses to expand beyond their existing model so that they can take advantage of the new opportunities created by AI and other technologies such as blockchain. An organisation adopting this business model perceives the increasing role of AI and automation as an opportunity for growth, not a threat. The ability of AI to scale more easily, along with specific applications of other technologies such as the internet of things (IoT), creates opportunities in adjacent areas for an organisation. A positive feedback loop of growth can be created, driven by technology, business model expansion, an increasing consumer base, and more data.

From the consumer's perspective, they want to find as many of the services they use in one place as possible, so they can save time and don't have to share their personal information with others. Consumers want a smooth, seamless customer journey, and that can only be achieved by having the necessary APIs with partners or covering more of the services consumers use. In an ideal scenario, the processing can be done faster in-house, such as when a banking app pre-decides what loan they will offer if we apply for it.

This model could be called the 'go big or go home' model, although a more cynical person might argue it's the 'get rich or die trying' model. The perception that the best defence is a good offence also applies here. While the previous two models can be seen to some degree as defensive, this one is in no way defensive.

A more extreme implementation of this strategy would involve an organisation transforming itself into the new platform for its sector of the economy. An example of this is the many banking apps that encourage users to link all of their bank accounts and operate them through a single platform. Deutsche Bank did this some time ago, and while it was seen as innovative at the time, it is now quite common. The combination of AI-driven automation and blockchain makes it easier to create the infrastructure for this than in the past.

This model has two main variations. In the most common manifestation of this model, the organisation keeps their existing business model intact and adds new processes and services on top of it. The second variation of this approach is to sacrifice part of the existing business while expanding to take advantage of new opportunities. The second variation is not a complete pivot to something new, as this is much rarer, although it does happen. Complete pivots usually happen with startups, or at least younger small or medium enterprises, and are much rarer with large, mature organisations. When pivots do happen with large organisations, they are usually something that was forced onto them because of a legal ruling or financial weakness. An example is a very large company in the UK that bought and sold second-hand cars online. They kept a very high volume of stock in their original model, but when they ran into financial trouble, they tried to turn into a platform for consumer-to-consumer sales. In this way, they did not need stock and just earned a commission.

Examples of the strategy to expand organically beyond the current model to fully utilise AI are not hard to come by. We can find them in many sectors of the economy. Many insurers, including Bupa, are providing free tracking devices, such as fitness trackers, so they can benefit from receiving more data. The insurer can learn how to manage risk better with the new data, but it also manages risk better for the consumer wearing the health device. Sensors utilising IoT are enabling many similar new services. Another example is insurers using IoT sensors to check if fruit in containers being shipped has not gone bad.

While the goal here is organic growth, this does not mean opportunities to collaborate with ecosystems from different sectors of the economy should not be explored. As the customer base and related data grows, there is more to offer potential partners.

The role of AI for an incumbent expanding beyond their current model

One of the benefits AI can bring is customisable services, so when more services are provided by an organisation, these can be bundled together to be made more appealing. With the breadth of services, the relationship with the consumer deepens. Ideally, the consumer starts to feel a stronger bond and behaves more like a citizen of that brand, not only giving money but also backing them up and supporting them when the opportunity arises (Su et al., 2025).

The organisation does not need to make a profit from each individual service as long as it is making some profit overall. Arguably, the biggest benefit is the extensive data collected, which creates a positive feedback loop of growth in customers, data, and machine learning accuracy. Access to more data enhances the ability to utilise machine learning. AI benefits from large-scale operations, and large-scale operations benefit from AI, so this model is a good fit for AI adoption and growth. To adopt this model, an organisation needs to build up their in-house AI capabilities and their ability to offer innovative services.

How to build trust when expanding beyond the current model to fully utilise AI

The broader and closer relationship with the consumer creates more opportunities to build trust. There is a larger bandwidth both literally and metaphorically between the organisation and the consumer. New forms of big data create new opportunities. There are opportunities for machine learning to identify less obvious relationships that can be taken advantage of for mutual benefit. For example, customers that type quickly have been associated with less risk by insurers in China.

While this closer relationship with more data and touchpoints creates new opportunities to build trust, it also creates more situations where there can be friction, disappointments, and a loss of trust. If an organisation wants to take advantage of the new opportunities but keep the additional risks at arm's length, startups can be used. These startups can be affiliated in some way, such as being partly owned. This strategy was implemented with many of the generative AI startups as there were very high risks involved.

Key concept: An incumbent expanding beyond the current model to fully utilise AI and new services gains new consumers and additional data. There is a larger bandwidth which creates opportunities for machine learning to identify less obvious relationships that can be taken advantage of for mutual benefit.

Leadership tip: To achieve organic growth driven by AI, the technology needs to be applied to profitable services faster than the competition.

Trust-building tip: Utilise the larger bandwidth between the organisation and the consumer to enable machine learning to understand the consumer's perspective on trust and build a closer, more trusting relationship.

8.2.4 Startup disruptor focused on one sector, optimised for AI from the start

These startups are often referred to as 'mobile-first' and 'born digital'. As digital transformation can take some time for large organisations, and they can face resistance when they try to change, this opens the door to startups that are created with a business model designed to fully utilise AI and automation. The fourth business model is very different to the third, as the goal is not to cover more and more services, but to cover a small number of services that can be simplified. The goal is to utilise AI faster to offer services more efficiently. This model is not simply about a new organisation – a disruptor entering a sector of the economy. There are at least three different ways a new company can enter a sector. This model is specifically about a new organisation being created, with a highly automated business model to cover a small number of services more cheaply than before.

While this is a startup, it may have a larger organisation behind it, not only supporting it financially, but it may have been conceived by a large organisation from the start. There are several reasons to use this strategy, but two stand out. The first is that, as the digital transformation is so disruptive and far-reaching, it is easier to create an organisation from scratch rather that gradually restructuring an old one. The second point is that an existing organisation may not be eager to change as they are very profitable the way they are, charging existing consumers higher prices than necessary. Therefore, the existing, incumbent organisation is kept as a cash cow and a new startup is created to be more efficient and attract new consumers. This explanation is to some degree an oversimplification, but this is the basic logic that is often behind what is happening.

The role of AI for a startup disruptor focused on one sector, optimised for AI

These startups are created with a clear business model in mind: utilising AI to achieve maximum automation and the lowest prices for consumers. The business as a whole, and the way it uses technology, must leave no room for another organisation to do it more efficiently and undercut them. A new technology is matched to a niche and a business model is built to bring the two together. By having a low headcount, scaling can be incredibly fast. While many think of flexibility when they think of AI, this is not always possible. As this model is highly automated and with a low headcount of experts, the processes are very rigid. Complex services often cannot be offered because they are hard to deliver and have legal implications that cannot be covered.

Typically, everything is done through a mobile app and the automation integrates all the sensors of the mobile device. Real-time data can be used to increase personalisation and flexibility. If the service is car insurance, a picture of the damage can be uploaded and machine learning processes it automatically and releases the compensation. In insurance, finance, and many other services, a low price and fast processing are the two most important issues for consumers. This is where this model excels. Many insurers that had invested millions trying to be leaders in technology had to then accept that their company will 'live or die' on a comparison website. They had to give up their plans and focus on low-cost, no-frills services. Unfortunately for insurance and many other services, it is a race to low prices, but also a race to the bottom in terms of service.

While many organisations say they are customer-focused when they are building a new business model, to get the most out of a new technology this is critical. From the various theories that help us understand our consumer and our relationship with them, the technology adoption model and its updates is the most useful here. The key to this model's success is the consumer adopting the new technology; they must find it useful and easy to use. The technology used must solve a real problem the consumer has, but it should also have a more caring side. In addition to processing an order or a claim, the AI can provide useful advice and tips. Many organisations use this in an intrusive way, making their nudges seem more like pushes, but it can be done in a constructive, win-win way. After a day of nudges, we can often end up feeling more shoved than nudged.

While this type of business is set up to utilise the latest AI, it does not necessarily mean it needs exotic, futuristic technologies. These types of companies have simple models and processes, so they can often utilise technologies off-the-shelf with limited customisation. The startup disruptor focused on one sector, optimised for AI, attempts to be the purest expression of the new technology's application. The business channels the technology; it does not expect the technology to bend to the will of the business.

How to build trust with the startup disruptor focused on one sector, optimised for AI

The clarity of this model is beneficial in building trust. On the other hand, as the priority is usually to automate and simplify things as much as possible, this model often runs into trouble with difficult cases and the quality can suffer. As the processes are automated and optimised for the typical scenarios, there is often no plan B if something goes wrong.

We discussed how the third business model had additional touchpoints with the consumer where trust could be built. This model is intended to be as 'light' and streamlined as possible, so the touchpoints are limited in time and duration. This is not necessarily a bad thing for trust, but a way must be found to maintain transparency.

As all the consumers are new, they will be going through the onboarding process. The onboarding process is often the hardest. This is not a rule, and the onboarding can be smooth for these born-digital disruptors, but what can happen is that if there is a hitch at any step, the whole process acrimoniously grinds to a halt. Frozen screens and not knowing what has happened is not a good look. If trust is reduced before any is built, it is a negative amount of trust and therefore distrust. Being customer-focused does not start once they have completed the onboarding process, but as soon as they start the onboarding process. Speaking as a consumer for a moment and not a researcher, I have learned everything I need to know about some organisations, such as estate agents, during the onboarding process, and I choose to never give them a single cent, even if my life depends on it. It can be very patronising and upsetting when an organisation is clearly using the onboarding process to harvest as much data as they can get away with and violate our privacy as far as possible. If that is what being a modern organisation is going to be about, that is a nightmarish vision of the future.

The new startup does not have a heritage and a track record to reassure stakeholders, but this can also be seen as an opportunity to create an appealing narrative for themselves. We see in the car industry that startups such as NIO have been able to communicate how passionate they are about electric cars while some of the older manufacturers that are trying to have many fingers in many pies are not coming across as genuinely passionate about them. Getting a clear message across and appearing to be authentic and trustworthy is just as much about what we are not, as well as what we are. A new company focusing on a small range of services should be able to make it clear what their values are, and what they are not.

Being a new company focused on a limited number of services makes collaborations easier in some situations, as potential collaborators will not see them as competitors. An insurer that only insures passengers of taxis and ride-hailing will not be seen as a competitor by the ride-hailing services themselves. The ride-hailing services may, however, see a larger tech-savvy organisation as a potential future competitor. For example, Tesla may have not been a direct competitor to ride-hailing services in the past, but it is not too much of a surprise, given their capabilities, that they launched a driverless taxi. With the driverless taxi they are now a direct competitor to the ride-hailing services, so they may be more reluctant to collaborate with them. Companies looking for organisations to collaborate with appreciate companies that are committed to 'staying in their lane'.

Key concept: These startups are created with a clear business model in mind, with the purpose of utilising AI to achieve maximum automation and the lowest prices for consumers. A new technology is matched to a niche and a business model is built to bring the two together.

Leadership tip: This business model needs to use AI to solve a real problem, offer the cheapest service, provide effortless onboarding, and be transparent despite limited contact with the consumer.

Trust-building tip: The clarity of this model is beneficial in building trust. There are fewer touchpoints with the consumer because of the narrow focus, so the technology should solve a problem, be transparent, and show a caring side.

8.2.5 Disruptor focused on tech adding a new service such as insurance

The fifth business model is about an existing tech-savvy organisation that already utilises AI extensively moving into a new sector. It was not so long ago that tech companies were experts only in technology, while other sectors of the economy, such as retail and banking, were the experts in their respective fields. Those days have gone. As technology cuts across all sectors, it opens the door to tech-savvy companies, and especially big tech. Specialised knowledge is still necessary in every sector, particularly for those that are heavily regulated, but it is not the barrier to entry it used to be. Tech companies are expanding into many sectors, eating away at the incumbents' share of the pie.

The prominent role of technology across user-facing and back-office processes accessing data and implementing AI means technology companies are in a strong position. It has become easier for tech companies to copy what retailers, banks, insurers, and others do, especially since they often run their operations on tech companies' cloud services. Many companies have handed over the blueprint of their operations and the data of what they do to big tech and kept nothing secret to keep a competitive advantage. In truth, often the only limitation to what tech companies can do is regulation. Tencent and Alibaba are examples of tech companies that have covered many different services but were also given some limitations by government regulation.

Regulation has an even more important role than in the past. As there are fewer barriers for big tech, it is the regulator that needs to decide what the demands should be from different sectors and what scrutiny each sector should have. An organisation should, and in most cases does, face very different scrutiny if they offer a simple app, are a retailer, a social media platform, or provide financial advice and financial services. While many understand that an organisation that has a dominant oligopolistic position in one sector of the economy has too much power, organisations that have a piece of the pie across many sectors also have too much power.

The role of AI for the model of a disruptor focused on tech adding a new service
The growing importance of AI and data opens the door to tech-savvy companies to enter new sectors of the economy. When tech companies move into sectors where they have no legacy, they can rearrange their processes to deliver their services with a focus on AI and data; they are just adding a new service to their portfolio of services. Some of these companies act as a platform for services to be added. This makes the implementation of the necessary technology much easier for both the front end and the back end.

Tech companies often have a competitive advantage on AI. This is not just because of the AI they are currently implementing – they may have better AI, and with the vast data and expertise they have, they are in a better position to keep developing it. Data collected while offering one service can help the machine learning get insight in another service in the portfolio. In addition to the importance of having as much data as possible, some AI implementations, such as large language models, are also very intensive in terms of processing power. Once again, having scale in the technology supporting the AI, such as the latest servers with the latest processors, is beneficial.

How to build trust with for the model of a disruptor focused on tech adding a new service
It was mentioned in the previous section that for a born-digital startup, by definition, all their customers will be going through the onboarding process. As a new organisation, those applying the fourth business model, they do not have any existing customers. So, while they are focused on efficiency, they have this burden. This is a financial burden, but also a burden in terms of making sure a strong relationship is built with the consumer or whoever is using their services, such as staff or a patient. The tech-savvy company moving into a new sector using the fifth business model brings their existing consumers with them. These existing consumers may have already provided sensitive personal information that they may be reluctant to share with organisations they have not shared it with before.

While an organisation active in one sector must build trust in the services of that sector, a tech-savvy company can build trust in one area where they are strong and transfer that trust to the areas where they are not so strong. For example, a traditional bank may feel the need to remind the consumer that their savings are guaranteed up to a certain amount by the financial authorities, so that even if the bank runs into trouble, they will not lose their money. A tech-savvy company may choose to point to their growth and user numbers to convince a consumer they can be trusted.

It might be tempting for a tech-savvy company to believe that, as this is not their core business, it does not have to be delivered to a high standard. A new incumbent, with no reputation to lose in a sector, should not accept a higher risk and use technology in new untested ways. The opportunity to enter a new area and gain consumers should not be seen as a raid or a smash-and-grab and should be done in a sustainable, trustworthy way. Just as there is trust transference from the tech-savvy company's existing operations to the new ones, there can be distrust transference if things go wrong.

Key concept: The growing importance of AI and data opens the door to tech-savvy companies to enter new sectors of the economy. They are just adding a new service to their portfolio of services. Tech companies arrange their processes to deliver the services with a focus on AI and data from the start.

Leadership tip: Tech companies have a competitive advantage on utilising AI. With the vast data and expertise they have, they are in a better position to keep developing it. Data collected while offering one service can help the machine learning get insight in another service in the portfolio. Other companies will struggle to keep up with the rate of innovation tech-savvy companies can achieve.

Trust-building tip: The tech-savvy company moving into a new sector using the fifth business model brings their existing consumers with them. While an organisation active in one sector must build trust in the services of that sector, a tech-savvy company can build trust in an area where they are strong and transfer that trust to the areas where they are not so strong.

8.2.6 Disruptor with extensive user or fanbase adding new services

The sixth model, just as the fourth and fifth, is an organisation coming in from outside the sector. It has some similarities to the other two models of disruptors entering a sector of the economy, but it also has some differences that make it necessary to look at it separately. This is the newest of the business models optimised for AI; previous versions of this theory did not include it.

In this business model, an organisation or famous individual that has an existing fanbase or user base adds a new service. They are not a tech company and do not have a competitive advantage in AI. Their strength is their existing user base and the strong emotional and trusting bond they have. In this model, an organisation finds a way to monetise an existing trusting relationship. In a similar way to the fifth model, the company entering a new sector brings their consumers with them. The Tesco supermarket offering car insurance is an example of this.

AI and other technologies such as blockchain make it easier to set up a new service. Typically, the goal is to set the service up quickly and in the simplest way. Therefore, best-of-breed, off-the-shelf solutions are used to replicate a model that has been proven to work. Therefore, while in terms of bringing its consumers with them and already having a trusting relationship, the sixth model is similar to the fifth in terms of how technology is used, it is actually more similar to the fourth model.

This model further illustrates the point that sometimes the best way to innovate with technology is to apply the latest technology quickly rather than to create new technology. By using advanced but commoditised technology, we can innovate faster in terms of business operations. If we already have an advantage – a unique selling point – we do not need it to come from the technology. The technology simply needs to match the competition.

This is the newest model of the six and it reflects the changing world we live in. In particular, it reflects what is most valuable in business today. The prevailing dynamic of the last couple of decades is that as technology becomes more capable and influential, tech companies keep taking a larger piece of the pie. However, in some cases now, it is not the technology that is most important but the data and the trusting relationships. This means individuals or organisations that create a fan base have no problem monetising it in various ways.

Donald Trump and Elon Musk are obvious examples of this, but this approach can also work for those with a lower profile. Donald Trump launched a social media platform, Truth Social, with the slogan 'Your voice, your freedom'. If anyone looks at this social media platform, it is clear that there is a coherent message and 'brand'. The coherence in the content from the platform and the followers should retain the trust that already exists between the supporters (or fans) and the platform owner. Donald Trump then launched a new digital currency initiative, World Liberty Financial. It is clear that additional services are being offered to a group of people with shared values that want to give their money to others with similar values.

While some might view these new ventures by Donald Trump cynically, seeing them as a ploy to profit financially from a relationship, they could also be regarded as positive steps aligned with the original vision and message. The original message of Donald Trump emphasised freedom of speech, which lines up well with Truth Social. The original message also emphasised financial growth for everyone, not just the 'elites', which may potentially be delivered by a new cryptocurrency and associated financial service. Therefore, it appears that there has been an effort to have a coherent message or brand across the new tech-based endeavours.

The role of AI for the disruptor with an extensive user base adding new services
As this model is not typically applied by tech companies, and those applying it do not have a competitive advantage in AI, they would generally avoid innovating in AI, customising AI themselves, or doing anything in-house. In a similar way to the fourth model, they prefer to cobble together the best-in-breed, off-the shelf services in a basic and reliable way. It is important to appreciate that sometimes the best way to innovate is with commoditised technology that can be applied quickly.

While the technology used is not necessarily innovative, the breadth of data collected can enable machine learning to gain useful insights from one part of the operation that can be utilised in another. The data collected is not only on the typical buying behaviour but also on more fundamental beliefs that can help machine learning gain a deeper insight into us.

How to build trust for the disruptor with an extensive user base adding new services

In terms of building trust, the sixth business model has similarities to the fifth, as the trust may be built elsewhere and transferred to the new service. Therefore, the priority is not to build trust but to maintain it. The values that built the trust in the first place need to be consistently replicated across all parts of the relationship.

The relationship is different to the typical dynamic of a company and a consumer, where the company tries to understand the consumer's needs and meet them. Everyone involved has already bonded on some shared values and an appreciation of each other. Additional services are being offered to a group with shared values that want to give their money to others with similar values. Some of us do not want our identity to be 'consumer of big tech company XYZ'. We want to be part of a community with some shared beliefs about how the world should be. Bonding on values can build very strong trust – far stronger than trust based on the typical operational dimensions of reliability, customer service, and value for money.

When an organisation is relying heavily on trust transference from one part of the organisation to another, instead of building trust, it is emphasising that the services in question are related. As with the fifth business model that relies heavily on trust transference, this can potentially backfire. Just as there is trust transference from the existing operations to the new ones, there can be distrust transference if things go wrong.

Key concept: A disruptor with an extensive user or fanbase adding new services is bringing its consumers with them and already has a trusting relationship with them. AI and other technologies such as blockchain make it easier to set up a new service. Typically, the goal is to set the service up quickly, in the simplest way, so off-the-shelf solutions are used to replicate a model that has been proven to work.

Leadership tip: Innovation usually starts from the technology side or the business side. It can start from seeing the potential in a new technology, or it can start from identifying a better way to organise the business operations. Increasingly, innovation can start from a trusting relationship. The trusting relationship can be the unique selling point – what makes the model special – and the rest of the operations and technology can be generic and unremarkable.

Trust-building tip: Trust may be built elsewhere and transferred to the new service, so the priority is not to build trust but to maintain it. The values that built the trust in the first place need to be consistently replicated across all parts of the relationship.

8.3 Business models not focused on AI but other technologies such as blockchain

There is no disputing that AI is driving the economy-bending digital transformation we are going through. In most cases, even when several other technologies are involved, it is AI that plays the decisive role in shaping the new business model.

AI, however, is not 'the only show in town' and there are new business models constantly emerging where the priority is to utilise other technologies. A new business model can also be created to leverage the unique characteristics of blockchain technology, such as decentralisation, transparency, and security. While there are business models focused on many different technologies, after AI, blockchain is the most transformative. This is not just because it is a very valuable and useful technology, but also because it can enable a very different way of operating. The new ways an organisation can create ecosystems with partners using blockchain is particularly interesting.

While AI and blockchain can be used for both good and evil, blockchain has a negative reputation with some people because it is associated it with meme coins and many crypto scams. None of this is because of the blockchain technology itself and is more to do with the fear of missing out and insufficient regulation. Ironically, what blockchain brings as a technology is order, transparency, and security, unlike AI, which is proving a much harder beast to tame.

The application that gets most attention is using blockchain to offer decentralised financial services, but there are many other applications. It has been particularly useful in tracking products across a supply chain, ensuring their authenticity and verifying they come from where they claim they do.

There are currently many successful implementations of blockchain across the private and public sector. In the public sector in Germany, councils are using blockchain to control what personal information is being shared with who in order to deliver services. In this way, citizens' personal information is kept as private as possible while providing them with the services they need. In the private sector in Germany, blockchain is being used to sell shares and manage their ownership. These two are good examples of how we can use blockchain to sufficiently decentralise and automate a service that is still centrally controlled. Blockchain is used to automate the granting of certain permissions, but it is by no means a revolution or a new world order.

We need to be able to understand the typical opportunities and challenges when implementing blockchain technologies or collaborating with organisations that use them. If we spend a little time to understand some blockchain business models, this will give us a good starting point. For most, it will be some useful general knowledge to boost their business acumen, but for others it will trigger a passion to make things better with blockchain. Blockchain is quite unusual in how it leaves some of us not only disinterested but angry about something we do not see the value in, while for others it triggers a passion – a hope – for a better, fairer world.

The business models of NFTs and fan tokens and how they build trust

We will look at an example of the business models using blockchain to sell tokens such as non-fungible tokens (NFTs). These are very interesting models that innovate on many different levels. They change the way we use technology and how we run a business, but also our relationships with each other. While blockchain does support trust and can be interpreted as a 'trustless technology' when it is applied in a real-world scenario, there is still a whole chain of trust necessary. Therefore, as with AI because of the critical, pivotal role of technology in these models, we also need to discuss how trust is built at the business-model level.

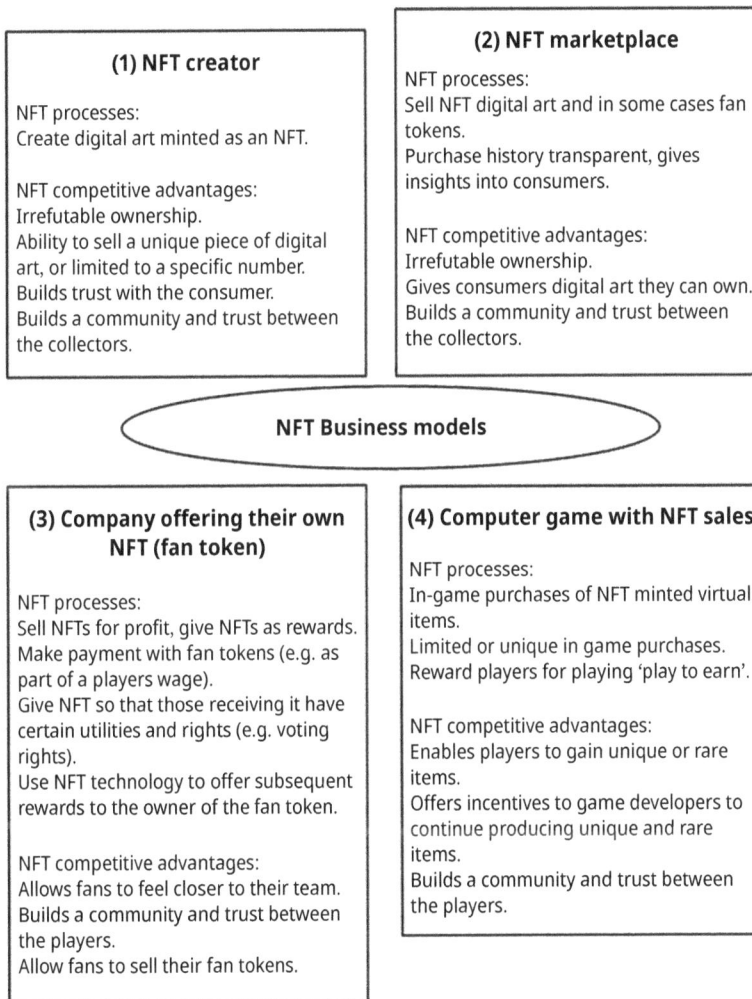

(1) NFT creator

NFT processes:
Create digital art minted as an NFT.

NFT competitive advantages:
Irrefutable ownership.
Ability to sell a unique piece of digital art, or limited to a specific number.
Builds trust with the consumer.
Builds a community and trust between the collectors.

(2) NFT marketplace

NFT processes:
Sell NFT digital art and in some cases fan tokens.
Purchase history transparent, gives insights into consumers.

NFT competitive advantages:
Irrefutable ownership.
Gives consumers digital art they can own.
Builds a community and trust between the collectors.

NFT Business models

(3) Company offering their own NFT (fan token)

NFT processes:
Sell NFTs for profit, give NFTs as rewards.
Make payment with fan tokens (e.g. as part of a players wage).
Give NFT so that those receiving it have certain utilities and rights (e.g. voting rights).
Use NFT technology to offer subsequent rewards to the owner of the fan token.

NFT competitive advantages:
Allows fans to feel closer to their team.
Builds a community and trust between the players.
Allow fans to sell their fan tokens.

(4) Computer game with NFT sales

NFT processes:
In-game purchases of NFT minted virtual items.
Limited or unique in game purchases.
Reward players for playing 'play to earn'.

NFT competitive advantages:
Enables players to gain unique or rare items.
Offers incentives to game developers to continue producing unique and rare items.
Builds a community and trust between the players.

Figure 8.3: The business models of NFTs and fan tokens and how they build trust (Zarifis & Cheng, 2022).

The interest in tokens including NFTs is growing, despite some inevitable ups and downs. The most important indication of their potential is not if their value is up or down this week, but the fact that they solve practical problems. Some examples of the practical problems blockchain and NFTs solve include proving the authenticity and ownership of digital art, automatically receiving royalties, sharing ownership, and transferring ownership transparently and securely. This innovation will have difficulties reaching a wider audience until more clarity is achieved on two main issues: what exactly the NFT business models are and how do they build trust.

Research finds that there are four NFT business models that are proven to work (Zarifis & Cheng, 2022). These four models are illustrated in figure 8.3 and summarized below:

(1) NFT creator
The NFT creator can create digital art that is then digitally minted as an NFT and sold on an NFT platform. The competitive advantages of using an NFT here include having proof of irrefutable ownership and the ability to sell a unique piece of digital art or one limited to a low number. The reliability and transparency of this technology builds trust with the consumer.

(2) NFT marketplace selling creators' NFTs
The purchase history of the consumers is transparent, so this gives insights into their interests. The competitive advantage of NFTs as part of this business model is once again the irrefutable ownership and that it gives consumers digital art they can own. As with the previous business model, a community and trust are built between the collectors.

(3) Company offering their own NFT, typically a fan token
This business model has several NFT processes. These are to sell NFTs for profit, give them as rewards, make payment with fan tokens, and give them so that the person receiving them has certain utilities and rights, such as voting rights. The competitive advantages of this technology as a fan token are that they allow fans to feel closer to their team and it builds a community and trust between the fans.

(4) Computer game with NFT sales
There can be in-game purchases of NFT-minted virtual items, limited or unique in-game purchases, and rewarding players for playing, known as 'play-to-earn'. This offers incentives to game developers to continue producing rare items, provides an ongoing revenue stream for existing games, and builds a community and trust between the players.

How to build trust with business models focused on blockchain

There are many different ways to implement blockchain technology, but when it is implemented in the ideal way, it supports trust in several ways due to the transparent record of what is happening. If we are not talking about a cryptocurrency such as Bitcoin, the ledger may not be available to everyone to review, but it should be accessible to stakeholders.

Trust building should have two priorities: the first is to communicate how the specific implementation of blockchain supports trust; the second is that trust must also be built in the aspects of the value chain not using blockchain. For example, blockchain can be used to prove the provenance of a physical product. It can be tracked along the supply chain all the way to the consumer, but the actual quality of the tangible product cannot necessarily be ensured. So, in this example, a good approach would be to communicate the benefits of being able to track the provenance, but also ensure through checks that the quality of the physical product is suitable.

Key concept: While it is AI that is driving most of the digital disruption, it can be valuable for a new business model to focus on the second most disruptive technology, blockchain. A business model can be created to leverage the unique characteristics of blockchain technology, such as decentralisation, transparency, and security. Blockchain solves real problems in many different industries, creates new opportunities, and can support trust.

Leadership tip: Traditionally, one of the roles of a leader is to be the face of the team to those outside, representing the team, and arranging collaborations. When trying to utilise AI, this often means securing sources of data. The role of blockchain in collaborations is different. Blockchain can be a useful platform for collaboration providing the infrastructure to collaborate in an automated, secure, and transparent way. This obviously applies to services, but it also applies physical, tangible products that can be tracked using a blockchain.

Trust-building tip: While blockchain does support trust and can be interpreted as a 'trustless technology', when it is applied in a real-world scenario, there is still a whole chain of trust necessary. Therefore, as with AI, because of the pivotal role of technology, we need to be clear at the business-model level how trust is built.

8.4 Summary

There's no complete script as far as a manager is concerned. — Alex Ferguson, football manager

There are business models that will help organisations already active in an area fully utilise AI, and there are business models for organisations to use the new opportunities created by AI to move into new areas. The six business models proven to be ideal for an AI-centric world are: (1) focus on one part of the value chain and disaggregate,

(2) absorb AI into existing model, (3) an incumbent expanding beyond the current model to fully utilise the opportunities of AI and access new data, (4) a startup disruptor focused on one sector, built from the start to be highly automated, (5) a disruptor focused on tech adding a new service such as insurance, and (6) disruptor that is not tech-focused but has an extensive user or fanbase. These models are illustrated in figure 8.4.

Some large businesses use a combination of these business models. They may operate one part of the business using the first model, narrowing their focus on the part of the value chain they feel strongest, and start a new business in a new sector for them in a similar way to the fourth business model.

Hopefully, these models appear to be logical, intuitive, or even obvious. As is often the case, however, there are far more ways that appear to make sense and could potentially work than those that are finally proven to work. It is important to look at these potential models with an open mind and brainstorm which one will work best. It is also important to recognise that there is rarely just one solution, and we must move beyond the over-simplistic approach of 'let's add AI to what we are doing'.

It is very hard in the age we live in to keep something secret, especially if it's something that gives us a competitive advantage. However, throughout history there have been leaders that could keep part of what gave them a competitive advantage secret. An example from history is John Walker, inventor of the friction match in the 1820s. He had to hire staff to scale up production of his invention, but he always did the final process himself, possibly using a secret ingredient. It is believed he did this to prevent competitors copying his invention for as long as possible. A modern example is the recommendation algorithm TikTok uses that is believed to be worth hundreds of millions. In other cases, leaders intentionally create an impression that there is something very special in what they are doing to misdirect competitors away from the logical steps that would lead to replicating their innovation. A true leader should add something truly special and unique – or something perceived to be truly special and unique – to a proven business model.

A business model does not constrain innovation and creativity but makes it easier. We must not feel that a business model, or any theory or science, limits us as humans. We should feel it liberates us to be more human. One of the basic needs of humans that is often overlooked is the need for beauty. Beauty in the broadest sense of the word. It could be something visually pleasing, music, or charming wordplay. Using AI to add beauty, or enable beauty to happen, will take an organisation to a higher level. Luxury brands build empires and fortunes based on beauty, and other organisations should also incorporate some. An example from history is when engineer Karl von Ghega created a rail journey from Graz in Austria to Trieste across the Alps. Not only did he achieve an incredible challenge for that time, but he also created the beautiful Borovnica Viaduct. A more recent example is how, at the 2024 Summer Olympics in Paris, AI was used heavily in new innovative ways, both to create beauty and to support and protect it. The ideal scenario is a combination of a proven business model with a sprinkling of something truly special and unique – and some beauty.

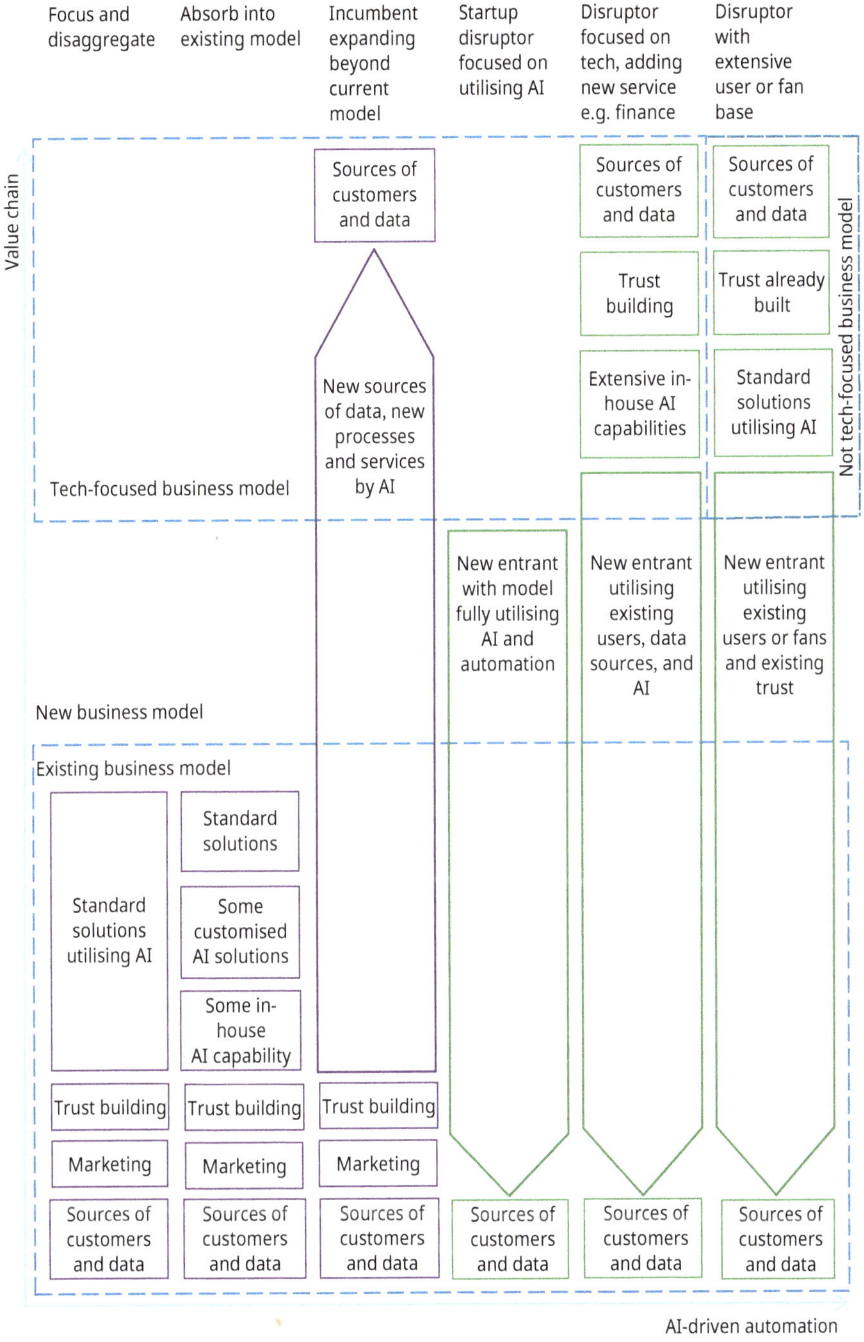

Focus and disaggregate | Absorb into existing model | Incumbent expanding beyond current model | Startup disruptor focused on utilising AI | Disruptor focused on tech, adding new service e.g. finance | Disruptor with extensive user or fan base

Value chain

Tech-focused business model

Sources of customers and data

Sources of customers and data

Sources of customers and data

Trust building

Trust already built

New sources of data, new processes and services by AI

Extensive in-house AI capabilities

Standard solutions utilising AI

Not tech-focused business model

New business model

New entrant with model fully utilising AI and automation

New entrant utilising existing users, data sources, and AI

New entrant utilising existing users or fans and existing trust

Existing business model

Standard solutions

Standard solutions utilising AI

Some customised AI solutions

Some in-house AI capability

Trust building | Trust building | Trust building

Marketing | Marketing | Marketing

Sources of customers and data | Sources of customers and data | Sources of customers and data | Sources of customers and data | Sources of customers and data | Sources of customers and data

AI-driven automation

Figure 8.4: The six business models to utilise AI and build trust (previously presented here and in Chapter 1).

The role of AI and blockchain in transforming business models

A leader that has prepared and has at least some insight on strategy to offer will also encourage a better engagement from all stakeholders in how to move forward. There is no simple solution that fits every situation, but there is a lot of evidence behind the business models discussed here. A leader relying on proven models will avoid feeling overwhelmed. The six business models to thrive with AI provide a strong foundation for leadership decisions.

In a similar way to the disruptive impact of the internet, the transition to a new business model can be a long journey. In some cases, AI and blockchain simply update a number of processes in a specific way, while in other cases, AI drives a broader automation in a similar way to the internet. Beyond the organisation, the value chain they are part of is also changing.

How to build trust in AI- and blockchain-based business models

To be successful, it is critical that the way trust is built is part of all business models. Building trust needs to be planned and baked in at the business-model level. Often, the mistake is made to see trust as an IT or marketing issue. Others make the mistake to think trust is only important for some front-end services. Not finding solutions to build trust at the business-model level and leaving it to a marketing or operations manager is not the right approach.

New sources of risk from AI and blockchain, and the changes to processes, must be identified and mitigated. We must decide by who, and how, trust needs to be built. Building trust across the value chain will enable the interlinking of processes. For the consumer, trust must be built from the start during the onboarding process. AI- and blockchain-focused models should be implemented in a way that users inside and outside the organisation can be encouraged to support this change.

Will the business model of incumbents and disruptors converge?

There are signs of convergence between the models of existing companies in a sector utilising AI and new organisations entering a sector (Zarifis & Cheng, 2021). First, there is convergence in technologies, such as the use of chatbots utilising AI. Second, there is a convergence in processes, for example, interaction with the consumer. Third, there is convergence in the strategy on costs and pricing.

However, there are areas where there seems to be a limit on convergence, which seems to suggest the business models of the incumbents and the disruptors will remain distinct. For example, the cost of attracting the consumer and profitability will most likely remain different. The new entrants can attract consumers more efficiently. A new entrant using the fifth and sixth business models do not need to make profit from the new sector of the economy they are entering as they make a profit from other services.

Despite some convergence, certain differences are likely to remain even after this transitionary period. This is because the models of incumbents and disruptors have distinct competitive advantages. Traditional incumbents no longer monopolise their sector of the economy, but they still have the existing user base and utilise the data they have collected. Technology-savvy companies that enter the sector have their own forms of engagement with their consumers, use different methods to evaluate risk due to their access to real-time data, and do not prioritise generating revenue but instead want to increase their user base, overcome barriers, and reduce the overall cost of their products and services.

Key concept: The six business models proven to be ideal for an AI-centric world are: (1) focus on one part of the value chain and disaggregate, (2) absorb AI into existing model, (3) an incumbent expanding beyond current model to fully utilise the opportunities of AI and access new data, (4) a startup disruptor focused on one sector, built from the start to be highly automated, (5) a disruptor focused on tech adding a new service such as insurance, and (6) a disruptor that is not tech-focused but has an extensive user or fanbase.

Leadership tip: A leader needs to understand how technology changes relationships and business models to be able to act. A leader that has broad horizons and is constantly comparing different leadership styles, different applications of technologies, different business models, and different contexts will be much stronger.

Trust-building tip: Building trust needs to be planned and baked in at the business-model level. New sources of risk from AI and blockchain, and the changes to processes, must be identified and mitigated. We must decide by who, and how, trust needs to be built.

8.5 Exercises

Exercise 8.1

AI-focused business model in banking and finance
There are business models that will help organisations already active in an area fully utilise AI, and there are business models for organisations to use the new opportunities created by AI to move into new areas. The six business models proven to be ideal for an AI-centric world are: (1) focus on one part of the value chain and disaggregate, (2) absorb AI into existing model, (3) an incumbent expanding beyond current model to fully utilise the opportunities of AI and access new data, (4) startup disruptor focused on one sector, built from the start to be highly automated, (5) a disruptor focused on tech adding a new service such as insurance, and (6) a disruptor that is not tech-focused but has an extensive user or fanbase.

There are examples of these business models across many sectors of the economy. One sector of the economy where these models are particularly prevalent is banking and financial services.

Questions

1) Find one company that matches each of the six business models that utilise AI in banking and finance. Do they match the model accurately, or are they a mixture of models? Can you identify ways they try to build trust, either directly or indirectly?

2) Find one company that matches each of the six business models that utilise AI in the sector of the economy you are most interested in. Do they match the model accurately, or are they a mixture of models? Can you identify ways they try to build trust, either directly or indirectly?

Exercise 8.2

Business models to utilise AI and other new technologies better
Scenario: Imagine you work for a company trading in foreign exchange (forex) in Cyprus. Most of your clients are from Cyprus, but there are some from other parts of the world. The company is doing well, but competitors are using technology better and gaining more market share.

Your organisation is considering two possible business models to utilise AI and other new technologies better. One is the second business model, to not make significant strategic changes but absorb AI into existing processes to make them more efficient. The other business model being considered is the third one, to expand beyond the current model to fully utilise the opportunities of AI and access new data.

Questions

1) To decide if the change is worth doing, the potential benefits must be more than the potential problems. Write down as many opportunities and threats as you can for these two models.

2) Based on the opportunities and threats you identified, which business model would you chose and why.

3) For the model you selected, how would you build trust?

Exercise 8.3

Business model for an AI startup

AI and other new technologies provide new opportunities for delivering health advice and services. Sectors of the economy where the risks are particularly high, such as health, involve more challenges for trust (Chen et al., 2017).

Questions

1) If you could create a startup in the health sector, what business model would you chose? Would you prefer to go it alone, or provide services to existing incumbent companies? Which strategy has the biggest risk and the biggest reward?

2) For the model you selected, how would you build trust? Would you focus on a small number of methods, or would you try as many as possible?

Space for your notes

References

Chen, L., Zarifis, A., & Kroenung, J. (2017). The role of trust in personal information disclosure on health-related websites. *Proceedings of the European Conference on Information Systems (ECIS)*, 771–786. http://aisel.aisnet.org/ecis2017_rp/50/

Su, L., Cheng, X., & Zarifis, A. (2025). Passengers as defenders: Unveiling the role of customer-company identification in the trust-customer citizenship behaviour relationship within the ride-hailing context. *Tourism Management, 107*, 105086. https://doi.org/10.1016/j.tourman.2024.105086

Zarifis, A. (2019). The six relative advantages in multichannel retail for three-dimensional virtual worlds and two-dimensional websites. *Proceedings of the 10th ACM Conference on Web Science (WebSci '19)*, 363–372. https://doi.org/10.1145/3292522.3326038

Zarifis, A., & Cheng, X. (2021). Evaluating the new AI- and data-driven insurance business models for incumbents and disruptors: Is there convergence? *24th International Conference on Business Information Systems (BIS 2021)*, 199–208. https://doi.org/10.52825/bis.v1i.58

Zarifis, A., & Cheng, X. (2022). The business models of NFTs and fan tokens and how they build trust. *Journal of Electronic Business & Digital Economics, 1*, 1–14. https://doi.org/10.1108/JEBDE-07-2022-0021

Zarifis, A., & Cheng, X. (2023). AI is transforming insurance with five emerging business models. In J. Wang (Ed.), *Encyclopedia of Data Science and Machine Learning* (pp. 2086–2100). IGI Global Scientific Publishing. https://doi.org/10.4018/978-1-7998-9220-5.ch124

Zarifis, A., & Cheng, X. (2025). The new centralised and decentralised Fintech technologies, and business models, transforming finance. In A. Zarifis & X. Cheng (Eds.), *Fintech and the emerging ecosystems: Exploring centralised and decentralised financial technologies*. Springer Nature. https://link.springer.com/book/9783031834011

Zott, C., & Amit, R. (2017). Business model innovation: How to create value in a digital world. *NIM Marketing Intelligence Review, 9*(1), 18–23. https://doi.org/10.1515/gfkmir-2017-0003

Chapter 9
Transactional leadership with servant or transformational styles for AI and trust

9.1 Introduction

Vision is not enough; it must be combined with venture. It is not enough to stare up the steps, we must step up the stairs. — Václav Havel, former president of the Czech Republic

The leadership method put forward here for AI

This book has not given oversimplified or patronising guidance on leadership. It has not offered a silver bullet that will solve all the problems we face in trying to fully utilise AI. We must resist the hypnotic charm of the over-simplistic answers often provided by influencers and stay in the real world with all its complexities. The real magnitude of the challenge posed by AI and trust have been presented in this book, and a practical structure to adapting to a leader's context has been offered. The guidance has been grounded in science and sources have been provided throughout. We must combine transactional, servant, and transformational leadership to get the most out of people and AI, including autonomous AI agents. Utilising the three core leadership styles, the successful leader in AI and trust has to think about what to do at each of the six typical steps of digital transformation, but also build their values – and even their character. As each stage has different priorities, a successful leader should have some long-term beliefs combined with constant tweaking and adapting.

The organisations that implement an AI-focused business model effectively will get some certainty from the model and gain an advantage over those that struggle to make the transition. There are six business models proven to be ideal for an AI-centric world (Zarifis & Cheng, 2023, 2025). Traditionally, some leaders were focused on day-to-day operational and tactical decisions, while others focused on more strategic decisions. In order to move towards an AI-centred organisation with trust in AI, the leader must identify, either on their own or with the help of others, what the ideal business model to aim for is and then build a consensus around it. These two steps are critical as they will trigger change and give that change a suitable destination to aim for. Failing to identify the right business model will keep the organisation stuck in uncertainty while other organisations outmanoeuvre them.

The stages of a project and the challenges at each stage

In the second chapter, we mainly looked at the stages of a typical project. While each project can be different, over thousands of projects, certain typical challenges have been identified for each stage. Just as a footballer practices for certain typical scenar-

https://doi.org/10.1515/9783111630137-009

ios, such as taking a penalty, a leader must build their knowledge and be prepared for the typical scenarios they will likely face at each stage. In a similar way to a footballer, but also a sailor or a chess player, they must also get into a position that will be beneficial in the subsequent steps. Several lists of challenges have been compiled over the years, but the ones here are up to date and take into account the technologies, such as AI, that. along with many other things, are disrupting the role of the leader and the critical role of trust.

Choosing the right leadership style and priorities at each stage of a project may complicate the leader's role, but getting these things right will save time, money, and drama in the long run. Throughout history, in order to get things done, we have typically organised ourselves into leaders and followers. We have achieved great things in this way, but there has always been a tension between the leader and the followers. From the time of Plato, many have tried to resolve this tension in the best way possible. There is not only no simple answer, but there is no single answer – simple or complicated – across a whole project or process of adopting an innovation.

In addition to the typical challenges teams often face when moving through a process to achieve a goal, we must pay particular attention to the challenges created by AI. Knowing how, and when, to build trust is critical (Zarifis & Fu, 2023; Zarifis & Cheng, 2024). Not only young inexperienced managers can fail due to their handling of AI and trust. Experienced managers that don't update their leadership style can also fail to get the most out of AI. To get the most out of technology we must also look at the stages of a project, their challenges, and provide practical guidance on what to focus on at each stage.

Traditional leadership approaches

In the third chapter we looked at the most influential traditional leadership approaches: autocratic vs. democratic, delegative, bureaucratic, and charismatic. The biggest mistake a leader can make in a time of dramatic change is to not move fast enough and adapt to the new unfolding situation. The second biggest mistake is to move forward too fast, discarding theories, values, processes, and leadership styles that are still useful. We have seen the main traditional leadership styles and identified how they can still be useful in certain scenarios, either on their own or when used to complement other leadership styles. These traditional styles have been proven to get results, but they are resonating less today than they did in the past. The world has changed. In most cases followers have options and will not endure a situation that they do not enjoy or does not satisfy them as it did in the past. The three more modern, more popular approaches today are harder to implement for the leader but resonate far better with the followers.

The best leadership style combinations and proven business models
To lead people today we must lead in AI, and to lead in AI we must lead in trust between people, and between people and technology. The following sections will focus on transactional and servant leadership's combined impact on AI and trust, transactional and transformational leadership's combined impact on AI and trust, and the six AI-focused business models a leader should choose from and how to adapt them.

9.2 Transactional and servant leadership's combined impact on AI and trust

The end result of kindness is that it draws people to you. — Anita Roddick, businesswoman, human rights activist, and environmental campaigner

A leader can have a much bigger impact if they are clear on what AI-focused business model they want to implement, however, for some organisations and in some contexts, this is not always clear. If the leader knows that the organisation should utilise AI more extensively but they are not clear on what the best approach to achieve this is, and they believe a lot of the insight on strategic issues can come from specialised experts inside the team that are not necessarily the most senior, then the servant approach should be combined with the transactional approach.

The transactional leadership style is defined as an approach where the leader makes a series of agreements with their followers on specific exchanges of value. An effective transactional leader goes beyond an over-simplistic understanding of this approach and is not limited to bargaining and agreeing a deal. They ensure that everything is in place for the follower to succeed and, importantly, they always fulfil their part of the agreement. This is a very beneficial leadership style that has a lot to offer for AI adoption and trust building, either on its own or in combination with other approaches. It is important to understand this leadership approach thoroughly, including the typical traits a leader applying this approach should have.

If we have successful leadership styles that focus on structure, such as bureaucratic, approaches that focus on the leader, such as autocratic, and approaches that focus on the follower, such as servant, why has an approach focused on the exchange of value become so popular? There are many reasons, but the main one is the nature of modern society and work. With the proliferation of short contracts and the gig economy, there are many business models that necessitate this approach. More broadly, even if we compare to ten or twenty years ago, money has become everything to more people than before. People want money, and they want it now. Trying to inspire with visions of a better future has become harder. Building long-term professional relationships is of little value to many workers in the transient world we live in, as they may not interact with that person again. It is also because of the reduced trust in society. Workers don't trust that they will be appreciated, and they don't trust they will get a promotion if they do their job well. All this leads to employees valuing short-term goals and immediate reward.

Servant leadership, with an emphasis on coaching, focuses primarily on followers' growth and well-being, in the hope that this will lead to better performance. By encouraging followers' personal growth, they satisfy their need for autonomy, competence, and relatedness (Chiniara & Bentein, 2016). The servant leader genuinely cares about their team and the other stakeholders, but they still care about having a high performance and achieving goals. Servant leadership works very well when the recruitment team manages to hire employees that value personal development and a little more freedom in how they will pursue goals. This leadership approach is one of the two that are most in tune with the zeitgeist of the time. It prioritises good values such as ethical behaviour and environmental sustainability. When applying this style, it is important to strike the right balance between giving colleagues some space to express themselves and still retaining sufficient authority. Servant leadership can be used on its own, but it is a very complementary approach to transactional leadership when trying to move towards an AI-centred organisation with trust.

Combining the two when implementing AI means the leader can be more specific for clear tasks and focus more on supporting the team for more vague tasks they do not fully understand. These approaches combined can build the ecosystem of partners sharing data and services that is often needed to get the most out of AI. Leaders need transactional leadership to satisfy and encourage a follower's self-interest and the servant or transformational approach to encourage them to transcend self-interest. Balancing the clarity of the short-term extrinsic motivation of transactional leadership with the longer-term intrinsic motivation of servant and transformational leadership is at the heart of effective modern leadership.

Trust-building tip: Transactional leadership can build trust very effectively due to the transparency it offers. When combined with servant leadership, the resulting approach should retain that transparency in what the follower should deliver and receive in return.

9.3 Transactional and transformational leadership's combined impact on AI and trust

If you think you're too small to have an impact, try going to bed with a mosquito. — Anita Roddick, businesswoman, human rights activist, and environmental campaigner

Depending on the leader and the situation, transformational leadership can be used either on its own or combined with other leadership approaches to fully utilise AI and build trust. If the leader has identified the AI-focused business model to aim for and believes convincing their team of its value will get them there, then the transformational leadership approach should be the one added to the transactional approach.

Transformational leadership prioritises creating a shared vision to change something, inspiring and motivating people to go beyond their narrow personal interests. This leader may not be an authoritative figurehead, but they embody the change they are promoting, and as a positive role model, they are emulated by their followers. If a transformational leader wants to promote more AI use, they should be knowledgeable on the topic and use it themselves extensively. Transformational leadership supports digital transformation with AI in two ways. Firstly, it encourages change. As we all have a limited bandwidth and there is conflicting information on AI, this leader selects an AI-focused business model and builds consensus around it. Secondly, by creating a resilient team, they are better prepared for the far-reaching implications of digital transformation.

Many often link a transformational leader with charisma, but authenticity – especially authenticity of the intention – is more important. Someone trying to masquerade as a transformational leader without authenticity will not get very far. For example, a politician promising anything and everything in well-scripted speeches, knowing they cannot deliver on those things, is not a transformational leader. They may have some stylistic similarities, and both get people motivated, but the transformational leader delivers on the change they talk about.

Transformational leadership is a very good fit for Generation Z and younger generations. However, there are some aspects of it that may be frustrating for these generations. Generation Z value having an overarching purpose and regular feedback. While transformational leadership offers the long-term vision and broader purpose, the lack of short-term targets being achieved may be disappointing to younger generations. If there are limited short-term targets, the feedback will not be about meeting targets and giving praise for meeting them. While transactional leadership is arguably the worst fit for this generation overall, from the three modern approaches, it is actually better for this generation in this aspect.

The dimensions of transactional leadership include articulating a vision, providing an appropriate model, gaining acceptance of the goals, creating a high performance, fostering individualised engagement and support, and being intellectually stimulating (Scheuer et al., 2022). The pioneers of transactional leadership state that, when applying this approach, there is no relationship between the two beyond the bargaining and the deal made (Burns, 1978). While most of those applying transactional leadership today do not apply it in such a dogmatic, narrow-minded way, being engaged and building strong personal relationships is clearly not the priority. As it is the leader that is pushing for more AI and automation that replaces some human interaction, it would be beneficial if it is the leader that covers the emotional void and isolation left over. Therefore, the leader in the age of AI needs to have some deep emotionally engaged relationships powered by servant or transformational leadership. These strong emotional bonds can complement the well-crafted exchange of value skilfully arranged with transactional leadership. Table 9.1 shows the questions a leader should ask themselves when choosing a leadership style.

Table 9.1: A two-by-two matrix of how to choose the leadership style to fully utilise AI.

Don't know AI business model, clear on digital transformation journey:	Don't know AI business model, not clear on digital transformation journey:
Transactional and servant	Servant
Know AI business model, clear on digital transformation journey:	Know AI business model, not clear on digital transformation journey:
Transactional	Transactional and transformational

Leadership tip: A positive consequence of the transformational leadership approach is that, to some degree, it compensates for the loss of humanness caused by the use of AI. A leader showing their human side is more transparent, so followers engage and trust them more. People need people. This is especially true in the age of AI.

Trust-building tip: If an agreement for one transaction of value is needed, such as sharing data with a competitor so that the services of both organisations engaged in the transaction run more smoothly, the leadership style should be transactional, and trust is built by crafting a clear, transparent, fair, sustainable, and robust agreement. Emotional engagement can be out of place and be counterproductive.

Trust-building tip: Unlike other approaches that rely on one or two methods to build trust, transformational leadership builds trust in multiple synergistic ways and creates a more holistic trust in all directions. People trust the leader, the plan, and themselves. When the leader and the plan are in the direction of using AI more, there is trust transference to AI. It is easier to have trust transference if there is a lot of trust.

9.4 The six AI-focused business models a leader should choose from and how to adapt them

The leader cannot become an expert on every technology being used, but they should be obsessed with learning as much as they can, especially about generative AI and blockchain. Before the leader inspires and creates a shared vision, they must understand their people, their context, the role of AI, and have some clarity on the business model and broader strategy. While it is perfectly fine to take a democratic approach to shaping the strategy with brainstorming and so on, the leader must bring some knowledge, business acumen, and intellectual ability to that process. Contrary to what some academics and practitioners say, a true leader must have a plan, and they usually live or die based on the merit of their plan.

The leader of digital transformation must identify the most suitable AI-focused business model and then keep the team focused on moving towards that model despite any uncertainty and challenges. The organisations that implements an AI-focused business model effectively will have a clear identity and make greater strides forward The six business models proven to be ideal for an AI-centric world are (Zarifis & Cheng, 2023, 2025): (1) incumbent focusing on one part of the value chain and disaggregating, (2) incumbent absorbing AI into existing model, (3) incumbent expanding beyond current model to fully utilise the opportunities of AI and access new data, (4) startup disruptor focused on one sector, built from the start to be highly automated, (5) disruptor focused on tech adding a new service such as insurance, and (6) disruptor that is not tech-focused but has an extensive user or fanbase.

From the six business models, three are for organisations that are already operating in a sector, such as insurance, and three are organisations that are moving into a sector that is new for them. There are two models that are typically more disruptive: the third model, an incumbent expanding beyond current model to fully utilise the opportunities of AI and access new data; and the fourth, a startup disruptor focused on one sector, built from the start to be highly automated. In the fourth, as it is a startup, all the employees will be new and there will be minimal or no organisational culture. A servant or transformational leader can create a shared sense of purpose among all these new colleagues. The six AI focused business models are illustrated in figure 9.1.

Trust-building tip: Identify the best business model that is optimised to benefit from generative AI and be clear how the followers fit into this model. Guide them through the digital transformation with clarity and transparency.

9.5 Summary

A modern leader should be knowledgeable on the leadership styles, the six stages of a typical project, understand the diffusion of innovation and technology adoption models, know the six AI-focused business models, and follow technology developments, especially on generative AI and blockchain. The steps to becoming a great leader in the age of AI are summarized in figure 9.2.

This book recommends using transactional leadership in combination with either servant or transformational leadership. While a leader can take lessons from all three approaches, the best balance for the current environment is transactional with servant, or transactional with transformational. Servant and transformational leadership approaches are very effective in motivating and inspiring people, but they are challenging to implement and do not necessarily fit every situation. Transactional leadership is usually practical and relatively easy to implement, but it lacks the motivation and the overarching vision the servant and transformational approaches offer.

A leader that has identified the AI-focused business model they want to move towards and believes the key to the success is to convince their team of the value of their plan should add the transformational to the transactional approach, If the leader knows that their organisation should utilise AI more extensively, but they do not have

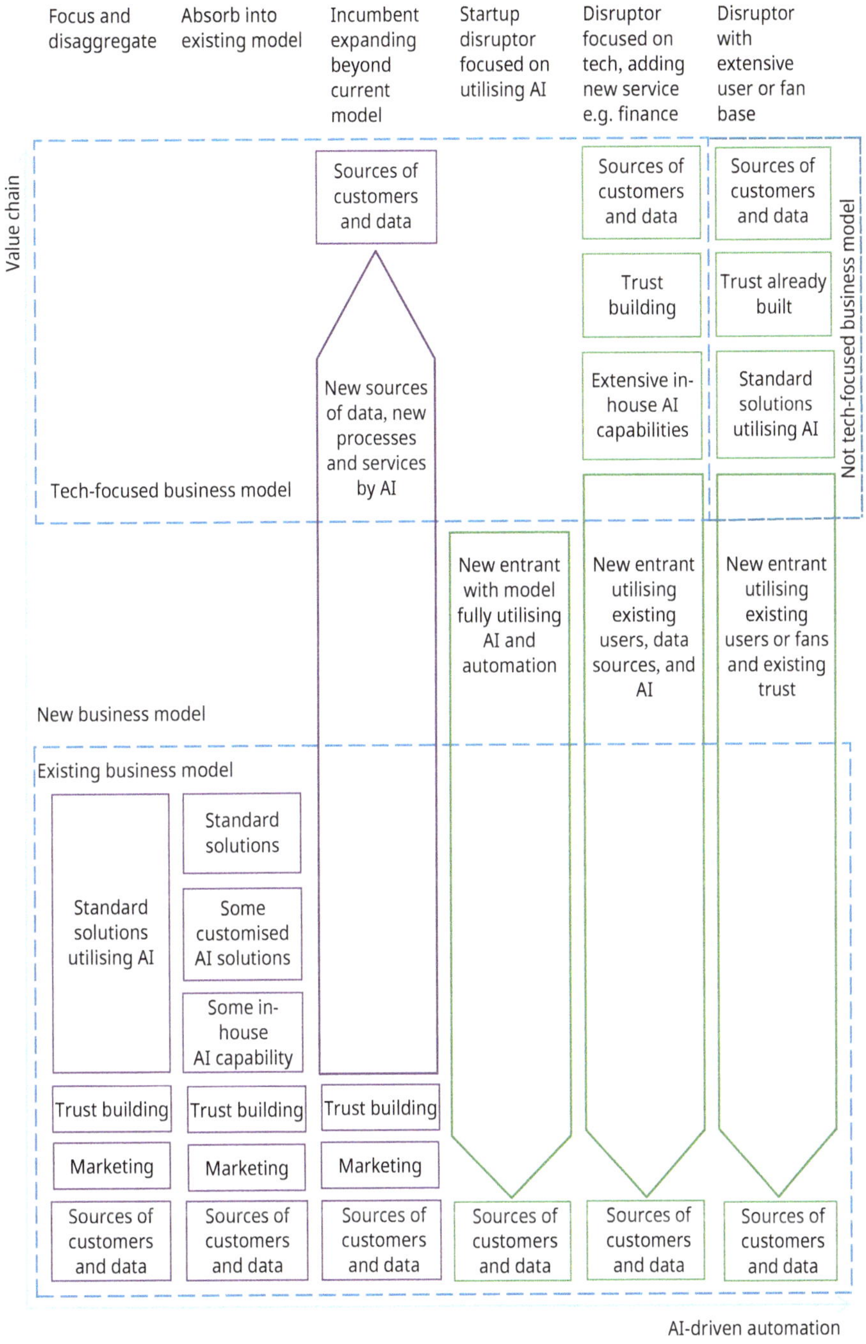

Figure 9.1: The six business models to utilise AI and build trust (based on Zarifis & Cheng, 2025; previously presented in Chapter 1 and 8).

```
┌─────────────────────────────────┐
│ (1) Learn leadership styles,     │
│     their traits, and the best   │
│     ways to combine two          │
│     leadership styles            │
└─────────────────────────────────┘
              │
              ▼
┌─────────────────────────────────┐
│ (2) Learn the typical stages of  │
│     a project and other key      │
│     processes such as the        │
│     diffusion of innovation      │
└─────────────────────────────────┘
              │
              ▼
┌─────────────────────────────────┐
│ (3) Evaluate the context         │
│     including the team, the      │
│     competition, the new         │
│     technologies                 │
└─────────────────────────────────┘
              │
              ▼
┌─────────────────────────────────┐
│ (4) Choose a business model and  │
│     a leadership style           │
└─────────────────────────────────┘
              │
              ▼
┌─────────────────────────────────┐
│ (5) Understand how to build      │
│     trust with the chosen model  │
│     and leadership style         │
└─────────────────────────────────┘
              │
              ▼
┌─────────────────────────────────┐
│ (6) Decide what to do at each    │
│     stage, not doing too much    │
│     or too little                │
└─────────────────────────────────┘
```

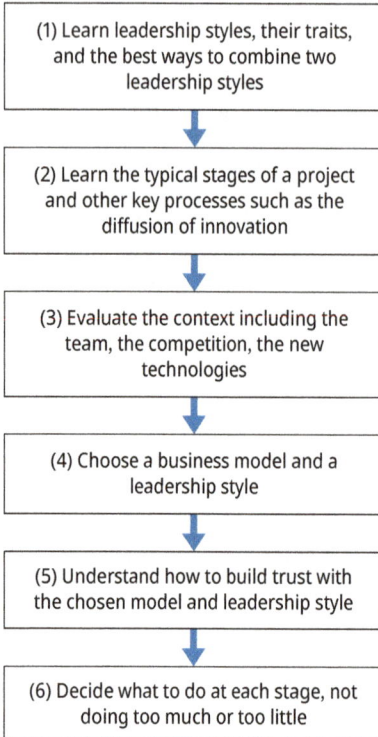

Figure 9.2: The six steps to being a great leader in the age of AI (previously presented in Chapter 1).

a clear plan and they want the team's input in choosing the new business model then the servant approach should be combined with the transactional approach.

Transactional leadership, despite its simplicity, can be the most powerful in building trust due to the transparency it offers. When combined with servant or transformational leadership styles, the resulting approach should retain that transparency in what the follower should deliver and receive in return.

In conclusion, to lead people today we must lead in AI, and to lead in AI we must lead in trust between people, and trust between people and technology. Many tell us it is all about the results, but the results must be achieved in a sustainable way, and the journey is just as important.

9.6 Exercises

Exercise 9.1

Reflecting on the three modern and five traditional leadership styles
Even with the best education and advice, in the end, the leader must decide for themselves what is a good fit for them and what they can pull off. It is worth reflecting on

the three modern and five traditional leadership styles and what their strengths and weaknesses are.

Questions

1) Which leadership style, or styles, do you believe is the best for you to apply and why? If you were a follower and you could choose the leadership approach your leader used, would it be the same choice? Is the best leadership approach the same from the perspective of the leader and the follower?

2) How would you use the leadership style you selected to build trust in generative AI?

3) How do you believe you need to improve your existing skills to implement this leadership style effectively.

Exercise 9.2

Leading mixed teams of humans and autonomous AI agents
Scenario: You work for a startup that is being set up to utilise AI better than the existing companies in their sector. They want to offer insurance to complicated large engineering and construction projects, such as offshore oil drilling, oil refineries, and large bridges. Most new startups have focused on utilising AI for simpler insurance, such as car insurance. Simpler insurance cases can be automated with the help of AI. These more complicated cases are far harder, if not impossible, to automate, as extensive negotiations with the various stakeholders are needed. This startup wants to gain an early mover advantage by finding an efficient and safe way to use AI more extensively for this purpose. Senior management believe that if this process cannot be fully automated with AI, mixed teams of insurance professionals and autonomous AI agents is the best approach. Leading mixed teams of humans and autonomous AI agents in such a project can be challenging (Zarifis & Cheng, 2024).

Questions

1) What are the additional risks, including risks to trust, of using mixed teams of humans and autonomous AI agents?

2) Which leadership style, or styles, would you apply if you were leading mixed teams of humans and autonomous AI agents?

Space for your notes

Recommended resources

https://www.youtube.com/@alexzarifis/videos
https://www.alexzarifis.com/blog/

References

Burns, J.M. (1978). *Leadership*. Open Road.

Chiniara, M., & Bentein, K. (2016). Linking servant leadership to individual performance: Differentiating the mediating role of autonomy, competence and relatedness need satisfaction. *Leadership Quarterly*, *27*(1), 124–141. https://doi.org/10.1016/j.leaqua.2015.08.004

Scheuer, C. L., Loughlin, C., & Woodside, A. G. (2022). Can you always catch more flies with honey than with vinegar? Applying an asymmetric approach to transformational leadership research. *Journal of Business and Psychology*, *37*(1), 191–213. https://doi.org/10.1007/s10869-021-09737-4

Zarifis, A., & Cheng, X. (2024). How to build trust in answers given by Generative AI for specific, and vague, financial questions. *Journal of Electronic Business & Digital Economics*, *3*(3), 236–250. https://doi.org/10.1108/JEBDE-11-2023-0028

Zarifis, A., & Fu, S. (2023). Re-evaluating trust and privacy concern when purchasing a mobile app: Re-calibrating for the increasing role of artificial intelligence. *Digital*, *3*(4), 286–299. https://doi.org/10.3390/digital3040018

Zarifis, A., & Cheng, X. (2025). The new centralised and decentralised Fintech technologies, and business models, transforming finance. In A. Zarifis & X. Cheng (Eds.), *Fintech and the emerging ecosystems: Exploring centralised and decentralised financial technologies*. Springer Nature. https://link.springer.com/book/9783031834011

List of figures

https://doi.org/10.1515/9783111630137-010

List of tables

https://doi.org/10.1515/9783111630137-011

List of boxes

https://doi.org/10.1515/9783111630137-012

Index

https://doi.org/10.1515/9783111630137-013

www.ingramcontent.com/pod-product-compliance
Lightning Source LLC
Chambersburg PA
CBHW061806210326

41599CB00034B/6901